Icons of Film

Film

The 20th Century

Edited by
Peter W. Engelmeier

With contributions by
Michael Althen, Sibylle Alverdes, Birgit Amon,
James Attlee, Marga Boehle,
Klaus Christoph Dahm, Peter W. Engelmeier,
Wolf-Christian Fink, Arnold Hohmann, Andrea Kaiser,
Horst Peter Koll, Josef Lederle, Hans Messias,
Ponkie, Michael Radtke, Susanne Rieger,
Heiko Rosner, and Georg E. Vogel

Prestel
Munich · London · New York

Peter W. Engelmeier

Raising the Curtain
on the First Century of Film

Movies can work wonders, as anyone who has sat in a dark cinema and been transported from the real world into a fantasy world knows. A well-told story combined with carefully composed images, a stirring score, and close-up shots, creates a perfect effect. Good movies can—and should—be wonderful dreams. And when legends are born, when a glamorous layer of exotic unreality lies gossamer-thin over material that has all the traits of the banal, then we have a cult film in the making. "Great cinema," those in the know will mutter, their eyes still glazed over from the rhapsodic experience of the previous night when they were dreaming the dream of the cinema, which —as New York poet Erica Joy Obert tells us— may feel more real than love itself.

It is no small task to compile a chronological retrospective of "great films" in a century when movies became an art form in their own right, a part of the societal fabric, and big business. This is especially true if the editor's own subjective favorites are not to influence the selection criteria.

To name those movies that proved to be outstanding to an informed public (and continue to do so into the twenty-first century), the editorial staff, my co-authors, my publisher, Jürgen Tesch—a real movie buff— and I wrestled with as much passion and insight as we could muster to form a definitive list that included less familiar gems such as *Broken Silence* and timeless visual treats such as *The Garden of the Finzi-Continis*. Surprisingly, we started out with well over one hundred films that had what it takes, be it story, production quality, direction, or cast performances. All too soon, however, one or the other was eliminated as arguments confronted personal criteria.

The result, I believe, is a book that you will be able to enjoy if you love film and the people connected to filmmaking. You may not find your favorite director. You may feel that *Pretty Woman* or *Titanic* could have been left out. You may ask yourself why some Olympians of the craft get to step into the limelight once more while others don't even get a front-row seat.

We start out with Charlie Chaplin's *The Kid*, described by my favorite critic, Ponkie, as "quintessential cinema: naïve and likeable." Bringing up the rear is *American Beauty*, which, like Chaplin's film *Modern Times* (also in this volume), is another working man's personal odyssey. It is the story of a contemporary man, who finds

himself caught in a suburban prison of mediocrity, told via the basic tools of icon-oclastic cinema (the kind that Pedro Almodóvar has been pulling out of his magic hat for years). Between these poles lies the full range of the art of cinema, a world full of contrasts, whose history wouldn't be complete without Jacques Tati, Akira Kurosawa, Pier Paolo Pasolini, David Lynch, Peter Greenaway, Bernhard Wicki, and several others. If their work is only mentioned in passing, or not at all, it is because of the restrictions which have to be imposed whenever such a selection is made.

Jacques Tati's *Mon Oncle*, 1958, Oscar 1959

The New York Times took the easy way out by seeking safety in numbers against possible omissions; it presented a mammoth list of the "1000 best films." *Time* magazine, on the other hand, decided to crown *Citizen Kane* the "Best Film of the Century," cau-tiously adding two runners-up—Truffaut's *Day for Night* and Polanski's *Chinatown*.

That's the nature of a selection process, and I feel that the attempt to distill the love for movies into several dozen works is as honest as it is explicable. In the thicket of ambitions, our selections offer the read-ers the opportunity to read, to look, and, perhaps, to contradict.

Tom Tykwer's *Lola rennt*, 1998

The experiential world of the cinema has one simple rule: turn the lights down low. This book hopes to remind you of memorable movies by presenting the most beautiful, the most important, the most moving, the most artistic, and the most daring films. Here are eighty-four portraits to remember and revisit.

Let the curtain rise for the highlights of a century of film!

Paul T. Anderson's *Magnolia*, 1999

Peter W. Engelmeier

Douglas, Mary, Charlie and Friends
or
How it Started so Silently and then Learned to Talk

Douglas Fairbanks, Mary Pickford, and Charlie Chaplin, 1917

Breathing life into motionless pictures was an ambition held by many during the second half of the nineteenth century, and inventors, scientists, designers, and engineers from many different countries set about turning that dream into reality. They were inspired by long-familiar inventions and optical toys such as the magic lantern, the camera obscura, the "wheel of life" (zoetrope) and, from around 1839 on, photography. Soon after the invention of photography attempts were made to bring static images "to life." Following experiments with serial photographs and the tachistoscope, a view box with a rotating drum, recording and projection equipment for moving pictures was manufactured.

Pioneers of cinematography were at work everywhere and almost every country had its own national device. Italy had its cinematografo, England its theatrograph, and Poland its pleograph; there was the kinetoscope of renowned American inventor Thomas Alva Edison and the bioscope of the German brothers Max and Emil Skladanovsky, who presented their "living pictures" in Berlin's Winter Garden on November 1, 1885. Unfortunately, all of these devices were but seven-day wonders, since they were technically inadequate or their inventors ran out of money. The bioscope,

with its complicated dual image projectors, had to give way to simpler technology.

Enter the Lumière brothers. Although they were not, strictly speaking, the inventors of cinema, the French brothers Louis Lumière (1864–1948) and Auguste Lumière (1862–1954) bear the honorary title of the "Fathers of the Cinema." The first use of their cinematograph, on December 28, 1895, at the Grand Café in Paris, is seen as the launch of the new medium. An amazed audience viewed eleven one-minute shorts projected by the most technically advanced device of its day. As the sons of a wealthy manufacturer, the Lumière brothers had the necessary financial backing to ensure success. The premiere netted a profit of thirty-three francs and, although takings soon increased, neither the Lumière brothers nor other filmmaking pioneers remotely recognized the artistic or commercial significance of their invention. Little did they realize that their moving pictures would change the world forever.

One hundred cameramen supplied the Lumières with footage from across the globe as early as 1889. Their short films dealt with important political or social events, such as the coronation of Tsar Nicholas II, or everyday scenes like "baby's breakfast" or "arrival of a train." In the case of the latter,

once the appeal of novelty had worn off, the public began to be bored by such commonplace events.

This was just the right moment for magician Georges Méliès (1861–1938) to come on the scene. If the Lumière brothers are regarded the pioneers of the documentary film, it is Méliès who best understood how film could be used for entertainment. Drawing from his background as a magician, he enthusiastically embraced the new medium and transported his audiences into a fantasy world. With his 1902 space-travel adventure, *A Voyage to the Moon*, the "magician of the screen" enjoyed a huge success—and invented the sci-fi film in the process. Méliès had been working in his own studio outside Paris since 1897 and had made around five hundred films. While working on his fantasy films, he developed around one hundred tricks, some of which, like multiple exposure, he discovered by chance. Despite his wealth of ideas, as a man of the theater he felt committed to the conventions of the stage. As his work was filmed using a static camera, from the perspective of a member of an audience looking toward the stage, the distance between the camera and the action never changed.

Méliès's space-travel adventures were a glimpse of futuristic screen spectaculars to

8

The first science-fiction film: *A Voyage to the Moon*, 1902

The prototype of the western: *The Great Train Robbery*, 1903

The embodiment of a screen goddess: Gloria Swanson

come, and other genres, too, developed during this early period of moviemaking. Different countries had their own specialities, although there were overlaps. Tiny Denmark, a moviemaking power to be reckoned with during the infancy of film, specialized in elegant drawing room dramas with hints of tragedy and eroticism. Contemporary observers described the proverbial "Danish kiss" in which the lips "meet passionately and protractedly." Movies like *Lion Hunt* (1907) or *White Female Slaves* (1913) were global successes. In 1910, renowned director Urban Gad introduced the beguiling Asta Nielsen to an enraptured public in *The Abyss*: the movie world had one of its first stars. If the Danes made melodramas in luxurious surroundings, the Italians turned to historical epics. *The Last Days of Pompeii* (1908) was the first in a series of super-spectacles. Other sensational hits were *Quo vadis?* (1913) and Giovanni Pastrone's *Cabiria* (1914) with Maciste, a character who appeared in other Italian muscle-man films made later.

From the beginning, the Americans had their own specialty. In 1903, Edwin S. Porter directed *The Great Train Robbery*, the first western. And then there were the cowboy stars: fearless Tom Mix and Bronco Billy who rode their way through hundreds of serial adventures and came out on top against the bad guys. As actor, director, and producer Gilbert M. Anderson commented: "We changed the horses, but not the sets."

Slapstick comedy became the other trademark of American movies. In slapstick, a team of clowns causes mayhem, indulges in pie-throwing and performs comic stunts before setting off on a wild chase. Mack Sennett and his "Keystone Company" gave rise to this boisterous genre after 1912. A slapstick staple were the bumbling Keystone cops and an array of bathing beauties, one of them being Gloria Swanson who went on to become a screen idol. Her seductive glamour and sex appeal in Cecil B. DeMille's feature film, *Male and Female*, made her the epitome of the wealthy and frivolous woman.

In France, on the other hand, the preference was for sophisticated comedy. Around 1908, the hugely popular Max Linder created the figure of the gentleman comic and dandy in his Max serial.

Very much in the tradition of the theater was the French *film d'art* that developed around 1907. The aim of its creators was to ennoble the "plebeian" medium of film. Their products were truly theatrical—academic and affected art films that were not received enthusiastically by the public. The best-known example of this genre is *L'Assassinat du duc de Guise* (1908). Even if *film d'art* flopped as a genre, its use of the best actors, great literature, and respected writers furthered the cause of film. Serious artists no longer looked down their noses at the new medium.

The French answer to pompous and emotive cinematic art works was not long in coming. In his film series, *Life as it is lived* (1911–13), Louis Feuillade attempted "to project realism onto the screen." Albert Capellani, whose *Les Miserables* of 1912, based on Victor Hugo's novel, became a worldwide success, was similarly concerned with realism. Feuillade, however, did not restrict himself to real life. Inspired by crime stories, he created the detective film. In 1913, he was the first to bring the mysterious figure of Fantômas (Master of Terror) to the screen, where he continues to make trouble to this day.

Russia and Germany missed out on the infancy of film, the former only waking up to the genre as a result of the 1917 Revolution. In Germany, *The Student of Prague* (1913) with Paul Wegener, caused a stir and presented the world with a German version of the fantasy film. German Expressionism was on the rise.

Director David Wark Griffith on set—to the left is his star Lillian Gish and the actor Howard Gaye

The Birth of a Nation (1915)—the poster for the revival of this successful movie in the 1920s

Intolerance (1916)—the epic was a monumental flop

Movies had by now taken their first steps, had been tried and tested in different genres, and had found admirers from all walks of life. It was now time to define a film language. The basics became evident in the work of two British filmmakers. As early as 1900, portrait photographer George Albert Smith had worked with close-ups and detailed shots and, in *Grandma's Reading Glass*, worked with a variety of framings. This early form of simple editing was also used by Smith's colleague, James Williamson. In his 1901 film *Attack on a Chinese Mission Station*, he showed an episode from the Boxer Rebellion. Both Lumière and Méliès would have used a static camera to show the mission house and its frantic residents under attack, and at some point British sailors would have stormed onto the scene to complete the rescue. However, Williamson's "parallel editing" includes changes of angle. The camera leaves the mission station before the attack is over and takes up the action elsewhere. The sailors are seen in the next shot, and the viewer knows that they will be going to the aid of the missionaries. Thus, the seeds are sown for the "last-minute rescue," one of

directors' favorite devices that, to this day, no dramatic film can do without. The British film pioneers, known in film history as the Brighton School, did not realize that they had invented film's very own narrative form using changes of angle and montage. This demanded that audiences see things in a new way—something that, in the beginning, they often found difficult to do.

The first fifteen years of the new medium saw highly creative attempts made by very different directors around the world. But it fell to the American, David Wark Griffith, to synthesize and perfect the new tricks and ideas. In effect, he catalogued cinematic forms and made conscious use of them in his own work. Just how deliberate he was is seen in a newspaper advertisement from 1913 in which he listed the novelties that went into his films: close-ups, detailed takes, panoramas, flashbacks, suspense shots, and a general restraint in dramatic expression. After an apprenticeship of six years, in which he made around five hundred films, he was ready for his masterpiece, *The Birth of a Nation*, 1915, which marked the arrival of artistically mature film. While this monumental, three-hour, civil war

epic was controversial for its racism, its place in the history of film is undisputed. Griffith, who called the film a "story in pictures," expertly employed the elements of film language that are valid to this day: atmospheric details, moving shots, close-ups, and cross-cutting, whereby scenes are edited and intermixed to give the impression that separate actions are happening concurrently. Parallel editing was perfected by Griffith in his next epic, *Intolerance* (1916). While *The Birth of a Nation*, with star actress Lillian Gish, became the most successful silent film ever, *Intolerance* flopped at the box office. Its failure meant bankruptcy for the Triangle Pictures Production Company whose artistic directors were Griffith, Mack Sennett, and Thomas Harper Ince. Ince, whose westerns made cowboy William S. Hart a star, had a more down-to-earth approach to filmmaking than his colleague Griffith. "Filmmaking is a bit like baking a cake... You need certain ingredients and have to know how to put them together."

Sennett, the third partner in the Triangle venture, was hugely successful with his slapstick comedies. Harry Langdon, Buster

Fantômas (1913)—the first police movie came from France

The man who never laughed: 'Buster' (Joseph Francis) Keaton

Always endeavoring to be all things to all people: Harold Lloyd, in a precarious situation

A French poster with 'Fatty' Arbuckle, ca. 1920

Keaton, Harold Lloyd, and Roscoe "Fatty" Arbuckle all trained under him, as did Charlie Chaplin who went on to become one of the biggest artists in the history of film. At the end of 1916, Sennett hired Chaplin for a weekly fee of 150 dollars. Four years later, Chaplin signed the so-called Million Dollar Contract with First National; he received an annual salary of one million dollars, becoming the world's highest-paid movie star. And at that point he hadn't even made his most famous movies. In the year that he spent under Sennett, Chaplin created the conditions for his later career and developed the essential features of what would become the legendary tramp figure.

Movies do not flourish in a vacuum, and from the start, substantial economic and political interests were linked to them. In 1895, Auguste Lumière expressed the opinion that his invention could "be exploited for a while as a scientific curiosity; beyond that it has no commercial future." Yet, the business opportunities afforded by their moving pictures must have dawned quickly on the Lumière brothers. Why else would they have put so much effort into setting up their own film studio employing so many people? As soon as it became obvious that money was to be made from the new invention, big investors got involved, heralding the end of the era of artisanal directors. The French understood how to take advantage of their leading position. Charles Pathé was the first to do so by securing a monopoly for his company between 1903 and 1909, not only in France but also throughout Europe and the United States. He rightly claimed that "while I didn't invent the movies, I did turn them into an industry." In 1910, a competitor named Gaumont emerged in France, eclipsing Pathé.

As an industrial product, the movies needed an audience—a big one. The fairground films from cinema's infancy, when shorts were a cheap form of entertainment for crowds in tents or in vaudeville shows, soon became obsolete. In the United States, moving pictures found their first home in penny arcades; after 1905, they were shown in the legendary nickelodeons, theater-style cinemas which charged an entrance fee of five cents (one nickel). Their number increased rapidly and, after 5 years, there were no fewer than 10,000. By 1914, there were around 60,000 movie theaters worldwide, and, by the 1920s, the first movie palaces were being built.

In the long term, the millions of fans who flocked to the movies were not satisfied with simple features. Movies became longer, the narratives more sophisticated. Australia, in fact, can claim to be the country that produced the first film of substantial duration, the hour-long *Story of the Kelly Gang* (1906).

World War I caused major disruption in film production and distribution. France was unable to market its products in Germany; Denmark, wholly dependent on exports, lost its markets and any significance it once had in the film world. Europe's supremacy dwindled, and the United States became the world's leading filmmaker.

The upturn in the movie industry in the United States led to a situation of savage competition. To bring things under control, leading producers, importers, and distributors formed the first movie trust at the end of 1908, the Motion Pictures Patent Company (MPPC). The trust attempted to control the whole of the American market, 11

Tickets for just 5 cents: The Nickelodeon, 1906

The beginning of a film metropolis: Hollywood in 1905

but independent producers resisted and, heeding the pioneers' motto to "Go West," moved out to California. The good weather undoubtedly facilitated outdoor movie making, but also the location put producers beyond the Movie Trust's sphere of influence, which did not extend to the West Coast of the United States. So it was that a Los Angeles suburb became the center of filmmaking—the much-loved, much-hated, Hollywood.

The first studio was built in 1911 on the corner of Sunset Boulevard and Gower Street. Hollywood became the world's movie capital thanks to producers such as William Fox, Carl Laemmle of Universal, and Adolph Zukor of Paramount, who coined the phrase "famous actors in famous films." These men, who had started as independents, began to establish bigger and bigger film studios themselves. In 1919, four top Hollywood artists moved against the power of the movie moguls, forming United Artists production and distribution company. The four founding members were producer David W. Griffith and actors Mary Pickford, Douglas Fairbanks, and Charlie Chaplin.

During World War I, Hollywood's products barely trickled into Germany and, following the entry of the United States into the war in 1917, they dried up altogether. Germany was thus completely cut off from its European and overseas movie suppliers. These lean years encouraged home-grown productions, however, consisting of patriotic works, sensational films, and comedies. On December 12, 1917, the major German studios formed the *Universum Film Aktiengesellschaft* (Ufa) at the behest of General Erich Ludendorff. The military's involvement was not altogether altruistic. It wanted to employ the medium of film for propaganda purposes, as indeed Germany's foes were doing. Ludendorff said that "the war has shown the immense power of images and film as a means of instruction and influence." The powerful film studio's influence waned in the last year of the war, but its heyday was to return between then and 1923. Censorship was abolished, and the German mark was weak in comparison to other foreign currencies. This meant that foreign films were expensive to buy, but that German ones were cheap to produce and export.

The immediate postwar period was also a highpoint for Swedish film, since the French movie industry was weakened and German films were finding only reluctant markets among Germany's former enemies. And with Victor Sjöström and Mauritz Stiller, Sweden had only two important directors of its own. Sjöström's works were imbued with admiration for Nordic nature, culture, and folklore, such as *The Outlaw and His Wife* (1918), with Mauritz Stiller's *Sir Arne's Treasure* as the second major success of the Swedish school. In contrast to Sjöström's slow moving, balanced framing, in this movie, Stiller made use of a quick succession of cuts and montage, elements that characterize his comedy *Erotikon* (1920). In 1923, Sjöström emigrated to Hollywood and was followed three years later by Stiller, accompanied by his "discovery," Greta Garbo.

Impressed though audiences had been by Sweden's reverence for nature, they found German Expressionism even more impressive. In 1920, Robert Wiene produced *The Cabinet of Dr. Caligari*, a film that was to have a lasting influence and which caused controversy. The action takes place

A masterpiece of Expressionist cinema:
The Cabinet of Dr. Caligari, 1920

Came to Hollywood with Ernst Lubitsch in 1923: Pola
Negri in *Madame Dubarry*, 1919

One of the first stars: Asta Nielsen in the early 1920s

exclusively among painted and bizzarely distorted geometric sets which are designed to accentuate the film's nightmarish quality. Paul Wegener intensified the Expressionist style, which had already characterized his *Student of Prague*, by setting his third *Golem* movie (*The Golem, How It Came Into The World*, 1920) in a Prague cityscape of crooked houses and wonderful but unconventionally shaped roofs.

The lavish décor and costumes used by Ernst Lubitsch drew public attention both to him and his stars. In 1919, he produced *Madame Dubarry* (Passion) with the Polish actress Pola Negri, with whom he emigrated to Hollywood in 1923, and *Intoxication* with Asta Nielsen. Nielsen's striking and sensitive acting ("I am what I act") influenced the development of cinematic art. She was one of the first actresses to adapt to the new medium of the silent film, eschewing exaggerated poses and over-elaborate facial expressions. Following her appearance in *The Abyss* (1910), she became one of Europe's biggest film stars. The popularity enjoyed by Henny Porten, on the other hand, an actress who played guileless, sweet lasses, was restricted to Germany.

It was the Italians who really developed the star cult. They prostrated themselves at the feet of their leading ladies, and movies were produced for the stars' sake alone. Lyda Borelli and Francesca Bertini were the first Italian movie stars to be worshiped like goddesses and whom the public flocked to see.

The United States had its stars, too. First, there were the cowboys and the clowns; then Douglas Fairbanks conquered the screen as a beaming and carefree swashbuckler. Pearl White was the very opposite of the refined Italian stars and rose to prominence as the intrepid heroine in serials such as *The Perils of Pauline*. Blond, sweet, and innocent Mary Pickford, on the other hand, was considered America's darling. That did not prevent the young lady from taking a hard stance: "I cannot afford to work for only 10,000 dollars a week," she proclaimed and upped her fee to astronomical heights.

From the star-cult to the studio system, from the western to the melodrama, from the close-up to the panorama: at a breathtaking rate, film in its first twenty-five years developed the elements that still

characterize it today. Only one thing was missing—sound. Yet it would be another (silent) decade before the moving pictures became the talking pictures.

At the start of the 1920s, American inventor Lee de Forest and German engineers Hans Vogt, Jo Engl, and Joseph Massolle first devised and developed new sound-recording techniques which were incorporated directly on film. Their new technology was first used by Warner Brothers in the 1926 movie *Don Juan*, in which recordings of songs were heard. The breakthrough came a year later with *The Jazz Singer*. Enthusiastic audiences were astonished by its mostly synchronized songs and its few lines of dialogue. Seventy-three years after that crackling debut, movies in the year 2000 have reached another visual and audio technological dimension. Ridley Scott's lavish, ancient Roman epic *Gladiator*, with its vast and perfect sound, stretches sensory perception to its very limits.

Towards the end of the 1920s, certain stars of the silent film struggled to maintain their screen idol status, among them Harry Liedtke in Germany and John Gilbert in America. While they had shown great 13

Don Juan, 1926

The poster for the first sound motion picture with music and talking scenes: *The Jazz Singer*, 1927

In the year 2000, this movie sets the standards for grandiose visual and audio effects: Ridley Scott's *Gladiator*

expressiveness in the silent film—Kurt Hickethier speaks of facial expressions and gestures that replace language—they were not up to the demands of the sound film. Others, whose careers did not make the transition to sound, were the clowns Buster Keaton and Harry Langdon.

Only a few stars of the silent era had what it took—including an acceptable voice—to adapt to the demands of the sound films and to be successful in them. One who did was Charlie Chaplin, who believed that "a good sound film is worse than a good play, but a good silent film is better than a good play." Self-assured Mary Pickford was another actress who succeeded in the talkies (*Coquette*, 1929; *Secrets*, 1933). As if she knew what lay ahead, she commented satirically in a *New York Times* interview that "it would have been more logical if the silent film had grown out of the sound film, not the other way around."

The Kid

USA, 1920
Running time: 55 minutes
Black and white
Directed and written by Charlie Chaplin;
cinematographer, Roland H. Totheroh;
music by Conny Schumann
With: Charlie Chaplin (The Vagabond),
Jackie Coogan (The Kid), Edna Purviance
(The Mother), Carl Miller (The Artist),
Tom Wilson (The Policeman)

Charlie Chaplin at his best—with a touch of sentimentality

The tramp who dreams of the poor as winged angels:
Charlie Chaplin and the "kid" (Jackie Coogan)

In the first minutes of the movie, Charlie Chaplin proclaims
to the viewers what they can expect: "A picture with a
smile and perhaps a tear."

>>> Charlie Chaplin, *Modern Times,* and Biography, see p. 30

In 1920, before becoming an independent producer as a founding member of United Artists, Charlie Chaplin, one of the greatest geniuses in the history of film, created *The Kid*. It was his first feature-length film after countless, brilliant slapstick shorts. More than any of his other works *The Kid* is a reflection of his own life experience: his firstborn child had died only three days after being born, and his first marriage to the underage Mildred, the mother of the child, had already fallen apart. A short while later her lawyers chased him across New York to seize the newly finished copy of *The Kid*.

In *The Kid*, we see Chaplin's penchant for sentimentality as in no other of his early films. His own childhood experiences of poverty and loneliness in London are transformed into an orphan fairy tale that would make anyone cry. The love, kindness and passionate care, which a bedraggled tramp bestows on an abandoned baby exemplifies true human virtue when contrasted with miserly social workers from a municipal orphanage, the administrator of the homeless shelter, and a bailiff.

The Kid is an enchanting tearjerker in which an unwed mother's pain is heartbreaking as she lays her baby in an expensive car parked in front of a villa (unaware that two bandits are about to steal the car and will drop the bothersome infant in front of a dilapidated shed in the next slum they pass through.) The tramp, who becomes an instant and ingeniously creative baby caregiver, is beside himself with happiness. His energy is tireless as he chases the social workers, who tear the child from his arms, through streets and across rooftops.

The fantasy sequences are telling and powerful, such as when the tramp dreams that the poor are winged angels whose feathers are being plucked out by the devil. Other scenes are hilariously funny in the best slapstick tradition, such as the fighting scene between street urchins in which brawn wins out over the law and brain beats brawn any day.

Never again did Jackie Coogan, the wonderful "kid" in the story, come close to achieving a similar impact as an actor—the beautiful baby grew into a homely adult, but the baby is immortal. This film is quintessential cinema: naive and likeable for its raw feelings and sense of justice and loss. Chaplin's very own *comédie humaine*.   *Po.*

In *The Kid* Charlie Chaplin draws on the poverty and
loneliness he experienced during his childhood in London

Nosferatu—A Symphony of Horror

Nosferatu—Eine Symphonie des Grauens
Germany, 1921/22
Running time: 84 minutes
Black and white, some scenes highlighted
in color
Directed by Friedrich Wilhelm Murnau;
written by Henrik Galeen, *from the novel*
Dracula *by* Bram Stoker; *cinematographers,*
Fritz Arno Wagner *and* Günther Krampf;
music by Peter Schirmann *and* Hans Posegga
With: Max Schreck (Count Orlok Nosferatu),
Gustav von Wangenheim (Thomas Hutter),
Greta Schröder (Ellen Hutter), Ruth
Landshoff (Lucy Westrenka), Alexander
Granach (Knock)

Friedrich Wilhelm Murnau

1888 Born on December 28 as Friedrich Wilhelm Plumpe in Bielefeld. Studied philosophy and art history in Berlin. His first U.S. film, *Sunrise,* was celebrated as a masterpiece.

1930 In collaboration with documentarist Robert Flaherty, made his last film, *Tabu,* in the South Pacific.

1931 Shortly before the premiere of *Tabu,* Friedrich Wilhelm Murnau died of injuries incurred in an automobile accident.

In the remake of the classic *Nosferatu,* Werner Herzog, staying close to the original, paid impressive homage to Murnau, placing the great Klaus Kinski in the lead role.

A fashionably Expressionist studio backdrop: a scene out of *A Symphony of Horror*

"You want to see a symphony of horror? You can expect more than that. Beware! Nosferatu is no joke...." This "warning," issued during the 1922 PR campaign for *Nosferatu* was serious. For Fritz Murnau's film was the first, great vampire adventure in the history of the genre. Ever since its release, the "undead" have populated the screen in innumerable variations, but it was Murnau who created the prototype, and his subtitle, *A Symphony of Horror,* warned viewers to expect more than run-of-the-mill shock effects. The movie has inspired and set the standard for all subsequent vampire films, including those featuring Bela Lugosi, Christopher Lee, and Klaus Kinski.

In Murnau's story, the vampire isn't called Dracula but Count Orlok—or "Nosferatu, the Undead." Murnau changed the character's name to conceal the fact that the script was largely based on Bram Stoker's *Dracula* novel, published in 1897, and the fact that he had not purchased the film rights. Not surprisingly, Stoker's widow promptly filed a successful lawsuit, and the film was slated for destruction. But even the on-screen undead aren't so easy to kill. Luckily, some copies of *Nosferatu* survived, and the original was restored in 1988.

In the film, characters are constantly on the move, such as Thomas Hutter (Gustav von Wangenheim), a secretary to a property broker in Wisborg, Germany who must leave to travel to distant Transylvania to sell a house to Count Orlok (Max Schreck). His journey is cursed from the outset, and things begin to seem more ominous as he draws closer to the count's castle in the Carpathians. The count—a grotesque, bald man with skeletal fingers—sees a picture of Hutter's wife Ella (Greta Schröder) and lecherously exclaims: "Your wife has a beautiful neck." He then departs for Wisborg with six coffins in tow. Hutter, who is well aware of Orlok's vampire identity, panics and rushes home by the overland route—arriving too late. The count has already wreaked havoc, in the form of pestilence and death, on Wisborg.

The dreaded Count Orlok cum "Nosferatu"

Poisonous bloodsucker or a lethargic ghost? Max Schreck in the main role as Nosferatu

For today's viewers, accustomed to blood-spattered gore, the film is perhaps less horrifying than it was so many years ago. But Murnau's artistry still makes viewers feel the "icy breath from the netherworld," as one critic put it. Extreme camera angles, strong contrasts of light and dark, the use of negatives, various shutter speeds, and ominous shadows create a truly demonic quality. Working against the Expressionistic trend of his day, Murnau dispensed with studio sets and props. Instead, he shot exclusively on location in Lübeck, Rostock, and the Carpathians, transforming the scenery of these locations into ghostly and alien visions.

P.W.E.

The Battleship Potemkin

Bronenosez Potjomkin
USSR, 1925
Running time: 75 minutes
Black and white
Directed by Sergei M. Eisenstein; *written by*
Nina Agadshanova-Schutko; *cinematographer,*
Edouard Tissé; *music by* Nikolai Krjukov *and*
Edmund Meisel; *edited by* Sergei M. Eisenstein
With: Aleksandr Antonov (Seaman Vaku-
linchuk), Vladimir Barsky (Commandor
Golikov), Grigori Alexandrov (Lieutenant
Giljarovsky), Aleksandr Levshin (officer),
Mikhail Gomorov (sailor)

Sergei M. Eisenstein

1898 Born on January 23 in Riga, Latvia. Studied engineering.
1918 Fought with the Red Army in the revolution.
1920 First projects as director and set designer at the Proletcult
      Theater in Moscow. Directed his first film, lasting three
      minutes, to be screened in the context of a stage
      production.
1924 *Strike*
1925 *The Battleship Potemkin*
1927 *October/Ten Days That Shook the World*
1929 *The General Line/Old and New*
1929–33 Various film projects in the U.S. and Mexico could
      not be completed.
1933 Returned to the Soviet Union but faced great difficulties
      in working there as well.
1938 *Alexander Nevsky*
1944–46 *Ivan the Terrible* (Parts I and II); Part III was never
      finished.
1948 Sergei M. Eisenstein died from complications of a heart
      attack on February 11 in Moscow.

In spite of his universal success with *Potemkin,* Eisenstein
only managed to complete four more films in the Soviet
Union (including two parts of the planned trilogy, *Ivan the
Terrible*); his time in America was full of disagreements, and
his Mexico film remained a mere fragment.

Aleksandr Rodchenko's poster for *The Year 1905* project, on which Eisenstein's masterpiece *The Battleship Potemkin* is based

In 1925, an unknown, young director named Sergei Eisenstein was instructed by the Central Executive Committee of the USSR to direct a film in memory of the (failed) 1905 revolution. It was a commissioned work with clear instructions as to tendency and ideology—hardly ideal conditions for artistic creativity. Yet Eisenstein managed to steer clear of embarrassing pathos or clumsy propaganda in *The Battleship Potemkin*, which still continues on its journey across cinema screens seventy-five years later.

The original project, entitled *The Year 1905*, was intended to present a panoramic view of the revolution. But Eisenstein changed the concept after he began shooting. The sailors' revolt at Odessa, an episode of no more than a page and a half in the original script, became the subject of the entire film and symbolic of the revolution as a whole.

After being served rotten meat, the sailors on board the Potemkin revolt. Their commander, Vladimir Barsky, wants to execute the leaders. With an inspiring speech, sailor Vakulinchuk (Aleksandr Antonov) convinces the firing squad to side with the mutineers. In Odessa's harbour, the town's population rises in support of the sailors. Unfortunately, Cossacks are sent in and a massacre ensues on the harbour steps. The crew of the Potemkin fire the ship's cannon at the town's military headquarters and set out to sea, aware of imminent attack by the Czarist Black Sea fleet. Yet, instead of engaging in battle, the sailors join in brotherly solidarity. Sergei Eisenstein researched the facts carefully but insisted that "what matter[ed was] emotional authenticity and not documentary veracity."

Accordingly, he structured his history of the revolution as a tragedy in five acts, giving the classic form a revolutionary content and a creative force that was completely new in film-making. The masses, not the individual, are the heroes of the film. The massacre on the steps of Odessa, during which stone lions seem to come alive in defence of the people by means of fine-tuned editing and rhythmic cuts from frame to frame, is one of the most famous scenes in cinematic history. "As the key element it defined the character of the entire film." In this scene, Eisenstein brilliantly put his theory of montage into practice. The caliber of the film was evident even in its day, and famous film critic Alfred Kerr considered it the "most profound cinematic experience of the 1920s."

B.A.

Massacre on the harbor steps of Odessa

The masses are the heros of the film:
mutineers on board the Potemkin

Metropolis

Germany, 1925/26
Running time: 93 minutes (orig. 149)
Black and white
Directed by Fritz Lang; *written by* Thea von
Harbou; *cinematographers,* Karl Freund *and*
Günther Rittau; *music by* Gottfried Huppertz
With: Brigitte Helm (Maria, robot), Gustav
Fröhlich (Freder Fredersen), Alfred Abel (Joh
Fredersen), Heinrich George (Groth, robot
supervisor), Rudolf Klein-Rogge (Rotwang,
inventor), Theodor Loos (Joseph), Helene
Weigel (worker), Fritz Rasp (Slim)

Fritz Lang

1890 Born on December 5 as the son of an architect in Vienna.
Trip around the world. Volunteer service in World War I.
After the war, worked as a scriptwriter.
1919 First own film: *Halbblut (Halfbreed)*
1921 *Between Two Worlds/Beyond the Wall/Destiny* (based
on the script by Thea von Harbou, whom he wed in
1922 and who was involved in all of his films until
their divorce in 1933)
1922 *Dr. Mabuse the Gambler/Dr. Mabuse/The Fatal Passions*
1924 *Die Nibelungen*
1926 *Metropolis*
1931 Lang established himself as a sound-movie director
with *M* (see p. 26)
1932 *The Last Will of Dr. Mabuse/The Testament of
Dr. Mabuse*
1933 Avoiding advances from the Nazis, Lang went by way
of Paris to Hollywood, where he directed films such as:
1936 *Fury*
1940 *The Return of Jesse James*
1953 *The Big Heat*
1956 Frustrated by working conditions in the U.S., he
returned to Germany. There in:
1958 the two-part adventure movie *Journey to the Lost
City/Tiger of Bengal* and
1960 *The 1000 Eyes of Dr. Mabuse* were released. Yet his
attempts to revive his prewar success in Germany
failed.
1963 Lang played himself in the Godard film, *Contempt*.
From 1963 on, he lived in retirement (practically blind
during his final years) in his home in Beverly Hills.
1976 Fritz Lang died in Beverly Hills.

"The artistic film tries for constant development, conquering
new fields of endeavor, encompassing universal values.
This is the criterion by which the film of tomorrow must be
judged—to be innovative."
Fritz Lang, *The Film of Tomorrow,* February 1925

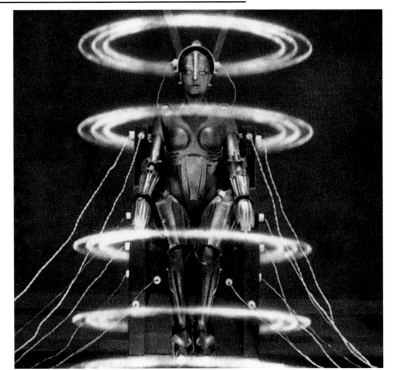

The robot (Brigitte Helm) is brought to life

For today's viewer, the present has caught up with this film's futuristic vision. In the silent movie era, Fritz Lang set his utopian tale of *Metropolis* in the twenty-first century. The German star director (*The Nibelungen, Dr. Mabuse*) wanted to put Hollywood in its place with this gigantic spectacle. The ambitious project consumed five million marks, instead of the budgeted one million, ended up as a box office flop, and brought the Ufa (Universum-Film AG) to the brink of ruin. But financial disaster could not diminish the artistic merit of the film. Even though *Metropolis* is often shown in brutally cut or even tinted versions, as a kind of cinematic "city of ghosts," Lang's visionary, imaginative film has had an enduring influence not only on science fiction as a genre but on horror films and music video clips to the present day. Lang's opus, shot in 1925–26 and premiered in Berlin on January 10, 1927, was controversial from the outset. The artistic dilemma of *Metropolis* was this: a simple story was dressed up in grandiose, fascinating style. It was made all the more questionable, politically and ideologically, by its Führer-like character, the "savior." (Not surprisingly, the Nazis immediately claimed the film as their own.)

In the utopian city of the title, Metropolis, the enslaved masses toil at the underground machine Molochs for the benefit of the rich who live a life of luxury above ground. Both worlds are ruled by Joh Fredersen (Alfred Abel). His counterpart is an angelic girl, Maria (Brigitte Helm), who preaches love to the workers and warns them against violence. To outwit Maria, an inventor named Rotwang (Rudolf Klein-Rogge) creates a look-alike robot (also played by Brigitte Helm) programmed to incite unrest in the masses. The real Maria and Frederson's son, Freder (Gustav Fröhlich), who is in love with the girl, are able to prevent disaster. A truce is achieved between the two worlds, and love bridges all differences: "The heart must mediate between brain and hands."

Lang later admitted that the central message of the film was "absurd." The trivial action was merely an excuse to create a stunning visual symphony with masterfully designed moving elements. The daring skyscraper and road constructions were shot with a revolutionary new process invented by one of the cameraman Eugen Schüfftan, employing mirror images of miniature models in life-sized scenes to create an illusion of gigantic buildings.   *B.A.*

The vision of a nightmare: the machine Molochs

The workers live and slave away in the underworld

Der blaue Engel
Germany, 1930
Running time: 108 minutes
Black and white
Directed by Josef von Sternberg; *written by*
Robert Liebmann *and* Josef von Sternberg,
based on the novel Professor Unrat *by* Heinrich
Mann; *cinematographers,* Günther Rittau
and Hans Schneeberger; *music by* Friedrich
Hollaender; *edited by* Sam Winston
With: Emil Jannings (Prof. Immanuel Rath),
Marlene Dietrich (Lola Lola), Kurt Gerron
(Kiepert), Rosa Valetti (Guste Kiepert), Hans
Albers (Mazeppa)

Josef von Sternberg

1894 Born on May 29 in Vienna. Grew up in Vienna and New York. Went to Hollywood in 1923. After a series of setbacks (films that were left unfinished, did not make it into the theaters, etc.).
1925 Debuted with *The Salvation Hunters*
1926 Breakthrough with *Underworld*, a gangster film in which von Sternberg employed highly innovative lighting and camera work.
1928 *The Last Command*. This film earned Emil Jannings the first Oscar in cinema history for best actor.
1930 At Jannings' suggestion, von Sternberg directed the first Ufa sound film in Germany, *The Blue Angel*. With his "discovery," Marlene Dietrich, he made six further movies in the U.S.:
1930 *Morocco*
1931 *Dishonored*
1932 *Blond Venus*
1932 *Shanghai Express*
1934 *The Scarlet Empress*
1935 *The Devil Is a Woman*
Only a few more films followed, at relatively long intervals, including
1939 *Sergeant Madden*
1941 *The Shanghai Gesture*
1953 After *The Saga of Anatahan/Ana-Ta-Han,* von Sternberg retired from the movie business.
1969 Josef von Sternberg died in Hollywood.

Marlene Dietrich:
"They Call Me Wicked Lola"

An actress's trademark, the figure of a glittering vamp, and a vehicle to fame for an inspired director: these are the important threads that run together in *The Blue Angel*, a gritty 1920s tale in Josef von Sternberg's film adaptation of Heinrich Mann's novel *Professor Unrat*.

Sternberg's *The Blue Angel*, which catapulted Marlene Dietrich from the bohemian scene in Berlin to Hollywood stardom, is one of those classics whose legends are more powerful than the film itself. Today, with a distance of seventy years, we can separate the old-fashioned elements from those that stand out as artistically timeless. At the time of its publication, Heinrich Mann's malicious tale of a provincial teacher, full of Wilhelmian hypocrisy and ruined by his erotic obsession for a nightclub singer, must have struck his readers—weaned as they were on Freud and psychoanalysis—like a grotesque figure in a panopticon. Although more recent, Emil Janning's performance as Professor Rath seems outdated; as he savors each and every expression and coquettishly poses as a tragic figure, Janning seems caught in the emotive pathos that characterized the silent movies. By contrast, Marlene Dietrich, with her lascivious casualness, is like a breath of fresh air.

When Professor Rath, nicknamed Unrath (the irony of which, however, is lost in translation—*Rat* meaning advice and *Unrat* garbage), catches his students in the demimonde establishment, the Blue Angel, gawking at the legs of an immoral *artiste* named Lola and listening to her cheeky songs, he preaches

unctuously of a life of virtue. He wants to cure his unruly charges of their "sinful behavior" but ends up falling under Lola's spell himself as he listens to her song "They Call Me Wicked Lola." Soon he is completely infatuated and becomes her lover and pathetic cuckold. He ends up traveling with the troupe as a clown—pitifully devoted to Lola while she openly flirts with Mazeepa (Hans Albers).

Sternberg's style is firmly based in the *chiaroscuro* of German Expressionism and full of teary-eyed sentimentalism, such as the professor's spiritual death in an empty classroom to the sound of a Glockenspiel playing the tune "Üb immer Treu und Redlichkeit" (Always Practice Honesty and Loyalty). The story is a tragedy of social descent and self-destruction. The film's rituals and world-famous poses, including the musical trademarks by Friederich Hollaender, have long since become separated from their context; they are ornaments in the history of film—the beginning of the Marlene myth, perpetuated and celebrated by Dietrich herself until her death in 1992.

The film may disappoint younger audiences, interested neither in its history nor in its reflection of the era. It comes to life only as a precious museum piece.   *Po.*

"Men gather around me
Like moths around a flame
And if their wings burn
I know I am not to blame."
Lola Lola (Marlene Dietrich)

The conflict looms: Marlene Dietrich as Lola Lola, Hans
Albers (center) as Mazeppa, and Emil Jannings as Rath

Still in a position of honor:
Professor Rath alias Unrath (Emil Jannings)

M – Eine Stadt sucht einen Mörder
Germany, 1931
Running time: 117 minutes
Black and white
Directed by Fritz Lang; *written by* Thea von Harbou *and* Fritz Lang, *based on a newspaper report by* Egon Jacobson; *cinematographer,* Fritz Arno Wagner; *music by* Edvard Grieg; *edited by* Paul Falkenberg
With: Peter Lorre (Hans Beckert, the murderer), Gustaf Gründgens (the criminal), Otto Wernicke (Inspector Karl Lohmann), Paul Kemp (pickpocket), Theo Lingen (con man), Theodor Loos (Chief Inspector Gröber), Inge Landgut (Elsie), Georg John (the blind beggar), Ellen Widmann (Mrs. Beckmann), Hertha von Walther (prostitute)

This is what a murderer looks like: Peter Lorre as the compulsive offender Beckert

EIN
FRITZ LANG
FILM
DER NERO
VERLEIH: VER. STAR-FILM G·M·B·H

The original poster (Germany), 1931

Director Fritz Lang was forced to change the film's original title "The Murderers Are Among Us", as the Nazi party suspected (correctly) that it was referring to them.

>>> Fritz Lang, *Metropolis,* and Biography, see p. 22

No viewer can escape the claustrophobic suggestiveness of this film. With his dark story of a hunt for a murderer, brilliantly directed in the shadows of the streets of Berlin, Fritz Lang created one of the highlights of film history. In the early thirties, the director was himself looking for new challenges. He wanted to get away from "such monster films as *Metropolis* and *The Woman in the Moon* and make a more intimate, profound film." He came up with the criminal theme of a child murderer for "M" by reading the daily papers and through in-depth research.

Lang was exploring new territory not only because of the theme. With "M" he also made the shift from silent film to "talking" pictures in 1931. And his cinematic genius is evident even in this first attempt. No director before (or after) treated sound as brilliantly. Lang wanted more than merely a realistic backdrop and used the soundtrack very consciously as a dramaturgical tool. The out-of-tune whistling of the murderer—whose trademark melody (a motif from Grieg's *Peer Gynt*) ultimately leads to his capture when a blind beggar recognizes him by the sound—is one example. In other instances, Lang meshes sequences by leaving a sentence unfinished at the end of one scene and immediately picking it up in the next. Lang's parallel montage is also legendary: in the middle of a conversation between policemen discussing how to proceed, Lang cuts to the criminals, who carry on seamlessly where the policemen left off (or vice versa).

The authorities and the underworld join forces to capture the psychopath who has cast all of Berlin into a state of fear and mass hysteria. The authorities, i.e. the police, do so because it is their duty, and the criminals because the increased police activities are interfering with their "business." Thus, the circle draws ever closer around the pervert who begins to look more and more like a hunted victim himself. His confession is deeply disturbing: "I always have to walk the streets, and I constantly feel that someone's following me. It's me! … But I can't… ! I can't escape from myself! Must, must continue on the path I'm being chased along!" Peter Lorre's screen debut as the tortured child murderer was so convincing that the image haunted him for the rest of his career. In the end, the criminals (led by Gustaf Gründgens) apprehend the murderer and sit in judgement of him. The police show up at the last minute and prevent a lynching. Off-screen we hear the voice of a mother: "We'll just have to look out more for the little 'uns."   *B.A.*

A psychotic child murderer has Berlin holding its breath

10000 M
Belohn
Wer ist d
Seit Montag, dem 11. Juni ds.
Der Schüler Kurt Klawitzky und
gewesen Müllerstr.
Aus verschiedene
ähnlichen
Jahres

USA, 1935
Running time: 97 minutes
Black and white
Directed by Mark Sandrich; *written by* Dwight
Taylor *and* Allan Scott, *based on the play* The
Girl Who Dared *by* Alexander Farago *and*
Aladar Laszlo; *cinematographers,* David Abel
and Vernon L. Walker; *music by* Irving Berlin;
edited by William Hamilton
With: Ginger Rogers (Dale Tremont), Fred
Astaire (Jerry Trevers), Edward Everett Horton
(Horace Hardwick), Helen Broderick (Madge
Hardwick), Eric Blore (Bates), Erik Rhodes
(Alberto Beddini)

Mark Sandrich

1900 Born on August 26 in New York. Studied mathematics.
1923 Entered motion pictures as a prop man. Began to work
as a director in 1927, principally making short comedies.
1933 *So This Is Harris* received an Oscar. The award led to
his directing features.
1934–38 Sandrich's lasting fame was ensured by five movies
made in collaboration with Fred Astaire and Ginger
Rogers:
1934 *The Gay Divorcee*
1935 *Top Hat*
1936 *Follow the Fleet*
1937 *Shall We Dance?*
1938 *Carefree*
From 1940 on Sandrich produced all of his films himself,
including:
1942 *Holiday Inn* (with Fred Astaire and Bing Crosby, whose
song "White Christmas" became a worldwide hit)
1943 *So Proudly We Hail* (a patriotic war melodrama)
1945 Mark Sandrich died during the filming of *Blue Skies* in
Hollywood. The film was completed by Stuart Heisler,
who was given credit for it.

The magic lives on: Ginger Rogers and Fred Astaire

The classic summary of Fred Astaire's talent during rehearsals: "Can't act. Can't sing. ...Can dance a little."

"I often find that I just have to dance," Fred
Astaire confesses to his partner Ginger Rogers.
To begin with, Ginger isn't thrilled by Fred's
confession. After all, the dance exercises in his
hotel room have interrupted her slumber. Thus
begins a banal love story full of romantic twists
and turns—and one of Hollywood's most
beautiful musicals, whose stars literally dance
their way into our hearts.

Top Hat was the fourth of nine films made by
the American dream dance couple Fred Astaire
and Ginger Rogers. The lively tale is considered
the pinnacle of their collaboration, the quintessential work of the Astaire-Rogers team.
Never did they dance more elegantly, more
energetically, and with more charm than in
this film, which became RKO's greatest box
office hit of the thirties. Hit hard by the de-
pression, the public was only too happy to
escape into a fantasy world full of *joie de vivre*
and carefree fun. The fact that the film's magic
has endured across decades is proof of the
allure of the on-screen pairing of Fred Astaire
and Ginger Rogers and their catchy, imaginative
dance sequences. Elegant Fred and tomboyish
Ginger merged into one. "She gave him sex, he
gave her style," as colleague Katharine Hepburn
said about the most famous dance couple in
film history.

Astaire, especially, revolutionized the genre
of the musical/dance film with innovative,
quirky, and intricate choreography. His films
were lavish in costume and set. Yet, compared
to the stylized orgies of a Busby Berkeley, the
Astaire-Roger musicals were always filmed in
ordinary settings, such as hotel lobbies, parks,
or bedrooms, which became the stages for

exciting dance routines. Another completely
new approach was the treatment of the musical and song numbers, which no longer interrupted the flow of the plot in the shape of
bombastic showstoppers but were integrated
into the action and carried the plot forward.
"In *Top Hat* every song grew from the scene itself," director Mark Sandrich explained. "If
one of the songs had been cut, then the
dialogue would have had to be changed as
well." Thus, the two sing and dance through
rain and shine, or lovingly in "Cheek to
Cheek" (or accompanied by other hit melodies
by Irving Berlin), through countless mix-ups all
the way to the happy ending in a Venetian
gondola.

Pure pleasure—for the viewer. Yet, every now
and then, we should remember that all these
images, which look so light and effortless on
the screen, were the result of incredibly hard
work and endless rehearsals. *B.A.*

The quintessence of all performances by Fred Astaire and
Ginger Rogers: perfection—lightness—elegance

USA, 1936

Running time: 87 minutes
Black and white
Directed, written, produced and music by
Charlie Chaplin; *cinematographers,* Roland
H. Totheroh *and* Ira Morgan
With: Charlie Chaplin (Charlie), Paulette
Goddard (Gamine), Henry Bergman (café
owner), Allan Garcia (factory owner), Chester
Conklin (mechanic), Stanley J. Sanford
(Big Bill, worker), Stanley Blystone (Sheriff
Couler), Sam Stein (foreman)

Charles Spencer Chaplin

1889 Born on April 16 in London into a family of indigent
artists. First stage appearance at age five. At 17,
became starring comedian in a vaudeville troupe.

1913 While on a U.S. tour Chaplin was discovered by Mack
Sennett, head of Keystone Pictures, and hired for
slapstick comedies.

1914 First scripts and directing work. Developed the
character of "The Tramp."

1915 *The Tramp* became the hero of the eponymous movie
and soon a cult figure.

1919 Founded the production company United Artists with
Mary Pickford, Douglas Fairbanks, and D. W. Griffith.

1920 *The Kid,* Chaplin's first feature film, became an
international success.

1925 *The Gold Rush*

1927 *The Circus*

1928 Chaplin received an honorary Oscar at the first Oscar
Award presentation.

1931 Since adjusting to "the talkies" proved difficult for him,
Chaplin launched *City Lights* as a silent movie—and
reaped a huge success.

1936 *Modern Times*

1940 *The Great Dictator*

1943 Chaplin wedded his fourth wife, Oona O'Neill; the
relationship lasted until his death.

1947 *Monsieur Verdoux*

1952 *Limelight.* That same year Chaplin left the U.S., where
he had become a *persona non grata* due to alleged
Communist sympathies, and settled in Switzerland.

1957 In reaction to being refused entry into the U.S., he
made the satire *A King in New York.*

1966 *The Countess From Hong Kong,* his last film.

1967 Returned to the U.S. Received a second honorary Oscar.

1975 Awarded a knighthood by the Queen of England.

1977 Charles Spencer Chaplin died in his home on Lake
Geneva.

 >>> *Charlie Chaplin, The Kid,* see p. 16

Gamine (Paulette Goddard) and Charlie (Charlie Chaplin)
and their proletarian struggle for survival

This Chaplin film, created between 1932 and
1936, is one of the crown jewels in the treasure
chest of film history. Flawless and timeless,
it makes others of its kind look second-rate.
Chaplin insisted, later in his life, that he never
cared for art, only for money, a preposterous
statement that can only be taken as confir-
mation of the lonely naiveté of the genius.
Intuition and hard-won artistry combined to
create the image of a character who has become an international icon of the twentieth
century.

Modern Times describes the odyssey of the
worker through the industrial era, where his
plight is, above all, one of relentless poverty
and impoverishment. Chaplin's tour de force
as a speedy assembly line worker, a dock worker, a night watchman in a department store,
and an overworked head waiter is also a mirror
of the American dream of limitless opportunity.
Where there is work, Charlie is ready to do it,
filled with ideals of bourgeois order and clean-
liness. And although the capitalist dream pre-
dictably remains out of reach for the dispos-
sessed, the tramp is pumped up with hope to
the very end. Sisyphus keeps on kicking to his
last breath.

Two basic scenarios are played out in several
variations in this cinematic metaphor of the
century: Charlie at work and Charlie in jail.
These key scenarios embody all of the traps of
capitalism and all of the neuroses of a brutal,
profit-oriented society. Chaplin's assembly line
scene is a timeless symbol of a human being as
a robot, another cog in a machine that literally

swallows him—and that the trauma leaves
him with an nervous tick that repeats the
rhythm of the machine. Meanwhile, the social
hierarchy forces everyone to kick the one
below him while the boss controls, and constantly increases, the speed from above.
These world-famous images of the tramp at
the assembly line are tragicomical symbols of
exploitation (including self-exploitation)
and of the bourgeois longing for conformist
happiness. (When Chaplin is arrested as a
Communist because he carries a red construc-
tion site flag, the comedy of errors turns
grotesque).

Chaplin executes this proletarian struggle
for survival (in cahoots with poor orphan girl,
Paulette Goddard) with unequalled, "roller-
blading" grace. This is a film of precise acrobatic elegance—of classic pantomimes: The
underdog losing his mind at the assembly line;
an unintentional cocaine trip; dodging the bill
out of sheer hunger and desperation; the nasty
revenge of the down-trodden; and the pathetic,
everyman's vision of "home," with its white
picket fence, little wife at the stove, and clean
curtains in the windows.   *Po.*

The classic pantomime with the eternal underdog

Slapstick odyssey of the worker:
Charlie Chaplin in a mechanical world

Bringing Up Baby

USA, 1938
Running time: 94 minutes (orig. 102)
Black and white
Directed by Howard Hawks; *written by* Dudley Nichols *and* Hagar Wilde, *based on a short story by* Hagar Wilde; *cinematographer,* Russell Metty; *music by* Roy Webb; *edited by* George Hively
With: Cary Grant (David Huxley), Katharine Hepburn (Susan Vance), May Robson (Aunt Elizabeth), Charles Ruggles (Major Applegate), Walter Catlett (Constable Slocum), Barry Fitzgerald (Mr. Gogarty)

Howard Winchester Hawks

1896 Born on May 30 in Goshen, Indiana. Studied engineering in New York. Served as a pilot in the World War I, then worked as an aeronautic engineer, test pilot, and racing driver.
Decided on a movie career (first as prop man, author, editor, director's assistant, then making own short films).
1926 Feature film debut: *The Road to Glory*
In almost 45 years of directing, Hawks achieved brilliant results in nearly every genre, for instance:
1932 *Scarface* (gangster movie)
1938 *Bringing Up Baby* (screwball comedy)
1939 *Only Angels Have Wings* (action film)
1940 *His Girl Friday* (comedy)
1943 *Airforce* (war movie)
1944 *To Have And Have Not* (suspense film)
1945 *The Big Sleep* (film noire)
1948 *Red River* (western)
1959 *Rio Bravo* (western)
1966 *El Dorado* (western)
1970 *Rio Lobo* was Hawks' farewell to filmmaking.
1974 Awarded honorary Oscar for his lifetime achievement.
1977 Howard Hawks died at age 81 in Palm Springs, California.

"Now it isn't that I don't like you, Susan, because, after all, in moments of quiet, I'm strangely drawn toward you, but—well, there haven't been any quiet moments."
David Huxley (Cary Grant)

In the style of the period: the American poster in 1938

In 1966, the German film-going public eagerly anticipated the comedy event of the century: a German version of a US production with the silly title *Leoparden küsst man nicht*—or *Don't Kiss the Leopard*. Afterwards, everyone swore that they had never laughed so hard. One of the most famous comedies in the history of film finally made its debut on German screens after a delay of nearly thirty years.

Howard Hawks's *Bringing Up Baby*, from 1938, has a crazy plot and is fast-paced and spiked with witty dialogues. In short, it is a classic screwball comedy. The madcap and completely unrealistic plot is carried out by the brilliant duo of Cary Grant and Katharine Hepburn—who made her debut as a comedienne with this film, finally overcoming her reputation in Hollywood as "box office poison." As the eccentric, capricious heiress, Susan (accompanied by her tame leopard cub and George, the terrier), she steps into the life of palaeontologist David Huxley, whose quiet days—and career as a museum scientist—are henceforth over.

The shy, inhibited professor is approaching the crowning moment of his life's work. He is about to receive a million dollars for his museum, but only if he can relocate a missing bone to complete the reconstruction of a

dinosaur. Not surprisingly, George, the terrier, has stolen the bone, leaving the professor to stumble from one mishap to another. Susan wants to help him relocate the bone, but in the process, Huxley loses his bride, windows are broken, clothes are torn, chickens and fire hydrants cause more confusion, and an eccentric aunt (May Robson) and pompous big game hunter (Charles Ruggles) appear on the scene. Amidst all this, Susan revels in the hopeless chaos she has created.

In one highlight, everyone ends up in the local jail, including the professor who has brought along Susan's lost, tame leopard on a leash—only it isn't "Baby" who's tagging along but a murderous beast escaped from the circus. Finally, Susan shows up at the museum with the lost dinosaur bone. And, although the gigantic dinosaur skeleton collapses when she tries to hand over the last missing piece, nothing can stand in the way of a happy ending: a glorious victory of exuberant *joie de vivre* over sterile, stuffy science. This crazy and enchanting madcap movie, by director Howard Hawks, not only an accomplished comedian but also a brilliant director of Westerns and mysteries, was admired and emulated by his colleagues and successors. Peter Bogdanovich's comedy of errors, *What's Up, Doc?*, is unthinkable without the Hawks predecessor.   *B.A.*

Still a little unsure about how to deal with spotted domestic animals: Cary Grant as David Huxley with "Baby" and Susan (Katharine Hepburn)

Cranky professor meets eccentric, young woman
(Katharine Hepburn, Cary Grant)

USA, 1939
Running time: 230 minutes
Color
Directed by Victor Fleming; *written by* Sidney
Howard, *based on the novel of the same name
by* Margaret Mitchell; *cinematographers,* Ernest
Haller *and* Ray Rennahan; *music by* Max
Steiner; *edited by* Hal C. Kern *and* James
E. Newcom
With: Vivien Leigh (Scarlett O'Hara), Clark
Gable (Rhett Butler), Olivia de Havilland
(Melanie Hamilton), Leslie Howard (Ashley
Wilkes), Thomas Mitchell (Gerald O'Hara),
Hattie McDaniel (Mammy)

Victor Fleming

1883 Born on February 23 in Pasadena, California.
1910 Entered moviemaking as a cameraman for D.W. Griffith,
      Douglas Fairbanks, and others.
      Photographer for the Secret Service during World
      War I. After the war, Fleming did a photo-documentary
      of President Wilson's European trip.
1919 Returned to Hollywood.
1920 Successful directing debut with the Fairbanks adventure
      film, *The Mollycoddle.*
1929 *The Virginian*
1933 *Bombshell* (with Jean Harlow)
1934 *Treasure Island*
1937 *Captains Courageous*
1939 Fleming's halcyon year as director of two opulent
      productions, *The Wizard of Oz* and *Gone With the Wind.*
1940 *Dr. Jekyll and Mr. Hyde*
1948 His final work, *Joan of Arc,* with Ingrid Bergman in the
      starring role.
1949 Victor Fleming died on January 6 in Arizona.

Despite a huge promotional campaign, the sequel to *Gone
with the Wind,* as a sentimental TV soap opera, was a flop.
In the leading roles, Joanne Whalley-Kilmer and Timothy
Dalton fell far short of their predecessors.

Hollywood's romantic picture of the American South:
Vivien Leigh as Scarlett

Gone with the Wind was enthusiastically received
at its world premiere on December 15, 1939
in Atlanta, Georgia. Today, its fame remains undiminished. The movie was a "dream factory"
product of gloss and glamour, a Hollywood
epic of superlatives on an unprecedented scale.
The story behind the making of the film is
almost as fascinating and expansive as the
Southern melodrama itself.

The entire enterprise can be attributed to
producer David O. Selznick, who acquired the
film rights to Margaret Mitchell's international
bestseller, *Gone with the Wind*, when it was
published in 1936. He paid 50,000 dollars for
the material—a record sum at the time—and
announced that he would transform the book
into the "greatest film of all times."

Selznick was obsessive and pedantic about
every detail. He wrote thousands of exacting
memos and went through scores of scriptwriters
and directors, including real professionals like
George Cukor, before finally settling on Victor
Fleming. Even the casting search for the film's
ravishing heroine was a huge event. Well-
known stars, from Katharine Hepburn to Lana
Turner to Bette Davis, auditioned for the role,
as did 1,400 aspiring hopefuls. The casting
hysteria reached a crescendo and shooting had

already begun when the virtually unknown
British actress Vivien Leigh was chosen as
Scarlett O'Hara. On the other hand, the man
who would play the debonair and brazen
Rhett Butler had been a foregone conclusion:
Clark Gable was the only actor considered.

The story covers twelve years in the life
of Scarlett O'Hara, a capricious and spoiled
southern belle. The narrative weaves it way
through plantation life in the Old South,
the Civil War (1861–65), and the period of
Reconstruction, during which the former glory
of plantation society finally fades. The historic
events are presented as a backdrop to the romantic life of Scarlett, a headstrong woman
who pursues her lifelong love, plantation owner
Ashley (Leslie Howard), despite his marriage to
Melanie (Olivia de Havilland) and in spite of
the romantic declaratons of daredevil, Rhett.

Gone with the Wind is great cinema, Hollywood at its best. The epic was praised as "the
greatest and most successful film of all times"
and received ten Oscars, including a surprise
award to Hattie McDaniel, the first black
actress to receive one of the golden statues.
Sadly, Clark Gable was left empty-handed
for the crowning performance of his career.

P.W.E.

Poster (USA), 1939

The dream couple: Rhett and Scarlett
(Clark Gable and Vivian Leigh)

Atlanta in flames

Ninotchka

USA, 1939

Running time: 108 minutes (orig. 110)
Black and white
Directed by Ernst Lubitsch; *written by* Charles
Brackett, Billy Wilder, *and* Walter Reisch,
based on an idea by Melchior Lengyel; *cinemato-
grapher,* William Daniels; *music by* Werner R.
Heymann; *edited by* Gene Ruggiero
With: Greta Garbo (Ninotchka), Melvyn
Douglas (Count Léon d'Algout), Sig Rumann
(Iranoff), Alexander Granach (Kopalski),
Felix Bressart (Bulianoff), Bela Lugosi
(Detective Superintendent Razinin), Ina
Claire (Countess Swana)

Ernst Lubitsch

1892 Born on January 28 in Berlin.
1911 Became an actor with the Max Reinhardt Ensemble at
the Deutsches Theater. In parallel with theater work,
was active in motion pictures, initially as an actor and
soon as author and director.
1918 Made a name for himself with *Gypsy Blood* and
The Eyes of the Mummy.
1919 Great breakthrough with *Passion* and *The Oyster Princess*
1923 Lubitsch received a Hollywood contract and, from then
on, worked with extraordinary success in the U.S.
1924 *Forbidden Paradise*
1932 *Trouble in Paradise*
1933 *Design for Living*
1934 *The Merry Widow* (one of his best-known film operettas)
1937 *Angel* (with Marlene Dietrich)
1938 *Bluebeard's Eighth Wife.* Lubitsch was accepted into the
French Legion of Honor.
1939 *Ninotchka*
1942 *To Be or Not to Be*
1946 Honorary Oscar
1947 Ernst Lubitsch died of a heart seizure during the filming
of *The Lady in Ermine* (which was finished by Otto
Preminger).

Poster (USA), 1939

"Garbo appears in her first comedy here and could have
no better director than the inimitable Lubitsch who presented a mirthful, delightful lark. ... Garbo is magnificent,
and so is the film."
The Motion Picture Guide

>>> Ernst Lubitsch, *To Be or Not To Be,* see p. 44

Greta Garbo as the faithful Communist, Ninotchka, and Bela Lugosi as Razinin

At the outbreak of the war, Americans wanted nothing to do with the Bolsheviks and, therefore, also with this film. When the war was over, protests arose from the Soviets, who felt discriminated against by the story. Unwittingly, Ernst Lubitsch had fallen between two fronts, and his film had become a political hot potato. Still, *Ninotchka* remains his most popular work, undiminished by the passage of time. With time, the famous and indefinable Lubitsch touch seems all the more light, elegant, and ironic—an inimitable ability to wrap inanities in a package of intelligence. His method of revealing all by insinuation even prompted colleague and admirer, François Truffaut, to remark that: "In the Lubitsch Emmenthal every hole is a stroke of genius."

In addition to his "touch," Lubitsch held another trump card: Ninotchka was the first comedy character played by remote screen diva, Greta Garbo. "Garbo laughs!" MGM's banner boasted above the studio star's smiling face. And laugh she does. At first, bonvivant French count Léon (Melvyn Douglas) fails in his attempt to coax a smile from the beautiful commissar, but when he falls off his chair in his frustration, her laughter rings out.

The elegant Parisian does more than make her laugh. He converts the commissar to western decadence—just as he had done with three Soviet functionaries sent to sell Countess Swana's jewels (Ina Claire) for the good of their country. The countess happens to be Léon's lover, and this hardly makes things

any easier. Since the three functionaries have slipped into a life of leisure and luxury, the dedicated, strict, and tough Ninotchka is dispatched to bring them back into line—and promptly falls in love with Léon herself. Nevertheless, she returns to Moscow with the jewels and the three functionaries. Later she is sent out once more, again on the trail of the delinquent trio. She travels to Constantinople, where Léon—and a happy ending—await her far from Moscow, Paris, or ideologies.

Although Lubitsch was adept at treating political ideologies with aloof elegance, he could hardly have been unaware of the seriousness of the situation. The native Berliner, who worked in Hollywood from 1922 on, cast German emigrants Sig Rumann, Felix Bressart and Alexander Granach as the three functionaries. The script was brilliant, full of sparkling dialogues on which Billy Wilder had collaborated. None of the sequels inspired by *Ninotchka* (*Comrade X*, 1940, *The Iron Petticoat*, 1956, and the musical *Silk Stockings*, 1957, with Cyd Charisse and Fred Astaire) can compete with the inspired and intelligent original. *B.A.*

"Garbo laughs!" Ninotchka (Greta Garbo) with (from left to right) Alexander Granach,
Felix Bressart, and Sig Rumann

Sparkling dialogue: Greta Garbo and Melvyn Douglas as Count Léon

Citizen Kane

USA, 1941
Running time: 117 minutes
Black and white
Directed by Orson Welles; *written by* Herman
Mankiewicz *and* Orson Welles; *cinematographer,*
Gregg Toland; *music by* Bernard Herrmann;
edited by Robert Wise *and* Mark Robson
With: Orson Welles (Charles Foster Kane),
Harry Shannon (Kane's father), Agnes
Moorehead (Kane's mother), Joseph Cotten
(Jed Leland), George Coulouris (Thatcher),
Dorothy Comingore (Susan Alexander),
Everett Sloane (Mr. Bernstein), Ray Collins
("Big Jim" Gettys), Paul Stewart (Raymond),
Alan Ladd (reporter)

Orson Welles

1915 Born on May 6 as the son of a prosperous inventor and a concert pianist in Kenosha, Wisconsin. Lost his parents at an early age.

1931 Went to Ireland. Bluffed his way into being accepted as an actor by a Dublin theater.

1934 First Broadway acting appearance, followed by acclaimed theater productions. Radio broadcasting activity.

1938 The radio play adaptation, *The War of the Worlds* (based on the H.G. Wells story), was so realistic that people believed a Martian invasion had actually taken place, and a widespread panic ensued.

1941 *Citizen Kane,* Welles' first work and a cinematic masterpiece

1941/1942 *The Magnificent Ambersons*

1946 *The Stranger*

1948 *The Lady From Shanghai* (with then-wife, Rita Hayworth), *Macbeth.* Enervated by working conditions in the U.S., Welles went to Europe for several years. He frequently took on acting roles (partly to finance his own productions), one of the most outstanding of which was his characterization of

1949 Harry Lime in *The Third Man.*

1949–52 *Othello* (Golden Palm, Cannes)

1955 *Mr. Arkadin/Confidential Report*

1957 *Touch of Evil* (made during a temporary return to the U.S.)

1962 *The Trial*

1965 *Chimes at Midnight/Falstaff*

1970 Honorary Oscar for his contributions to motion pictures

1972 "Life Achievement Award" of the American Film Institute

1973 With *F for Fake,* ended his directing—but not acting—activity
In the late 1970s, returned to the U.S.

1985 Orson Welles died on October 10.

> "Not that Charley Kane was ever brutal; he just did brutal things. Maybe I wasn't his friend, but if I wasn't, he never had one...."
> (Joseph Cotten, in his role as Leland)

>>> Orson Welles, *The Third Man,* see p. 52

His word is law: Kane (Orson Welles; center) with Jed Leland (Joseph Cotten) and Bernstein (Everett Sloane)

Xanadu is the name of an extravagant mansion in Florida, a monumental castle built to satisfy the insatiable ego of a man whose profitable goldmine earned him a life of wealth and influence. This is the domain of Charles Foster Kane, a powerful "rags to riches figure," driven by the desire to set something in motion, to create something, and to be loved.

Thirty-seven radio stations and newspapers in the United States spread Kane's message. A tycoon whose word is law, Kane has two failed marriages behind him and faces death alone. When he does die, he utters a single, cryptic word: rosebud. Thus, ends the life of a newspaper man "who wanted to make history."

What the word signified—the name of Kane's childhood sled—is revealed at the very end of this grandiose puzzle, but viewers in 1940 would have recognized early on who Kane represented. The obvious parallels between Welles' broken hero and American media mogul, Willam Randolph Hearst, sparked an anti-*Citizen Kane* campaign in all of Hearst's publications that damaged ticket sales. Welles did receive an Oscar for best script, perhaps the Academy's way of protesting Hearst's attacks; however, in retrospect, it is difficult to understand why the film received only one award.

Kane, a Croesus without a trace of the erotic, wears the grimace of hate better than any other despot of the black-and-white genre. He is interpreted by Orson Welles in nuanced and vivid scenes that credibly depict his tormented, egomaniacal inner life ("He never believed in anything other than Charly Kane") and his inability to realize political ambitions. Revealing close-ups, artfully arranged details, and monumental, wide-angle shots graphically illustrate each situation. Dialogues etch themselves into our minds: "If the headline is big enough, it makes the news big enough," says Kane.

When Orson Welles made his debut as a director and actor—he gave a powerful and wonderfully wicked performance in the title role—he was only twenty-five years old. From the great tradition of the American 1940s, he extrapolated a masterpiece in black and white that continues to fascinate viewers today. *Time* magazine proclaimed the dark tale the best film of the century and "a tragicomic vision of media power". The somber epic represents an era in which artistic cinema with a political accent could produce the likes of Orson Welles.

P.W.E.

The publisher and despot King Kane with his first wife, Emily (Ruth Warrick)

Arsenic and Old Lace

USA, 1941
Running time: 115 minutes
Black and white
Directed by Frank Capra; *written by* Julius J.
and Philip G. Epstein, *based on the play of
the same name by* Joseph Kesselring; *cine-
matographer,* Sol Polito; *music by* Max Steiner;
edited by Daniel Mandell
With: Cary Grant (Mortimer Brewster),
Priscilla Lane (Elaine Harper), Josephine
Hull (Abby Brewster), Jean Adair (Martha
Brewster), Raymond Massey (Jonathan
Brewster), John Alexander (Teddy Brewster),
Peter Lorre (Dr. Einstein), Jack Carson (O'Hara),
Edward Everett Horton (Mr. Witherspoon)

Frank Capra

1897 Born on May 19 in Palermo. When Frank was six,
his family emigrated to Los Angeles. Attended the
California Institute of Technology. Beginning in 1922,
Capra attempted to carve out a niche for himself in
motion pictures (among other things as a gag writer
and director for the comedian Harry Langdon).

1934 First big success: *It Happened One Night* won the five
most important Oscars. There followed a series of
social comedies:

1936 *Mr. Deeds Goes to Town*

1939 *Mr. Smith Goes to Washington*

1941 *Meet John Doe* and

1947 the Christmas story *It's a Wonderful Life*

1941 Capra's last great commercial success was the black
comedy *Arsenic and Old Lace* (premiered in 1944)

1961 After *Pocketful of Miracles* Capra retired from
moviemaking.

1982 Received the 'Life Achievement Award' of the American
Film Institute

1991 Frank Capra died in La Quinta, California.

Reverend Harper: "Have you ever tried to persuade [your
nephew] that he wasn't Teddy Roosevelt?"
Abby Brewster: "Oh, no."
Martha Brewster: "Oh, he's so happy being Teddy
Roosevelt."

Abby and Martha (Josephine Hull and Jean Adair) have only the best intentions for Mr. Witherspoon (Edward Everett Horton)

"I was doubled over in laughter," enthused Ida
Lupino of the *Saturday Evening Post*, summing
up what made Frank Capra's *Arsenic and Old
Lace* so successful. It's simply hilariously funny.
Everything works in the genial farce based on
Joseph Kesselring's stage play of the same name,
from the dark and morbid humor of the story
to the timing and the cast. Capra did the right
thing by taking on most of the original cast
of the successful Broadway production, adding
a leading star for box office allure. The star
was Cary Grant, whom Capra described as
"Hollywood's greatest farceur," which is why
he was able to convince Warner Brothers to
pay the required 100,000 dollars for the star.

Grant plays theater critic Mortimer Brewster
who is forced to realize that his dear little aunts
are sending aged gentlemen into the great beyond by means of poisoned elderberry wine—
an act of pure compassion, as they put it. In
his role as the overwhelmed and befuddled
nephew, torn between shock and love for his
aunts, the experienced comedian pulls out all
the stops; he does double takes, pulls faces,
chuckles, gurgles, squeals, and stutters. What
might seem embarrassing or exaggerated in
different circumstances fits the bill perfectly
in this instance. The scene in which Grant
discovers a corpse in the window seat is unforgettable. He tries, in vain, to explain to
his endearing aunts (Josephine Hull and Jean
Adair) why it simply isn't right to kill people:
"It's not only against the law. It's just not
done. At first it's only a bad habit, but then
it becomes a vice."

Capra shot the film in 1941 in a mere
four weeks because the two lead actresses were
granted only four weeks' holiday from the
Broadway show. Another stipulation was that
the film be released into the cinemas only
after the Broadway show had closed. When
the screen adaptation finally opened on
September 23, 1944, the success was overwhelming. Capra was already Hollywood's best-
paid director and one of its most celebrated.
His comedy *It Happened One Night* (1934) with
Claudette Colbert and Clark Gable had won
in the top five Oscar categories, box office hits
such as *Mr. Deeds Goes to Town* (1936) and
Mr. Smith Goes to Washington (1939) followed.

Things become precarious for Cary Grant (center),
Peter Lorre (right), and Raymond Massey (with rope)

A wedding that almost goes wrong: New York theater critic, Mortimer Brewster (Cary Grant), wants to marry Elaine Harper (Priscilla Lane) as inconspicuously as possible

While these films extolled the good in man —Capra aptly captured the American spirit of the 1930s and 1940s—*Arsenic and Old Lace* inspired the exact opposite. With murdering aunts, a crazy mass murderer, and a sadistic, drunken doctor (frighteningly well played by Peter Lorre), Capra toys with the contrast between middle-class comfort and raw horror, achieving the most wonderful effect. This is one of many reasons why the macabre comedy has lost none of its spunk over the years.   *S.Al.*

Casablanca

USA, 1942

Running time: 102 (or 82) minutes
Black and white
Directed by Michael Curtiz; *written by* Philip
G. Epstein, Howard Koch *and* Julius J. Epstein,
based on the play Everybody Comes to Rick's
by Murray Burnett *and* Joan Alison; *cinematographer,* Arthur Edeson; *music by* Max Steiner;
edited by Owen Marks
With: Humphrey Bogart (Richard "Rick"
Blaine), Ingrid Bergman (Ilsa Lund), Paul
Henreid (Victor Laszlo), Claude Rains
(Captain Louis Renault), Peter Lorre (Ugarte),
Conrad Veidt (Major Strasser), Sydney
Greenstreet (Señor Ferrari)

Michael Curtiz

1888 Born as Miháli Kertész on December 24 in Budapest.
1913 After a six-month internship at the Nordisk Studios in Copenhagen, returned to Budapest and made nearly 40 films (almost all of which have been lost).
1919 When a soviet republic was declared in Hungary, he fled the country and began directing films in Austria and Germany, such as:
1924 the monumental opus, *Moon of Israel.* America began to take notice.
1926 Brought to Hollywood by Warner Brothers. Over the next decades, Curtiz would make more than 100 movies for this studio, including the world-renowned Errol Flynn adventures
1935 *Captain Blood*
1938 *The Adventures of Robin Hood*
1940 *The Sea Hawk*
1942 His masterpiece, *Casablanca*
1945 *Mildred Pierce*
1949 *Flamingo Road*
1954 Curtiz left Warner Brothers and began to work for other studios, directing such films as:
1955 *We're No Angels*
1961 *The Comancheros* (his final film).
1962 Michael Curtiz died on April 11 in Hollywood.

"Ilsa, I'm no good at being noble, but it doesn't take much to see that the problems of three little people don't amount to a hill of beans in this crazy world." (Rick to Ilsa)

Memorable scenes and unforgettable lines: "If that plane leaves the ground and you are not with him, you will regret it. Maybe not today, and maybe not tomorrow, but soon and for the rest of your life."

What a film! What a piece of extravagant, old-fashioned, black-and-white magic from the dream factory! Even today, viewers are deeply moved by scenes in *Casablanca* that tug at their heartstrings with near magical power. Directed by Michael Curtiz and produced in the United States in 1942 by Hal Wallis—under almost amateurish conditions—the 102-minute film revolves around "love" on a grand scale. It is also a film about solidarity within a chaotic struggle for political power. These combined themes are what have made *Casablanca* the ultimate cult movie.

In the film, screen idols Ingrid Bergman and Humphrey Bogart are caught up in a sentimental plot that owes its magnetism more to interpersonal relationships than to factual events. It isn't necessary for viewers to know or even acknowledge the very real, French colonial background of the melodrama. (In fact, the entire film was shot on studio sets.) *Casablanca* can be enjoyed apolitically, as a nostalgic, black-and-white love story. The melancholic looks and gestures grip viewers more than those in any other movie of the time, making it easy to admire this classic masterpiece of modern filmmaking for its amorous, heroic, and poetic elements alone. Perhaps this is why the film's score, by Max Steiner, has become a trademark, especially the piano solo "As Time Goes By" performed by Dooley. Many fans of *Casablanca* also love the film's deceptively simple dialogue, written by Julius J. Epstein, Philip G. Epstein, and Howard Koch and based on the play *Everybody Comes to Rick's* by Burnett/Alison. Many exchanges are as witty as they are ironic:
Renault: "And what in heaven's name brought you to Casablanca?"
Rick: "My health. I came to Casablanca for the waters."
Renault: "What waters? We're in the desert."
Rick: "I was misinformed...."

Viewers today may not realize that Bogart was second in line, after Ronald Reagan, to play Rick. However, had Reagan played the part, as originally intended, the melodramatic, political romance would never have become such an uninhibited celebration of mysterious "manliness."

"I have only one goal," wrote Curtiz in 1941 about his work in progress, "to make the film to the best of my ability so that it will be worth its ticket...." The director could hardly have known that there was no cause for worry. As soon as the lights came up after the first screening on September 22, 1942, the word was out: "We've produced a hit!" The following

Poster (France), 1942

The love story between Rick (Humphrey Bogart) and Ilsa (Ingrid Bergmann) ends abruptly

day a telegram reached the studio's New York sales department: "Casablanca: truly wonderful…brilliant film…stunning cinematography …Certain, that this will be one of the hottest box office hits of the past two or three years… Rest assured: this film is top-notch…."

The première took place in New York in 1942, eighteen days after the Allies landed in Casablanca. The cinema release in January 1943 coincided with the Casablanca conference of Anglo-American heads of state. The reaction in Germany after the television broadcast of the unedited version in 1973 was equally euphoric: "Noble, surreal emotions give this film a glow that surpasses any reality and is nowhere more uplifting or more catching than in a cinema…."

P.W.E.

To Be or Not To Be

USA, 1942

Running time: 98 minutes
Black and white
Directed by Ernst Lubitsch; *written by* Edwin
Justus Mayer, *based on a story by* Ernst Lubitsch
and Melchior Lengyel; *cinematographer,*
Rudolph Maté; *music by* Miklós Rózsa *and*
Werner R. Heymann; *edited by* Dorothy
Spencer
With: Carole Lombard (Maria Tura), Jack
Benny (Joseph Tura), Robert Stack (Stanislav
Sobinski), Stanley Ridges (Professor Siletsky,
a spy), Felix Bressart (Greenberg), Tom Dugan
(Hitler)

Careful not to make the wrong move: Carole Lombard and Jack Benny in a perilous situation

A theatrical affair: Carole Lombard as Maria Tura

Horror was never so clever as in Ernst Lubitsch's caustic satire, *To Be or Not to Be.* In its time, however, Lubitsch's juxtaposition of comedy with horror was met with incomprehension. Shot in late 1941, the film is set in Warsaw of 1939. At the time of its première in March 1942, America had been in World War II for three months, thus its public, not to mention its critics, wasn't prepared to laugh about Hitler or the Nazis. Lubitsch was lambasted for trivializing the Nazi threat to the point of tastelessness. Thus, twenty years passed before this masterpiece—the only major anti-Hitler movie of the period, aside from Charlie Chaplin's *The Great Dictator*—was finally appreciated for what it is.

Lubitsch's film is literally about being and not being, about the vanity of actors, and about Nazis who behave like play-actors. The central character is actor Joseph Tura (Jack Benny), who delivers the famous monologue "To Be or Not to Be" in his role as Hamlet. Each time he gives the speech, a gentleman in the audience leaves the theater. Tura has no idea that this man is having an affair with his actress wife Maria (Carole Lombard), who outshines her husband on and off stage. When German troops march into Poland, the actors spring into action to prevent an informer from handing a list of Polish resistance fighters to the Nazis. Their theater is transformed into a pseudo Gestapo headquarters, where they stage an anti-Nazi play outfitted in SS uniforms. The slapstick farce—teeming with secret agents, Gestapo chiefs, and several *Führers*—turns into a game of life and death that ends with the entire troupe escaping to England. Yet, even though

Tura now plays Hamlet in Shakespeare's homeland, each time he throws himself into the famous monologue, the gentleman leaves the theater.

In the film, a Nazi officer remarks that what Tura "did to Shakespeare, we are now doing to Poland!" This joke, more than any other aspect of the film, prompted a storm of protest, even among Lubitsch's friends. In his own defense, Lubitsch responded: "What I attacked in this movie were the Nazis and their ridiculous ideology. I also sent up the attitude of actors, who always remain actors even in the most dangerous situations and, in my view, that is a realistic observation."   *B.A.*

Joseph Tura:

"Now listen, you. First you walk out on my soliloguy, and then you walk into my slippers. And now you question my patriotism. I'm a good Pole—I love my country and I love my slippers!"

>>> Ernst Lubitsch, *Ninotchka,* and Biography,
see p. 36

"To be or not to be"—Jack Benny as Hamlet is highly irritated when Sobinski (Robert Stack, left) leaves the theater

Tom Dugan as Hitler and his actor colleagues working on a comedy to discredit the Nazis

For Whom the Bell Tolls

USA, 1943

Running time: 130 minutes (orig. 170)
Directed by Sam Wood; *written by* Dudley
Nichols, *based on the novel by* Ernest
Hemingway; *cinematographer,* Ray Rennahan;
music by Victor Young; *edited by* Sherman
Todd, John F. Link
With: Gary Cooper (Robert Jordan), Ingrid
Bergman (Maria), Vladimir Sokoloff (Anselmo),
Arturo de Cordova (Agustin), Akim Tamiroff
(Pablo), Joseph Calleia (El Sordo), Feodor
Chaliapin (Kaschkin)

Sam Wood

1883 Born on July 18 as Samuel Grosvenor Wood in
Philadelphia. Real estate agent; entered the film
business in 1908, initially as an actor, then, in 1915,
became an assistant to director C.B. DeMille.
1920 Began his own directing
1933 *Hold Your Man*
1937 *A Day at the Races*
1940 *Our Little Town*
1943 *For Whom the Bell Tolls*
1945 *Saratoga Trunk*
1949 *Ambush,* his last film; that September, Sam Wood died
in Hollywood.

Maria (Ingrid Bergman)

"...it is produced as magnificently as any film has ever been.
Photographed largely in the High Sierras in Technicolor that
is breathtakingly fine, it has the hard texture of granite, the
rough and vivid colors of all outdoors...some of the close
shots of the characters have the brilliance of Goya paintings.
It's a shame, to put it bluntly, that in it art is so long and
life so short." **The New York Times,** July 15, 1943

46 | 47

Eternity in one brief moment: Gary Cooper as Jordan and Ingrid Bergmann as Maria

opposite page:
Jordan, mortally wounded,
secures the withdrawal of his
comrades (Katina Paxinou and
Arturo de Cordova) with
Maria (Ingrid Bergman)

For the author, the two stars were ideally cast.
Even as he wrote *For Whom the Bell Tolls,*
Ernest Hemingway pictured beautiful Ingrid
Bergman in the role of Maria and Gary Cooper
the perfect leading man. After Hemingway had
seen the film he complimented Cooper: "You
played Robert Jordan exactly as I imagined
him, tough and with an iron will. Thank you!"
Hemingway's great novel about the Spanish
civil war appeared in 1940 and contained
many of the author's personal experiences.
Paramount immediately snatched up the film
rights for a record sum of 150,000 dollars. But
this quick action was followed by one delay
after another, to the benefit of the film as it
turned out. Instead of Cecil B. de Mille, the
master of the melodrama who would have
treated this material in his usual manner, prag-
matic and experienced Sam Wood took over
directing. Wood was already shooting the outdoor scenes in the Sierra Nevada Mountains,
when Vera Zorina, who had been retained by
the studio for the leading role, was fired and
replaced by Ingrid Bergman.

With the dream couple complete, one of
the most beautiful love stories in film is told
against the background of the Spanish civil war.
Yet, the historic dimension remains strangely
out of focus, the word "fascist," for example,
is mentioned only once, and Franco not at all.
While critics have attacked this suppression

of the political context, it allows the melodramatic love story to unfold all the more fully.

American Robert Jordan is fighting on the
side of the Republicans in Spain. He is dispatched to blow up a bridge with the help of
a guerrilla group among whom he meets
Maria, a girl who was raped by fascists after
they had murdered her parents.

Robert and Maria fall deeply in love. Robert
resists at first, cautioned perhaps by his fear
that he may not survive the attack on the
bridge. Despite being aware that the struggle
for freedom may well be in vain, he refuses to
give up. Robert Jordan is not in any way weak-
willed. Instead, he tries to pack a life's worth of
experience into the three days remaining to
him and Maria. We see their love blossom in
tender and touching scenes, such as when she
asks him if noses don't get in the way when
kissing, and in the famous sleeping bag scene
under the stars. Both discover eternity in the
moment. Then Robert blows up the bridge.
Mortally wounded, he ensures the escape of
his comrades and Maria who is reluctant to
leave.

Since the war, Wood's sweeping 170-minute
epic has more often than not been screened in
heavily cut versions.   *B.A.*

Children of Paradise

Les Enfants du Paradis
France, 1943–45

Running time: 190 minutes
Black and white
Directed by Marcel Carné; *written by* Jacques
Prévert; *cinematographer,* Roger Hubert; *music
by* Maurice Thiriet, Joseph Kosma, Georges
Mouqué; *edited by* Henri Rust, Madeleine
Bonin
With: Arletty (Garance), Jean-Louis Barrault
(Baptiste), Pierre Brasseur (Frédéric), Maria
Casarès (Natalie), Marcel Herrand (Lacenaire),
Louis Salou (The Count), Pierre Renoir (shop
owner), Jane Marken (Madame Hermine)

Marcel Carné

1909 Born in Paris on August 18 as the son of a cabinet-
maker. After an apprenticeship with his father, became
an insurance agent and took courses in cinema
technique.
1928–36 Assistant to directors such as René Clair and
Jacques Feyder. Worked part time as a film critic.
1936 Film debut with *Jenny,* marking the beginning of a
longtime collaboration with poet and scriptwriter
Jacques Prévert. There followed such films as:
1938 *Port of Shadows* (with Jean Gabin), *Hôtel du Nord*
1942 *The Devil's Envoys*
1943–45 *Children of Paradise*
After 1945, Carné was unable to match his prewar
success, even though he continued to make films into
the 1970s.
1953 *The Adulteress*
1954 *L'Air de Paris* (with Jean Gabin)
1958 *The Cheaters*
1995 Awarded the European Film Prize, the Felix
1996 Marcel Carné died at age 87.

The first poster issued in France, 1945

With masterpieces, such as *Port of Shadows* (1938), *Hôtel
du Nord* (1938), and *Daybreak* (1939), Carné is considered
one of the main representatives of "poetic realism" in France
during the 1930s. His movies, which often portray the lives of
common people, are pervaded by pessimism and fatalism.

The audience in the "Funambules" theater

The première of *Children of Paradise*, on March
9, 1945 in liberated Paris, showcased cinema
as *gesamtkunstwerk*. The film, which took two
years to complete under appalling conditions,
represented the best of French cinema, proof
that the country's film industry had survived
the years of war and occupation.

Children of Paradise is an art film in the best
tradition of the "actors' cinema." It is also an
inspired creation by longtime creative duo
Marcel Carné (director) and Jacques Prévert
(scriptwriter). Finally, as a three-hour long
cinematic homage to the great literary epics
of the nineteenth century, it is the cinematic
equivalent of and successor to Dumas, Balzac,
and Hugo.

Carné's film brings to life Shakespeare's
credo that "All the world is a stage." It takes
place in early nineteenth-century Paris, where
mimes, crooks, thieves, murderers, and lovers
live their lives in the "Funambules," a cabaret
on the Boulevard of Crime, as if they were
characters in a great epic. Actress
Natalie loves Baptiste, an intro-
verted mime who only has eyes
for the beautiful Garance, whom
he admires with ardent yet unrequited passion. Garance, on the
other hand, is a child of the
streets who freely bestows her
favours on Lacenaire, an elo-
quent crook, Frédéric, a passionate but unstable actor, and
Count de Montray, her noble
protector.

The roles in this panoramic
vision of the *condition humaine*
are clearly defined. People love
(tragically), desire (in vain), and
plot (successfully). The inevitable
denouement is murder. Each

A passionate appeal: the daydreamer and
melancholy pantomime, Baptiste

character fulfills a role that is immediately understood by the viewer. As a result, a character
may disappear from the screen for half an
hour and then fit into the story again, seamlessly. So when the camera slowly pans towards Baptiste and zooms in on his eyes, we
immediately read their message: love is tragic.

The most wonderful aspect of this film is
its complicity with the audience: *we* are the
children of paradise. The audience in the top
rows of the "Funambules" watches the same
story unfold at four *sous* a ticket. Whenever
the emotional melodrama threatens to flip into
tragedy, the ribald and sensual cabaret show
helps to lift it above cliché. The film is a carnival
of vanities and jealousies that captivates our
hearts, since even the acts of common criminals
are motivated by great emotions. All of the
characters speak of love; all evoke the power
of passion. Even so, the greatest moments in
Children of Paradise occur when the slick dialogue stops and the film reverts to the silent
movie use of pantomime. Then we see in
Baptiste's eyes the eternal story of love for
whose sake the cinema was born.   *K.D.*

Marcel Herrand as the intellectual anarchist, Lacenaire,
Arletty as the beautiful femme fatale, Garance, and Jean-Louis
Barrault as the effusive Baptiste

Gilda

USA, 1946
Running time: 110 minutes
Black and white
Directed by Charles Vidor; *written by* Marion
Parsonnet, *based on a story by* E. A. Ellington;
cinematographers, Rudolph Maté *and* Marlin
Skiles; *music by* Morris W. Stoloff; *edited by*
Charles Nelson
With: Rita Hayworth (Gilda), Glenn Ford
(Johnny Farrell), George Macready (Ballin
Mundson), Joseph Calleia (Obregon), Steven
Geray (Uncle Pio), Joseph Sawyer (Casey),
Gerald Mohr (Capt. Delgado), Robert Scott
(Gabe Evans)

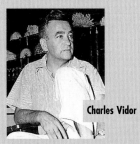

Charles Vidor

1900 Born on July 27 in Budapest as Károly Vidor. After the
First World War, began his motion picture career in
Berlin with Ufa, where he became an assistant director.
1924 Went to the U.S., initially as a Wagner singer, but
found the attraction of Hollywood irresistible.
Directing debut with *The Mask of Fu Manchu* (for which
he received no screen credits).
1937 *The Great Gambini*
1943 *The Desperadoes*
Directed two of his best films with Rita Hayworth:
1944 *Cover Girl* and
1946 *Gilda*
1951 *Thunder in the East*
1954 *Rhapsody*
1956 *The Swan*
1957 *A Farewell to Arms*
1959 During the filming of outdoor scenes for the Liszt
biography, *Song Without End*, Charles Vidor died on
June 4 in Vienna; the film was completed by George
Cukor.

The lascivious diva: Rita Hayworth

"I never really thought of myself as a sex symbol—more
as a comedian who could dance."
Rita Hayworth

She slaps him, he slaps her: Gilda (Rita Hayworth) and Johnny (Glenn Ford)

It is the most famous and seductive striptease
in film history. To the tune of "Put the Blame
on Mame," Rita Hayworth sensuously slides
long black satin gloves off her arms. Although
no other piece of clothing drops, the scene is
unbelievably erotic. The captivating Hayworth
played the part of a lifetime in the title role
of the melodrama *Gilda*. In the 1940s, the red-
haired beauty was America's top sex symbol,
a "love goddess," seductive and breathtakingly
beautiful. As a pin-up girl, her image was re-
produced five million times and glued onto
every American soldier's locker. In *Gilda* her
aura was at its most magical.

King Vidor directed the dark drama about
a threesome, which contemporary critics
misinterpreted as "hardly exciting" or even
"boring." They must have been wearing blind-
folds to miss Rita/Gilda parading her beauty
in a series of gorgeous, strapless evening gowns!
No doubt, the plot is confusing and even trashy.
Nevertheless, a cast of excellent actors performed in perfect Hollywood *film noir* style,
and the film soon reached cult status. A cliché
crime story on the surface, the layers under-
neath explore hate, love, passion, friendship
among men, and loyalty.

Gilda is married to elegant Ballin Mundson
(George Macready), who runs a casino in Argen-
tina. He tries to compensate for his feelings of
inadequacy by carrying a walking stick with a
sword hidden inside. From the nightlife of
Buenos Aires, he hires gambler, Johnny Farrell
(Glenn Ford), as his nightclub manager. Farrell
recognizes Gilda as his former lover. This time

around, however, he resists her temptations
(for which she even slaps him across the face).
He remains loyal to his friend and boss Mundson, even after Mundson's death. Farrell ends
up marrying Gilda—but only to punish her for
constantly betraying Mundson—and Gilda's
life becomes a living hell.

Then Mundson, believed dead, resurfaces.
Having been embroiled in dealings with a Nazi
cartel, he had faked his own demise. Returning
to kill his wife and his friend for what he as-
sumes to be their betrayal, he is shot himself by
an employee of the casino. The local inspector,
hot on Mundson's trail throughout the story,
lets everyone off the hook. Subsequently,
Johnny and Gilda decide to start their ex-
plosive relationship over again, even though
their love turns all too quickly to hate and
then from hate back to love.

Hayworth was identified with her role as
Gilda more than with any other. The glamour
goddess was born: "Every man I know fell in
love with Gilda and woke up next to me."

B.A.

"Put the Blame on Mame": the famous glove strip

The Third Man

England, 1949
Running time: 108 minutes
Black and white
Directed by Carol Reed; *written by* Graham
Greene; *cinematographer,* Robert Krasker;
music by Anton Karas; *edited by* Oswald
Hafenrichter
With: Joseph Cotten (Holly Martins), Alida
Valli (Anna), Orson Welles (Harry Lime),
Trevor Howard (Calloway), Ernst Deutsch
(Kurtz), Paul Hörbiger (Porter), Erich Ponto
(Dr. Winkel), Hedwig Bleibtreu

Carol Reed

1906 Born on December 30 in London.
1924 Start of his (modest) acting career.
1927 Began collaboration with Edgar Wallace as a theater
      actor and producer.
1932 Became a dialogue director for the Ealing Studios in
      London.
1934 Directing debut with *Midshipman Easy/Men of the Sea,*
      which received little attention.
1939 Breakthrough with *The Stars Look Down.* During World
      War II, made propaganda and documentary films:
1945 *The True Glory* (Oscar for best documentary)
1946 *Odd Man Out*
1948 *The Fallen Idol*
1949 *The Third Man*
1952 Raised to the British peerage.
1956 *Trapeze*
1959 *Our Man in Havanna*
1968 The musical *Oliver* was awarded six Oscars
1976 Carol Reed died in London.

Who is lying and why? Scene with Joseph Cotten

"His career demonstrates that a director who limits himself to solving technical problems quickly lapses into the
decadence of the inappropriate effect."
Film historian Andrew Sarris on why the quality of Reed's
films diminshed after the 1950s

Hard shadows, hard light: Harry Lime (Orson Welles) in Vienna

"No movies about rubble!" shouted the German
postwar public, preferring to escape from urban
scenes of ruin and destruction into an imaginary
world of green meadows and idealized game-
keepers. It is surprising, then, that a British
"rubble" film set in depressing postwar Vienna
—divided into sectors and already feeling the
chill of the Cold War—conquered the cinemas
in 1949 and was decorated with the Palme
d'Or at Cannes. The film in question is Carol
Reed's *The Third Man,* based on a book by
Graham Greene and permeated by sewers and
cemeteries.

Two years earlier, Reed had received acclaim
for his passionate Irish drama, *Odd Man Out.*
Yet, rumors circulated that he was dismissing
The Third Man as a failure. As the legend goes,
on his last evening in Vienna he happened to
hear Anton Karas playing the same tune over
and over again on his zither in a local wine bar.
In a last effort to rescue the film, he brought
the musician into the studio on the next day.
Whatever the true sequence of events may have
been, *The Third Man* is recognized around the
world by the zither motif played by Anton
Karas. The character of the city, whose crumbling feudal walls and chiaroscuro stairs recall
an old, run-down courtesan, is beautifully
captured by the simple, lightheartedly vulgar,
hurdy-gurdy sound of Karas's zither.

As we're still wondering who's lying and
why—and what really happened to Harry
Lime who's just been buried—powerful, almost
demonic, images pass before our eyes and are
etched on our memories. These include a
screaming caretaker (Paul Hörbiger—the very

personification of sentimental, old-fashioned
Viennese movies), a figure in the shadows of a
gateway, and a pair of shoes with a cat circling
around them (the cat, we know, doesn't let
anyone other than Harry Lime touch her).

American writer Holly Martin (Joseph
Cotton) is searching for his friend Harry Lime
(Orson Welles), but someone else lies in Harry
Lime's grave. When Holly finally meets up
with his old friend at the giant Ferris wheel in
Vienna's Prater amusement park, Lime is not
only very much alive, he has become a ruthless
pusher of penicillin—a cynic of the new era.

Harry makes use of the only route that still
links the occupied sectors in Vienna, the sewer
system. Holly's walks to meet with British
military officer Galloway (Trevor Howard)
are breathtakingly suspenseful, just as Harry's
dubious pusher friends (Ernst Deutsch, Erich
Ponto) are shady characters right out of a
thriller. The last walk from Harry Lime's grave
(the real one this time) through a central
cemetery leads Holly past Harry Lime's girlfriend (Alida Valli). She doesn't even glance
at him—she's just like the cat.   *Po.*

A film like no other?

Sunset Boulevard

USA, 1950
Running time: 110 minutes (short version: 104)
Black and white
Directed by Billy Wilder; *written by* Charles
Brackett, Billy Wilder, *and* D. M. Marshman, Jr.,
based on the story A Can of Beans *by* Billy
Wilder *and* Charles Brackett; *cinematographer,*
John Seitz; *music by* Franz Waxman; *edited by*
Doane Harrison *and* Arthur Schmidt
With: Gloria Swanson (Norma Desmond),
Erich von Stroheim (Max von Mayerling),
William Holden (Joe Gillis), Nancy Olson
(Betty Schaefer), Fred Clark (Sheldrake), Cecil
B. DeMille (Cecil B. DeMille), Buster Keaton
(Buster Keaton)

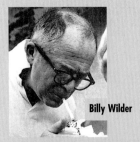

Billy Wilder

1906 Born on June 22 as Samuel Wilder in Sucha (Galicia).
Graduated from high school in Vienna. Worked as a
reporter in Vienna and Berlin, where he also earned
money as a professional dancing partner before
beginning to write scripts.

1929 Became known in through his collaboration on the semi-
documentary film, *People on Sunday*.

1933 Being of Jewish descent, Wilder left Nazi Germany,
by way of Paris and Mexico, for the U.S. His family,
remaining behind, died in concentration camps.
Difficult beginnings in Hollywood. Moved in with actor
Peter Lorre. Wilder's fortunes began to change when he
met scriptwriter Charles Brackett. The two collaborated
on many scripts, including those for the Lubitsch movies

1938 *Bluebeard's Eighth Wife* and

1939 *Ninotchka.* Their teamwork continued when, in 1942,
Wilder began his directing career with *The Major and
the Minor.* Subsequent films included:

1944 *Double Indemnity*

1945 *The Lost Weekend*

1948 *A Foreign Affair*

1950 *Sunset Boulevard*
Break with Brackett. On his own (often as producer as
well as director) Wilder now made films such as:

1955 *The Seven Year Itch*

1957 *Witness for the Prosecution*

1959 *Some Like It Hot*

1960 *The Apartment*

1961 *One Two Three*

1963 *Irma la Douce*

1981 Wilder ended his great career with the killer comedy
Buddy, Buddy. His accomplishments were honored by a
total of six Oscars.

2000 Awarded the Order of Merit of the Federal Republic
of Germany.

"We didn't need dialogue. We had faces."
(Norma to Joe Gillis on silent film stars)

>>> Billy Wilder, *Some Like it Hot,* see p. 82

How does one write a
comeback? Nancy Olson
as Betty Schaefer and
William Holden as Joe,
the successful screenwriter

Billy Wilder's classic has lost none of its op-
pressive power. This dark, tragic, macabre, and
yet comic study of the shifting boundaries between dream and reality is a story about the
power of illusion (on the screen) whose narrator,
as it were, speaks from beyond the grave. As
the film opens, Joe Gillis (William Holden) is
already dead, a corpse floating in the swimming
pool of a villa on Sunset Boulevard, Hollywood's
legendary residential mile where the great stars
live in opulent houses. This particular villa,
which Gillis had discovered by chance, seems
to belong to a different, bygone era—as does
its solitary owner, silent-film diva Norma
Desmond (Gloria Swanson), who is looked
after by her devoted servant Max (Erich von
Stroheim).

Against all common sense, Desmond is
preparing to launch her comeback on the big
screen, and Gillis, a down-and-out scriptwriter,
is reeled in to help her achieve this goal. Both
become entangled in a fatal relationship of
mutual dependency. Gillis becomes the aging
diva's employee, lapdog, and lover, and the
diva, in turn, looses all sense of reality. In
the end, she shoots Gillis. The next morning
her house is crowded with policemen, photog-
raphers, and tabloid journalists for whom
Desmond makes her last grand entrance.
Deluded, she believes that she is once again
the focus of a big film scene, radiant in the
light of flashbulbs and floodlights.

Desmond's dramatic loss of touch with
reality carries the viewer along in a maelstrom
that sweeps away anything real. Wilder's idea of
casting former silent movie star, Gloria Swanson,
as Norma Desmond was truly inspired. When

Desmond watches her "own" silent movies in
her memorabilia-stuffed villa, excerpts from
Queen Kelly—a silent film from 1928 directed
by Erich von Stroheim with Gloria Swanson in
the title role—flicker across the private screen
in her living room.

Space and time dissolve in Wilder's relentless reckoning with spiritual vacuity, people's
illusions, and self-deceit. This is masterfully
reflected in the complex dramaturgy of the
web of relationships and meanings. Desmond's
old car and villa are reflections of herself, while
the swimming pool is an existential symbol that
is omnipresent. Wilder's treatment is sophisticated down to the smallest detail, particulary
his inclusion of Buster Keaton in Norma
Desmond's morbid card circle. In this "talkie,"
Keaton, the star of many silent movies, says
only one word: "Pass!" More than merely an
interjection in a card game, this monosyllabic
utterance is a bitter commentary on time.
Time passes and dissipates. In the end, we,
too, pass and die.   *H.P.K.*

Losing touch with reality—dramatically: the has-been film star Norma Desmond (Gloria Swanson) with Joe Gillis (William Holden)

Illusions and delusions: "I am still big. It is the films that have become small," says Desmond (Gloria Swanson)

A Streetcar Named Desire

USA, 1951
Running time: 127 minutes
Black and white
Directed by Elia Kazan; *written by* Tennessee
Williams *and* Oscar Saul, *based on the play of
the same name by* Tennessee Williams; *cinematographer,* Harry Stradling; *music by* Alex
North; *edited by* David Weisbart
With: Vivien Leigh (Blanche DuBois), Marlon
Brando (Stanley Kowalski), Kim Hunter
(Stella Kowalski), Karl Malden (Mitch), Rudy
Bond (Steve Hubbell), Nick Dennis (Pablo
Gonzales), Peg Hillias (Eunice Hubbell)

Elia Kazan

1909 Born on September 7 as Elia Kazanjoglou to Greek
parents in Constantinople (Istanbul).

1913 His family emigrated to the U.S.

1930–32 Attended the Yale School of Drama, then joined the
Group Theater in New York. Directed highly successful
stage productions of plays such as Tennessee Williams' *A
Streetcar Named Desire* and Arthur Miller's *Death of a
Salesman.*
Worked on movies in parallel.

1944 Feature film debut with *A Tree Grows in Brooklyn*

1947 Co-founder of the Actors Studio in New York. Headed
by Lee Strasberg, the Studio would shape an entire
generation of American film actors and actresses—
Marlon Brando, James Dean, Caroll Baker, Natalie
Wood, Warren Beatty. That same year Kazan received
his first Oscar for *Gentleman's Agreement*

1951 *A Streetcar Named Desire*

1952 *Viva Zapata!*

1954 *On the Waterfront* (awarded eight Oscars)

1955 *East of Eden* (with James Dean)

1956 *Baby Doll*

1961 *Splendor in the Grass*
In the 1960s Kazan's success began to dwindle.

1963 *America, America*

1969 *The Arrangement*

1976 After *The Last Tycoon* he retired from the movie
business.

1999 Elia Kazan was awarded an honorary Oscar for his life's
work. Although artistically uncontested, this decision
triggered great controversy in view of Kazan's behavior in front of the Committee for Un-American
Activities, where he had accused many people in the
movie business of being Communists or Communist
sympathizers.

"He is like an animal. He has an animal's habits. There's
even something subhuman about him. Thousands of years
have passed him right by, and there he is! Stanley Kowalski,
survivor of the Stone Age, bearing the raw meat home from
the kill in the jungle."
(Vivien Leigh as Blanche DuBois to Kim Hunter as Stella)

No Oscar for the brutal macho: Marlon Brando and Vivien Leigh

A Streetcar Named Desire signaled the end of film
censorship in Hollywood. For half a century,
the industry had ensured that its output was
suited for the entire family. Insanity, homosexuality, sexual obsession, and rape were not
considered family themes. But they formed the
core of Tennessee Williams' steamy, feverish
story about a Southern family and made the
leap from liberal Broadway to the conservative
screen. When it was released, six years after
the end of World War II, the film shattered
any remaining belief in the moral mandate of
the medium. Despite numerous cuts, *A Streetcar
Named Desire* unleashed a media scandal in 1951.
However, its twelve Oscar nominations—and
four awards—proved that the public was more
open than its self-appointed guardians.

The film revolves around Blanche DuBois
(Vivien Leigh), an impoverished woman from
a "good" family who comes to New Orleans to
stay with her sister (Kim Hunter) and brother-in-law, Stanley Kowalski (Marlon Brando).
Blanche is a habitual liar whose delusions—
about her past, her true age, and the reason for
her sudden visit—unravel when they collide
with Stanley's raw animal instinct. The film
oozes with sexual energy amid images of the
American South, Stanley's sweat-soaked T-shirt,
and Blanche's careful rituals of dressing and
undressing. This is cinema as evening-long
foreplay.

Although Marlon Brando was the only one
of the four main actors who did not receive
an Oscar, the role of Stanley made the twenty-seven year old an erotic icon. "I like to be comfortable," says Stanley as he lifts his wet T-shirt
off his muscular torso. Brando plays the character as a brutal, sensual macho who enjoys
his wife's sexual dependence. He quickly sees
through his sister-in-law's sexual hysteria
and sets out to systematically destroy her. The
desire stated in the film's title is explored as
daringly as the wholesome 1950s would allow.

In 1993, Elia Kazan's masterpiece of psychological realism was re-released, this time in a
director's cut that included four minutes of
explicit dialogue which had been cut to appease churchgoers. Even so, the edited version
of *A Streetcar Named Desire* is just as morally
subversive and emotionally disturbing today
as it was half a century ago.   *K.D.*

Fleeing to her sister: Blanche
(Vivien Leigh) and Stella (Kim Hunter)

Tormented erotic icon: Marlon Brando with Vivien Leigh

High Noon

USA, 1952

Running time: 85 minutes
Black and white
Directed by Fred Zinnemann; *written by* Carl Foreman; *cinematographer,* Floyd Crosby; *music by* Dimitri Tiomkin; *edited by* Elmo Williams
With: Gary Cooper (Will Kane), Grace Kelly (Amy Kane), Thomas Mitchell (Jonas Henderson), Lloyd Bridges (Harvey Pell), Katy Jurado (Helen Ramirez), Lon Chaney, Jr. (Martin Howe), Lee Van Cleef (Jack Colby), Otto Kruger (Percy Mettrick), Henry Morgan (William Fuller), Ian MacDonald (Frank Miller), Eve McVeagh (Mildred Fuller), Jack Elam (Charlie), John Doucette (Trumbull)

Fred Zinnemann

1907 Born on April 29 in Vienna. After law studies, decided to enter motion pictures, beginning as an assistant cameraman in Paris and Berlin.
1929 The Berlin collage *People on Sunday* done in collaboration with Billy Wilder and Robert Siodmak.
Before the year was over Zinnemann emigrated to Hollywood and worked in various film jobs to survive.
1937 MGM hired him as director of short films.
1938 His short *That Mothers Might Live* won an Oscar.
1942 Feature film debut with *Kid Glove Killer.*
1944 *The Seventh Cross*
1947 *The Search* (made in war-torn Germany)
1952 *High Noon*
1953 *From Here to Eternity* (received eight Oscars)
1955 *Oklahoma!*
1959 *The Nun's Story*
1966 *A Man for All Seasons* (awarded the Oscar for best film)
1972 *The Day of the Jackal*
1976 *Julia* (with Jane Fonda)
1982 *Five Days One Summer.* After this love drama in a mountain setting proved a box office disappointment, Zinnemann retired from moviemaking.
1997 Fred Zinnemann died in London.

>>> Fred Zinnemann, *From Here to Eternity,* see p. 62

Walking with his head held high: Gary Cooper as Will Kane

Some teenagers in the fifties were thoroughly cured of their desire to see *High Noon.* Their teachers recommended the movie—which was often billed as the matinee on holidays —praising its virtue and civic value and reminding their students that "it [was] more than a western." Nothing could have sounded more suspect to young ears and less conducive to inquiring minds.

The pedagogic label stuck to Fred Zinnemann's film for a long time, especially in Germany. To civic educators who appropriated the film's message, marshall Will Kane (Gary Cooper) was a responsible democrat who didn't run from danger but faced it bravely, and, if necessary, alone. Thus, teenagers didn't discover that *High Noon* was, and continues to be, one of the greatest westerns of all time until much later. Nor did they find out how Kane's marriage to Quaker Amy (Grace Kelly) and his resignation of his marshall's badge, were steps away from the barbarity of frontier justice towards a more civilized life.

Kane's fate is that no one in his town, Hadleyville, is prepared to fight alongside him against the four-man strong Miller gang. The good townspeople cowardly shirk their responsibility, even mocking the marshall's stubborn insistence on confronting the Millers. Deserted and awaiting the train that will bring the Millers into town, the lawman sits down to write his last will and testament. All the while, he remains true to the motto that "a man's got to do what a man's got to do," even if he is afraid.

Zinnemann tells this story in a pared-down fashion, where real-time events take some 105 minutes, in near complete congruence over 85 minutes. He does not take advantage of the usual western gags, like chase and hunt, nor does he allow landscape to play a major role. The tension of the film depends entirely upon the passage of time. At the outset, it seems to stretch endlessly; however, towards the end, seconds pass quickly. The hands of the town clock provide the rhythm for the images, culminating in the showdown when, suddenly, time seems to stand still.

If this film has a political message, it probably relates to the atmosphere in Hollywood during the time in which it was shot. Those were the days of senator McCarthy's witch hunt, during which many were willing to denounce others, but too few were willing, or brave enough, to fight the official. Carl Foreman, who wrote the script for *High Noon,* was one of those few brave enough to resist. His courage landed him on the infamous "black list." *A.H.*

Who's going to face the Miller's? Gary Cooper!

Showdown: Grace Kelly as Amy

USA, 1952
Running time: 100 minutes
Directed by Stanley Donen *and* Gene Kelly;
written by Betty Comden *and* Adolph Green;
cinematographer, Harold Rosson; *music by*
Arthur Freed *and* Nacio Herb Brown; *edited*
by Adrienne Fazan
With: Gene Kelly (Don Lockwood), Donald
O'Connor (Cosmo Brown), Debbie Reynolds
(Kathy Selden), Jean Hagen (Lina Lamont),
Millard Mitchell (R. F. Simpson)

Stanley Donen

1924 Born on April 13 in Columbia, South Carolina.
1940 Dancing debut on Broadway
1949 Beginning of his movie career as co-director with Gene Kelly. Donen also worked independently in the musical genre.
1954 *Seven Brides for Seven Brothers*
1957 *Funny Face*
Subsequently: he directed sophisticated comedies and thriller-comedies like:
1958 *Indiscreet*
1963 *Charade*
1978 *Movie Movie*
1983 With *Blame It on Rio,* he drew the line under his cinema career.
In the 1990s Donen returned to staging Broadway musicals and worked as a television director, as in:
1999 *Loveletters*

Gene Kelly

1912 Born on August 23 as Eugene Curran Kelly in Pittsburgh, Pennsylvania. Successful Broadway career as dancer and choreographer.
1942 First movie appearance in *For Me and My Gal.* His finest achievement as actor/dancer/choreographer would come with Vincente Minnelli's musical *An American in Paris* (1951).
1949 *On the Town,* the first of three dazzling musicals directed in collaboration with Stanley Donen.
1952 *Singin' in the Rain*
1955 *It's Always Fair Weather*
1961 Kelly made the transition from musical to feature film director with *Gigot*
1968 Resounding success with the musical *Hello Dolly!*
1996 Kelly died on February 2 in Beverly Hills.

In 1951, Hollywood presented an honorary award to Gene Kelly "in appreciation of his versatility as an actor, singer, director, and dancer, and specially for his brilliant achievements in the art of choreography in film."

Dream-factory mockery: Kelly as Don Lockwood with Cyd Charisse

Heaven and earth have opened their gates. It's pouring buckets, and Gene Kelly is splashing and dancing in the puddles, singing at the top of his voice and fairly bursting with joy. He's "Singin' in the Rain" to tell the whole world of his new found happiness in love. The production seemed to be under a lucky star from the start, and the film is still celebrated as the best musical of all times. Everything works, from the songs and musical arrangements (with two exceptions, all composed by Arthur Freed and Nacio Herb Brown for different Hollywood films), to the brilliant, glamorous dance scenes, to the up-beat direction by Stanley Donen and Gene Kelly, who shared the task. In contrast to

The original poster (USA), 1952

many other musicals, a convincing plot takes us back to an era when talkies were beginning to take over silent movies. The dream factory created its own send-up in this funny and satirical look at itself and its history.

Don Lockwood (Gene Kelly) and Lina Lamont (Jean Hagen) are a celebrated screen couple of the silent film era. To keep up with the times, their producers decide to change the actors' silent love drama into a catchy musical. No problem for Don, but a big problem for Lina, whose annoying pip-squeak of a voice simply won't make it with the public. But Lockwood has a solution. He convinces a dancer named Kathy (Debbie Reynolds), with whom he immediately falls deeply in love, to do the voice over for Lina. The premiere is a great success, Don exposes Lina's bluff, and Kathy gets to stand in the limelight.

Just as Kathy succeeds in the script, so Debbie Reynolds achieved her breakthrough with this film. Jean Hagen is also hysterically funny as the over-the-top, silent movie diva. In addition to the legendary rain scene, for which the studio was literally drenched in water, a great dance number—*Broadway Ballet*—guest starring Cyd Charisse is one of the highlights of the film. The scene was studied for four weeks, and shooting took two full weeks. "He brought dance down from its pedestal," said Cyd Charisse about her partner Gene Kelly, who had become known as "the American in Paris" because of his rain escapades. Kelly had a similar view of himself and his athletic, acrobatic dance style. The "Marlon Brando of Dance," as he saw himself, characterized his great colleague Fred Astaire as "elegant and aristocratic," but of himself said: "I am much more plebeian." *B.A.*

Gene Kelly singing in the rain: perhaps the most memorable dancing scene in the history of film

From Here to Eternity

USA, 1953
Running time: 115 minutes
Black and white
Directed by Fred Zinnemann; *written by* Daniel
Taradash, *based on the novel by* James Jones;
cinematographer, Burnett Guffey; *music by*
Morris W. Stoloff; *edited by* William A. Lyon
With: Burt Lancaster (Sergeant Milton
Warden), Montgomery Clift (Robert E. Lee
Prewitt), Frank Sinatra (Angelo Maggio),
Deborah Kerr (Karen Holmes), Donna Reed
(Lorene), Philip Ober (Captain Dana Holmes),
Mickey Shaughnessy (Sergeant Leva), Ernest
Borgnine (Sergeant "Fatso" Judson), Jack
Warden (Corporal Buckley)

Burt Lancaster and Deborah Kerr in their legendary love scene on the beach in Hawaii

Cast against "type"—Donna Reed and Montgomery Clift

The preparation phase of this fim was so chaotic that it is a small miracle that it was produced at all. The fact that it turned into an enduring masterpiece is a characteristic of Hollywood, despite its flops and other disasters, and is surprising because the film was a plain black-and-white production in an era dominated by Technicolor and Cinerama.

It all started with James Jones's book, *From Here to Eternity*, a hefty tome that was as powerful and explicit in content as in tone. Columbia Chief Executive Harry Cohen had acquired the film rights, and author Daniel Taradash managed to create a script that satisfied both the toughness of the material and the need for "hygiene" in Hollywood's dream factory of morality.

Next came the casting drama. Director Fred Zinnemann threatened to resign if he couldn't get Montgomery Clift. Showstar Frank Sinatra, whose career had reached a low, dispatched his wife, Ava Gardner, as an ambassador to capture the role which, although he earned only a mere 8,000 dollars, finally put him on the map as a serious actor. Many of the lead actors were second casting choices: Burt Lancaster replaced Edmond O'Brian, Deborah Kerr stepped in for Joan Crawford, and Donna Reed for Julie Harris—the list goes on and on.

The performance of the entire cast is excellent, even though, or perhaps because, some played "against type." As a result, a dense web of relationships between conflicting personalities and figures is woven on the screen.

Soldier Prewitt (Montgomery Clift) has been sent to the US unit stationed at Pearl Harbor on Hawaii. Prewitt is a talented trumpet player and boxing champion who, having been involved in a tragic accident, stubbornly refuses to bolster the failing ranks of the company's boxing team. But when his friend Maggio (Frank Sinatra) is tortured to death by a sadistic sergeant (Ernest Borgnine), Prewitt kills the sergeant and deserts to hide with his girlfriend (Donna Reed). He rejoins his unit when the Japanese attack Pearl Harbor (on December 7, 1941), only to be killed himself. Burt Lancaster plays the model soldier who has an affair with the wife (Deborah Kerr, usually so cool and ladylike, shown here in a completely new and sensual light) of his incompetent and brutal superior (Philip Ober).

Despite its open criticism of barrack drills and hazing, the eight-time Oscar winning film is best remembered for the love scene between Burt Lancaster and Deborah Kerr. With the Pacific surf lapping over them, the two stars exchange the longest, most passionate, and most legendary kiss in the history of film. *B.A.*

>>> Fred Zinnemann, *High Noon,* and Biography,
see p. 58

Caught up in entangled relationships: Prewitt (Montgomery Clift) with his friend Maggio (Frank Sinatra)

La Strada (The Road)

La Strada
Italy, 1954
Running time: 102 minutes
Black and white
Directed by Federico Fellini; *written by* Tullio
Pinelli, Federico Fellini; *cinematographer,*
Otello Martelli; *music by* Nino Rota; *edited*
by Leo Catozzo
With: Giulietta Masina (Gelsomina), Anthony
Quinn (Zampano), Richard Basehart (Matto),
Aldo Silvani (Colombiani), Marcella Rovere
(widow), Livia Venturini (nun)

Federico Fellini

1920 Born on January 20 in Rimini.
1938 Moved to Florence and Rome then the following year;
       worked as a comic illustrator, journalist, and author for
       radio and movie scripts. Met Roberto Rossellini which
       led to collaboration in the latter's neo-realistic classics
       Open City (1945) and *Paisà* (1946)
1950 Directed his first movie together with Alberto Lattuada:
       Variety Lights
1953 *The Young and the Passionate/The Loafers*
1954 *La Strada* (with his wife Giulietta Masina in the female
       leading role). Received an Oscar for the best foreign
       film.
1957 Second Oscar for *The Nights of Cabiria*
1959 *La Dolce Vita*
1963 *8-1/2* (Oscar)
1973 *Amarcord* (Oscar)
1985 *Ginger and Fred*
1990 Directed his last movie at the age of 70: *The Voice of*
       the Moon
1993 Before his death on October 31 in Rome, Federico Fellini
       received an honorary award at the Oscars

>>> Federico Fellini, *La Dolce Vita,* see p. 76

Death on a country road: The Great Zampanó (Anthony Quinn) kills his rival, Il Matteo (Richard Basehart)

In the early fifties the Great Zampanó (Anthony Quinn) travels through the Po valley as a fairground artist. He specializes in feats of strength and looks and acts accordingly. One day, a poverty stricken girl, Gelsomina (Guilietta Masina), is offered to him for sale. He agrees to the shady deal, and the naive young woman begins to accompany his act on the trumpet. She even harbors some hope that she will be able to soften the ruffian's heart but discovers a kindred spirit in a ropewalker—Il Matteo (Richard Basehart)—who is the exact antithesis of the muscle man. The stage is set for conflict between the two male protagonists, yet Zampanó's actions are less driven by jealousy than by sheer possessiveness. On a country road, the tensions erupt into a fight, and Zampanó kills the gallant rival who has true affection for Gelsomina. The young woman loses her sanity, and the unfeeling ruffian continues his travels on his own. Later on, however, when he hears about his former partner's death, he collapses on the beach and the misery of his existence seems to overwhelm him in a single moment. *La Strada* is a story of becoming human, and, although the film is rooted in the tradition of neorealism, leftist Italian critics claimed that it betrayed the innovative style. Neorealism, however, tended towards the emotive and succeeded in plucking at viewers' heartstrings by siding with the victim. Fellini's film, which received more than fifty international awards, entered the names of its leading actors into the annals of film history.

The film works so well because Giuletta Masina (the director's wife) gives an impressive performance as the pure-hearted fool who stumbles through a chaotic world, knowing only how to speak from the heart. For such a creature, the world is indeed a bad place to be. Her powerful characterization is enhanced even further by her huge eyes which look in despair and, sometimes, in disbelief, at what goes on.

Worlds apart: Gelsomina (Giuletta Masina) and
Zampanó (Anthony Quinn)

Giulietta Masina as the naive clown, Gelsomina, with the traveling circus artist, Zampanó (Anthony Quinn)

La Strada is an important part of the cultural cinematographic heritage of the twenieth century because it convinces by means of its sympathetic perspective. In fact, Fellini was labeled "Catholic" because of the film's many spiritual references, a rash judgement that was revised years later upon the release of his *La Dolce Vita*.   H.M.

Rebel Without a Cause

USA, 1955
Running time: 106 minutes
Directed by Nicholas Ray; *written by* Stewart
Stern; *cinematographer,* Ernest Haller; *music by*
Leonard Rosenman; *edited by* William Ziegler
With: James Dean (Jim), Natalie Wood (Judy),
Sal Mineo (Plato), Jim Backus (Jim's Father),
Corey Allen (Buzz), Ann Doran (Jim's Mother),
William Hopper (Judy's Father), Dennis
Hopper (Goon), Rochelle Hudson (Judy's
Mother), Virginia Brissac (Jim's Grandmother)

Nicholas Ray

1911 Born Raymond Nicholas Kienzle in Galesville, Wisconsin. Studied architecture.
1932 Moved to New York; several years of cooperation in the theater with Elia Kazan and John Houseman both as actor and director.
1947 First film direction for *They Live by Night*
1949 *Knock on Any Door*
1950 *In a Lonely Place*
1954 *Johnny Guitar* (cult western)
1955 *Rebel Without a Cause*
1957 *The True Story of Jesse James*
1960 *King of Kings*
1962 *55 Days at Peking*
   After this grand-scale production, Ray, who was a pioneer and defender of the filming of literary works, drew the necessary conclusions from long-term fights with producers and turned his back on Hollywood. He lectured in New York.
1974 Directed one part of the episode movie *Dreams of 13*
1977 Appeared as an actor in *The American Friend* (by Wim Wenders)
1979 Acted in *Hair* (by Milos Forman)
1979 Ray died of lung cancer.

Buzz Gunderson:
"You know how to chicky-race don't you?"
Jim Stark:
"Yeah, it's all I ever do" [Buzz leaves.]
Jim Stark:
[to Plato] "What's a chicky-race?"

The "new guy" in High School, Jim (James Dean), becomes involved in a stabbing incident

World War II was won, and the Korean War was over. America licked its wounds, McCarthy campaigned against "subversives," and the country basked in the glow of its invincibility. Americans were the kings of the world, and they knew exactly what they were doing. That is, until a strange little book hit the stores. Called *Catcher in the Rye*, by eccentric author Jerome D. Salinger, the book drove the younger generation wild. The teenagers who were supposed to inherit a better world preferred "uncivilized" Rock 'n' Roll to Pat Boone. Was there hope of salvation for these crazy kids?

Salinger tells the story of sixteen-year-old Holden Caulfield who refuses to accept the conservative values of his parents, whose rituals seem antiquated and devoid of humanity. Four years after *Catcher in the Rye* was released, Holden Caulfield was made manifest, on-screen, by bad-boy James Dean. In the role of Jim Stark, Dean gave the quintessential performance of the restless teenager who hides behind a facade of casual indifference while yearning for love and recognition.

After the release of *Rebel Without a Cause*, directed by Nicholas Ray in 1955, the red windbreaker became a symbol of youthful rebellion for years to come. Even today, the film forms the core of the Jimmy Dean triptych. The loneliness that marked Dean's role as a wayward rancher's son named Cal, in Elia Kazan's *East of Eden*, grew to iconic proportions in *Rebel Without a Cause*. He was the perfect role model for a generation caught between the suburbs and Rock 'n' Roll.

In the film's opening scene, a drunk Jim Stark slouches on a curb, holding onto a toy monkey. The conflict at work in his character is obvious: his suit marks him as an adult, but his movements are those of a frightened child. Jim suffers because of his father's weakness and is determined not to become like him. To this end, he seeks out one daredevil challenge after another, and also falls in love with Judy (Natalie Wood). A third teen rounds out the plot: outsider Plato (Sal Mineo) comes from a wealthy home and approaches Jim with obvious romantic intentions. A fateful night brings the three young people together, one of whom does not survive to see the morning.

James Dean and Natalie Wood

Jim (James Dean) finds love and understanding in Judy (Natalie Wood)

Strangely, all three leading actors died under unusual circumstances. Dean died in a fatal car crash, Wood drowned off Catalina Island, and Sal Mineo was stabbed to death in a Los Angeles park. But the movie that brought them together has lost none of its edge, and its message transcends changing times and tastes. While some of the dialogues may sound dated, the emotions expressed in them are eternal. Each one of us has been Jim Stark at some point in our life.   *H.R.*

Wild Strawberries

Smultron Stället
Sweden, 1957
Running time: 92 minutes
Black and white
Directed and written by Ingmar Bergman;
cinematographer, Gunnar Fischer; *music by*
Erik Nordgren; *edited by* Oscar Rosander
With: Victor Sjöström (Professor Isak Borg),
Bibi Andersson (Sara), Ingrid Thulin
(Marianne Borg), Gunnar Björnstrand (Evald
Borg), Julian Kindahl (Agda), Max von Sydow
(Akerman), Gunnel Lindblom (Charlotta)

Ingmar Bergman

1918 Born on July 14 in Uppsala as the son of a strict,
       Lutheran minister. Studied literature and produced
       plays for various theaters in Stockholm.
1944 Wrote first script and worked as assistant director for
       Alf Sjöberg's *Torment/Frenzy*
1955 *Smiles of a Summer Night* (his first big success and
       international recognition)
1956 *The Seventh Seal*
1957 *Wild Strawberries* (Golden Bear, Berlin)
1959 *The Virgin Spring* (Oscar, best foreign language film)
1961 *Through a Glass Darkly* (Oscar for best foreign
       language film)
1963 *The Silence* produced a scandal because of sex scenes
       too liberal for the audience of the time.
1965 *Persona*
1972 *Cries and Whispers* (Oscar, best camera)
1973 *Scenes From a Marriage* (shortened movie adaption of
       a TV series)
1976 Bergman was wrongly accused of tax fraud in Sweden
       and moved to Germany.
1978 *Autumn Sonata.* Returned to Sweden.
1982 *Fanny and Alexander.* Bergman left the movie world
       with this grand-scale family history, which was
       awarded 4 Oscars. He continued to work intensively
       for the theater and directed TV movies.
1998 Won a special award for his œuvre on the 50th anni-
       versary of the Cannes Festival

Igmar Bergman worked with a regular team of actors
and technicians. These included the actors Liv Ullmann,
Bibi Andersson, Ingrid Thulin, Harriet Andersson, Max von
Sydow, and Gunnar Björnstrand, as well as cameraman
Sven Nykvist.

An uncomfortable conversation: Marianne (Ingrid Thulin) and her father-in-law (Victor Sjöström)

In 1958, forty-year-old, internationally renowned, Swedish director Ingmar Bergman
made one of the most beautiful films about
the central theme in his work: the tension between old age and youth and between man
and woman, framed in the age-old dichotomy
of God and Death. *Wild Strawberries* has become a cinematic classic, and it includes all
the facets of the magic world of imagery that
made Bergman films part of the collective sub-
conscious. Five years later, he shocked viewers
with *The Silence*, the first radical instance of
an existential disaster film.

Ingenius, neurotic, sensitive, steeped in his
European heritage, and burdened by the weight
of Scandinavian Puritanism, Bergman was a
virtuoso of the dream image, able to show, like
no other, the tortured soul caught between
religion, drive, and violence. He was sometimes
foolishly criticized for being a too serious,
heavy-footed seeker of meaning. Yet, watching
Ingmar Bergman's films is like taking a trau-
matic journey through the inner worlds of
the twentieth century which, ultimately, offers
only the refuge of the imagination and dream-
scapes, the magic treasure chests of childhood.
(The director came full circle with this idea in
his late masterpiece *Fanny and Alexander*.)

Suffering caused by bourgeois fears and
the claustrophobic life in a vicarage, as well
as the humiliations of life in a joyless society
of repentant sinners, became elements in
Bergman's particular artistic vocabulary and
inexhaustible sources of creativity. Fear leaps
from his images, as in one unforgettable scene
in *Wild Strawberries* in which the professor
has a disturbing dream the night before his

anniversary celebration at the university.
A coach carrying a coffin rattles through narrow,
cobblestoned streets and bumps against a light
post, causing the coffin to tumble onto the
street. This surreal sequence acts as a portent
of his fate. His frigidity is cast back onto his
face during the ice-cold conversations he held
with his son and daughter-in-law. He sees himself at a younger age passing the sites of his
youth as he travels to his old university town
where the wild strawberries grow—the basis
for all subsequent symbols in the film. He
finally recognizes himself for the cool, pedantic intellectual he has been all his life.

Like a sleepwalker, the protagonist stumbles
from faded memory to faded memory. The
film is simutaneously a search for the self and a
balancing act between dream and reality whose
style—which Bergman changes whenever he
feels like it, with tremendous individuality but
never without reason—is truly captivating,
both visually and intellectually. His coded layers
of dream sequences and the overlapping realities
are unforgettable. Memorable, too, is Viktor
Sjöström as the old man in a typical Bergman
ensemble.   *Po.*

A trip into the past: the professor and Sara (Bibi Andersson)

Taking stock of his life: Victor
Sjöström as Professor Isak Borg

The Cranes are Flying

Letjat zhuravli
USSR, 1957
Running time: 95 minutes
Black and white
Directed by Mikhail Kalatozov; *written (in Russian with English subtitles) by* Victor Rozov, *based on his play; cinematographer,* Sergei Urusevsky; *music by* Moisei Vaynberg; *edited by* M. Timofeyeva
With: Tatyana Samoilova (Veronica), Alexei Batalov (Boris), Vasily Merkuryev (Fyodor Ivanovich), Alexander Schvorin (Mark), Sonhola Kharitonova (Irina), Konstantin Nikintin (Volodya)

Mikhail Kalatozov

1903 Born on December 15 in Tibilisi (Tiflis), Georgia.
1925 Started his movie career in Tibilisi as an actor, cameraman, and director.
1930 First big success with the documentary *Salt for Swanetia* (camera and direction).
       Kalatozov's work was criticized for being "formalistic" and "negativistic." He took over an administrative position for the studio
1941 *Wings of Victory*
       During World War II, served as Soviet cultural ambassador to the United States (Los Angeles), then head of Soviet movie production.
1953 *Hostile Whirlwinds*
1954 *True Friends*
1957 *The Cranes Are Flying* (Golden Palm, Cannes)
1959 *The Letter That Was Never Sent*
1969 The international production *The Red Tent* (with Sean Connery) was his last movie.
1973 Mikhail Kalatozov died in Moscow.

Letter from Alexei Batalov to the author, Georg E. Vogel, dated February 16, 2000

"…I find that Boris in the film is not me but, rather, represents those who fought and suffered and died for me and the others."

Tatyana Samoilova as Veronica

Stalin, the almighty dictator, died in 1953. For a short period of time, the iron grip he had kept on cultural life relaxed a little. During this brief spell—when the Soviet Union was a "political no man's land," it was possible to make more controversial films. Director Mikhail Kalatozov seized the moment in 1957 to realize his passionate anti-war film, *The Cranes are Flying*. At last, he was able to dispense with idealized armies of workers and soldiers—the mainstay of Soviet cinema—and focus on the ravages of war in the lives of individuals.

As the film opens, we meet a young couple, Boris and Veronica. The two lovers think only of their love for each other, and of how they will spend the rest of their lives together. In rapturous fervor, their eyes follow the progress of a group of cranes flying high above. But their dreams of love and happiness are shattered all too soon. War is declared, and Boris signs up as a volunteer. Veronica interprets his decision as a betrayal of their love; her reaction indirectly causes Boris to leave for the front without a proper good-bye.

The ensuing months are a time of endless waiting for Veronica. There is no news from Boris. Gradually, the vivacious girl grows more and more despondent. In her hopelessness, she makes a fatal mistake by marrying Boris's brother, who has been wooing her persistently. Her married life is even more dreary and devoid of hope. Torn apart by feelings of guilt, Veronica withdraws into herself, and the marriage falls apart.

One day a soldier who has just returned from the front comes to see her. He was in the same unit as Boris, and he informs her that Boris was killed in battle. Veronica listens silently. She doesn't shed a tear because she is convinced that her lover will soon come back to her. Sadly, when the transports return from the front and Boris is not among the survivors, Veronica realizes that she will have to go through the rest of her life without him. Once again the cranes are flying, and the story comes full circle.

This moving story represents the stories of millions who suffered similar fates, painting a stark image of the senselessness of war. *The Cranes are Flying* is one of the most sensitive anti-war films ever made. Here, we witness the devastation wrought by war, not on bloody battlefields but in the suffering of those left behind—especially women. The film also reveals how unjust it would be to condemn a person for making poor decisions in difficult circumstances. The demoralizing conditions of Veronica's life leave little room for virtuous principles. For his masterpiece, Mikhail Kalatazov received the Palme d'Or in Cannes in 1958.

G.E.V.

Poster made for the German screening, 1958

Boris and Veronica (Alexei Batalov, Tatyana Samoilova):
happy and carefree, gazing at the cranes passing overhead

Mark (Alexander Schvorin), Boris' unpopular brother

Cat on a Hot Tin Roof

USA, 1958

Running time: 109 minutes
Directed by Richard Brooks; *written by* Richard Brooks *and* James Poe, *based on the play of the same name by* Tennessee Williams; *cinematographer,* William Daniels; *edited by* Ferris Webster;
With: Elizabeth Taylor (Maggie Pollitt), Paul Newman (Brick Pollitt), Burl Ives (Big Daddy Pollitt), Judith Anderson (Big Mama Pollitt), Jack Carson (Cooper Pollitt), Madeleine Sherwood (Mae Pollitt)

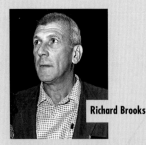

Richard Brooks

1912 Born May 18 in Philadelphia. Sports reporter in New York.

1942 Moved to Los Angeles. Wrote movie scripts and novels (among others the novel, *The Producer,* 1951).

1950 First directorial work for the film *Crisis*

1952 *Deadline USA* (with Humphrey Bogart)

1955 *The Blackboard Jungle* made him famous in Hollywood. After that, literary adaptions became his trademark. He wrote the scripts himself based on the originals:

1957 *The Brothers Karamazov* (based on Dostojevsky)

1958 *Cat on a Hot Tin Roof* (based on Tennessee Williams)

1959 *Elmer Gantry* (based on Sinclair Lewis)

1961 *Sweet Bird of Youth* (based on Tennessee Williams; Oscar for best script)

1964 *Lord Jim* (based on Joseph Conrad)

1967 *In Cold Blood* (based on Truman Capote)

1977 *Looking for Mr. Goodbar*

1981 *Wrong Is Right*

1985 With *Fever Pitch* Brooks bid farewell to the movies.

1992 Richard Brooks died.

Big Daddy (Burl Ives, center) turns sixty-five: things come to a head

Those were prudish times and homosexuality was definitely a taboo topic. It is difficult for today's viewers, accustomed to a diet of daytime TV tell-all talk shows, to reconstruct just how provocative a film such as *Cat on a Hot Tin Roof* was in the 1950s. Even in the original stage version, author Tennessee Williams beat about the bush and director Richard Brooks, who specialized in film adaptations of literary pieces, watered the story down for the screen version. Still, although much is veiled, obscured, and insinuated rather than stated, the film remains a moving, gripping, and captivating melodrama to this day—even for today's viewers, no matter how used they may be to disclosures.

This is mostly due to Brooks's exceptional direction of a star-studded cast. Elizabeth Taylor plays Maggie, the "cat," prickly, temperamental, passionate, sensual, and desperately fighting for the love of her husband, Brick (Paul Newman). Since the suicide of his friend Skipper, who, one can only guess, must have been his lover, the latter has fallen into a state of apathy and alcoholism. He no longer sleeps with his wife, who has no greater desire than to share her bed with him again. At the grand plantation home of Brick's father, events come to a head. "Big Daddy" (Birl Ives) is celebrating his sixty-fifth birthday; he and "Big Mama" (Judith Anderson) are the only two among the company who are unaware of his incurable cancer and that this may be his last birthday. Their eldest son, Cooper (Jack Carson), his perpetually pregnant wife, Mae (Madelaine Sherwood), and their brood of "neckless monsters" all have their eyes set on the inheritance. In a no-

holds-barred fight between father and son, Brick shatters the web of lies, while Maggie finds her own path to truth by means of a lie: she makes Big Daddy happy by telling him that she is pregnant—leaving her and Brick to do whatever it takes to make the lie come true.

If Tennessee Williams set himself the goal to "fashion a play like a noose with which to capture human truth," then Richard Brooks more than met the challenge in his direction of the cast. Elizabeth Taylor's work is admirable, especially since her husband, Mike Todd, died in a plane crash just ten days into the shooting schedule. "I could keep the tears back and function only as Maggie," Liz explained. It was a "relief to be able to play someone else. The rest of the time, I was just a robot." The film was nominated for six Oscars. Although it received none of the sought-after statuettes, it became the biggest box office hit of the year.

B.A.

Brick: "Now, you keep forgetting the conditions under which I agreed to stay on living with you!"
Maggie: "I'm not living with you! We occupy the same cage, that's all!"

Like a prowling cat: Elizabeth Taylor as Maggie

The Big Country

USA, 1958

Running time: 166 minutes
Directed by William Wyler; *written by* James
R. Webb, Robert Wilder, *and* Sy Bartlett, *based
on the novel* Ambush at Blanco Canyon *by*
Donald Hamilton; *cinematographer,* Franz
Planer; *music by* Jerome Moross; *edited by*
Robert Belcher, John Faure *and* Robert Swink
With: Gregory Peck (James McKay), Jean
Simmons (Julie Maragon), Carroll Baker
(Patricia Terrill), Charlton Heston (Steve
Leech), Burl Ives (Rufus Hannassey), Charles
Bickford (Major Henry Terrill)

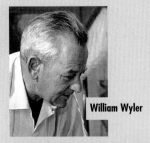

William Wyler

1902 Born on July 1 in Mulhouse, France. Studied the violin in Paris.
1922 Started film career; Universal boss, Carl Laemmle, a distant relative of his family, offered Wyler a job in his studio. Intern and assistant director (for, among others, the silent movie version of *Ben Hur*). Directs a series of short films.
1929 First feature film: *The Love Trap*
1936 Changes to MGM
1937 *Dead End*
1938 *Jezebel*
1939 *Wuthering Heights*
1941 *The Little Foxes*
1942 for both *Mrs. Miniver* and
1946 *The Best Years of Our Lives* (Oscar)
1953 *Roman Holiday*
1955 *The Desperate Hours*
1958 *The Big Country*
1959 *Ben Hur* (brings a third Oscar for Wyler)
1967 *Funny Girl*
1969 *The Liberation of L.B. Jones.*
1976 Life Achievement Award of the American Film Institute for his life's work
1981 William Wyler died in Beverly Hills, California.

Gentleman cowboy: James McKay (Gregory Peck)

A sailor in the Wild West: former sea captain James McKay (Gregory Peck), a gentleman from Baltimore, travels west. He wants to marry rancher daughter Pat Terrill (Caroll Baker), whom he met during her school time in New England. Going West to marry is not exactly a typical beginning for a western, but director William Wyler wasn't aiming for a typical "shoot-em up" Cowboy story when he captured his *The Big Country* in panoramic screen vision. In the 1950s, the genre was aiming higher: a western with class, good for the image and good for business.

The Big Country is a classic of what came to be called the "Noble Western." On the vast family ranch of his bride, the East Coast gentleman is soon drawn into a tumultuous clan dispute between his (future) father-in-law Major Terrill (Charles Bickford) and a neighbor (Burl Ives). At issue is a water hole that belongs to neither man but to a pretty teacher, Julie Maragon (Jean Simmons). On top of everything, bridegroom McKay comes under fire because he refuses to participate in the usual macho rituals of the Wild West—brawls, fisticuffs, shooting, and drinking. His attempts at mediation are seen as proof of his cowardice, and

soon he is a figure of ridicule to both his fiancée and ranch foreman Steve Leech (Charlton Heston), who also has his eye on the rancher's daughter. The only person who understands outsider McKay is Julie. Thus, events follow a fateful but predictable path in which peace comes about only after the two old tough guys have killed each other; Pat gets her foreman and James McKay the pretty teacher.

The Big Country is a pacifist western in which the will to peace and common sense prevail over revolvers and fist fights. Yet, despite the best intentions, even this soft take on an old theme can't get by without at least some fighting. The fistfight between Peck and Heston, by moonlight and without witnesses, has become legendary. As the story goes, the cameras kept rolling for fourteen hours before perfectionist Wyler was happy with the result. With an excellent cast, a good script, beautiful landscape shots, and a memorable sound track, Wyler made a western to satisfy every fan of the genre. Even viewers who aren't necessarily Wild West fans love this film, precisely because the story goes beyond the usual framework of the genre. Unfortunately, the masterpiece came up short at Oscar time, with only Burl Ives receiving recognition for his supporting role. Charlton Heston benefited in another way. Wyler was so taken with the actor that he offered him the title role in *Ben Hur*, for which Heston did finally get his Oscar.   B.A.

>>> William Wyler, *Ben Hur*, see p. 80

Jean Simmons in the role of self-confident teacher, Julie

Riding high through the Wild West: Gregory Peck and
Carroll Baker as engaged couple, James and Patricia

La Dolce Vita

Italy/France, 1959
Running time: 177 minutes
Black and white
Directed by Federico Fellini; *written by* Federico
Fellini, Tullio Pinelli, Ennio Flaiano, *and*
Brunello Rondi; *cinematographer,* Otello
Martelli; *music by* Nino Rota; *edited by* Leo
Catozzo
With: Marcello Mastroianni (Marcello
Rubini), Anita Ekberg (Sylvia), Anouk Aimée
(Maddalena), Yvonne Furneaux (Emma),
Alain Cuny (Steiner), Walter Santesso
(Paparazzo), Adriano Celentano (Sänger),
Lex Barker (Robert), Alan Dijon (Frankie Stout)

The paparazzo is invented: Mastroianni as gossip columnist, Marcello Rubini

The arrival of a film star: Anita Ekberg and the notion of
la dolce vita

There is a scene that has made film history
like no other, helping to create the myth of
the cinema as a dream factory. Late at night,
a seductive American film star Sylvia (Anita
Ekberg), climbs into the Trevi fountain in the
heart of Rome. She's dressed in an evening
gown and casually flirts with gossip columnist,
Marcello (Marcello Mastroianni). As always,
Marcello is right where the action is, but somehow he remains an outsider. The Marcello
character and his function are a narrative tool.
He is the useful fool—too intelligent, however,
to not suffer from his position—who simply
doesn't have what it takes to be a writer.

Frederico Fellini's bitter satire from 1959
provides an episodic look at decadent Roman
society hiding from its disgust with life behind
ever new distractions—all the while aware of
the futility of it all. Life is a mousetrap, even
if the moment can be made bearable through
sexual escapades. But moralist Fellini doesn't
allow his characters any way out, and every
escapist attempt is followed by a hangover
worse than the last one.

Fellini's three-hour film describes the life
of a weak man who feels that he has mastered
the rules of the game in the society in which
he lives. His suffering springs precisely from
the fact that he has mastered the game only
too well. This is a world in which lies and
death are everywhere.

The opening sequence contains a figure of
Christ flying across the Eternal City by helicopter. The figure's hands are raised in blessing,
but clearly this Christ has only an "overview,"
he can no longer reach people's hearts. This is
the background for another scene in which
children claim to have witnessed an apparition
of Mary at the city gates. Yet, the "miracle"
soon deteriorates into an ostentatious media
event.

Even people whose integrity seems un-
questionable despair over the situation, such
as a German writer Steiner, the hero Marcello
tries to emulate. Steiner commits suicide after
having killed his two children—a desperate act
that fails to inspire a new attitude. Society has
a new subject for gossip and paparazzi swarm
the scene. Since Fellini's film, "paparazzo," the
name of the photojournalist in *La Dolce Vita*,
has been adopted into everyday language.

La Dolce Vita was a cruel reckoning that
polarized the critics and viewers of its day because, in typical Fellini fashion, the only good
characters were petty thieves and whores.
In other words, the heroes are those who
acknowledge their own corruption and try
neither to cover it up nor to justify it, recog-
nizing instead that it is part of a system that
is corrupt. At least their hearts are in the right
place.
H.M.

>>> Federico Fellini, *La Strada,* and Biography,
see p. 64

Pure decadence: Film star Sylvia (Anita Ekberg)
in the Fontana di Trevi

A Bout de Souffle

France, 1959
Running time: 88 minutes
Black and white
Directed by Jean-Luc Godard; *written by*
François Truffaut; *cinematographer*, Raoul
Coutard; *music by* Martial Solal; *edited by*
Cécile de Cougis
With: Jean-Paul Belmondo (Michel Poiccard),
Jean Seberg (Patricia Franchini), Van Doude
(journalist), Liliane David (Liliane), Claude
Mansart (second-hand automobile dealer),
Henri-Jacques Huet (Antonio Berruti)

Jean-Luc Godard

1930 Born on December 3 in Paris as the son of a doctor.
Grew up in Switzerland. Started studying ethnology at
the Sorbonne in Paris, which was overshadowed by his
interest in film.
1950 Founded *Gazette du Cinéma* with Eric Rohmer and
Jacques Rivette.
1952 Was accepted into the ranks of movie critics of
Cahiers du Cinéma; contact with François Truffaut
and Claude Chabrol.
1954 First (documentary) short film: *Opération béton*
1959 Sensational movie debut with *Breathless*
(Silver Berlin Bear)
1960 *Le Petit Soldat* (banned by French censors because of its
critical stance towards the Algerian war)
1961 *A Woman Is a Woman* (with his first wife, Anna Karina,
as lead actress)
1963 *Contempt*
1965 *Pierrot le Fou* and *Masculine Feminine*
1967 *La Chinoise* (with his second wife, Anne Wiazemsky);
special jury prize in Cannes.
The protest movement of the late 1960s politicized
Godard and several projects were not completed.
1972 *Tout va bien* (with Yves Montand and Jane Fonda)
1975 *Numéro Deux*
1980 *Every Man for Himself*
1983 *First Name Carmen* (Golden Lion, Venice)
1990 *New Wave* (with Alain Delon)
1991 *Germany Nine Zero*
1993 *Woe Is Me*
1995 *J.L.G./J.L.G.* (Godard's self-portrait)
1996/97 Acted in *Nous sommes tous encore ici*
(produced by his third partner, Anne-Marie Miéville)
1999 *Éloge de l'amour*
2000 *Pour une histoire du XXIème siècle*
2000 *Origine du XXIème siècle*

"It doesn't matter where you take your ideas from. The
only thing that matters is where you take them to." Godard

The first flirt: Michel (Jean-Paul Belmondo) and Patricia (Jean Seberg) meeting in Paris

"This makes me puke," are Michel Poiccard's
(Jean-Paul Belmondo) last words after being
mortally wounded by a policeman's bullet.
"What's he saying?" asks Patricia (Jean Seberg),
his American girlfriend and police informant.
"He says, you make him puke," translates the
inspector. Patricia, looking straight into the
camera, asks: "What's that? Puke?" So ends
Godard's first film—shot on a small budget in
four weeks—which has long since attained
cult status, revolutionized the cinema, and
made Godard a guru.

A Bout de Souffle was a sensation that left
the film world breathless. In the late fifties,
Godard—along with colleagues François
Truffaut, Claude Chabrol, and Jacques Rivette—
set out to overthrow the "calcified" cinema and
conservative "serious films" of the postwar era
and became a leading figure of the New Wave.
"There were too many rules," he commented
in retrospect, long after ensuring that these
rules and regulations had lost their validity. It is
difficult for viewers today to comprehend what
was then perceived as new, different, exciting,
and even scandalous. But Godard's iconoclasm
and radical innovations in the language of film
were at first accepted by young filmmakers and
auteurs, only later did they enter the realm of
the commercial film world. When *A Bout de
Souffle* hit the screens, everyone believed that
the cinema had been reinvented.

Godard's tale, based on an idea by Truffaut,
is fairly conventional. It revolves around car

thief Michel Poiccard
(Belmondo in the part
that made him a star) who,
while on the run, shoots
and kills a policeman. In
Paris, he takes refuge with
an enchanting American
student named Patricia,
makes love to her, talks to
her about books, sex, and
death, is betrayed by her,
and shot by the police.

What matters more
than the story's subject
matter is *how* the story is
told. Shot live on location
with a handheld camera
—Godard made do without
artifical light—and edited
in an abrupt and seemingly
erratic manner, the story is
presented in fragments. Since 1995, the filmmakers of the group "Dogma," led by Lars
von Trier (see p. 176), have been working in
a similar fashion but more radically and with
greater stringency.

In 1983, director James McBride remade
Godard's classic. Entitled *Breathless*, with
Richard Gere and Valérie Kaprisky, the film
is but a pale imitation of the great original,
no more than entertaining fluff. Godard's film,
on the other hand, mirrored the spirit of a
generation and thus has lost none of its impact
and freshness. Perhaps one really does have to
be "a madman or a liar," as Godard's colleague
Claude Sautet put it, "to recognize the significance of this unique and grandiose film."

P.W.E.

Looks are deceiving: Patricia is about to leave Michel

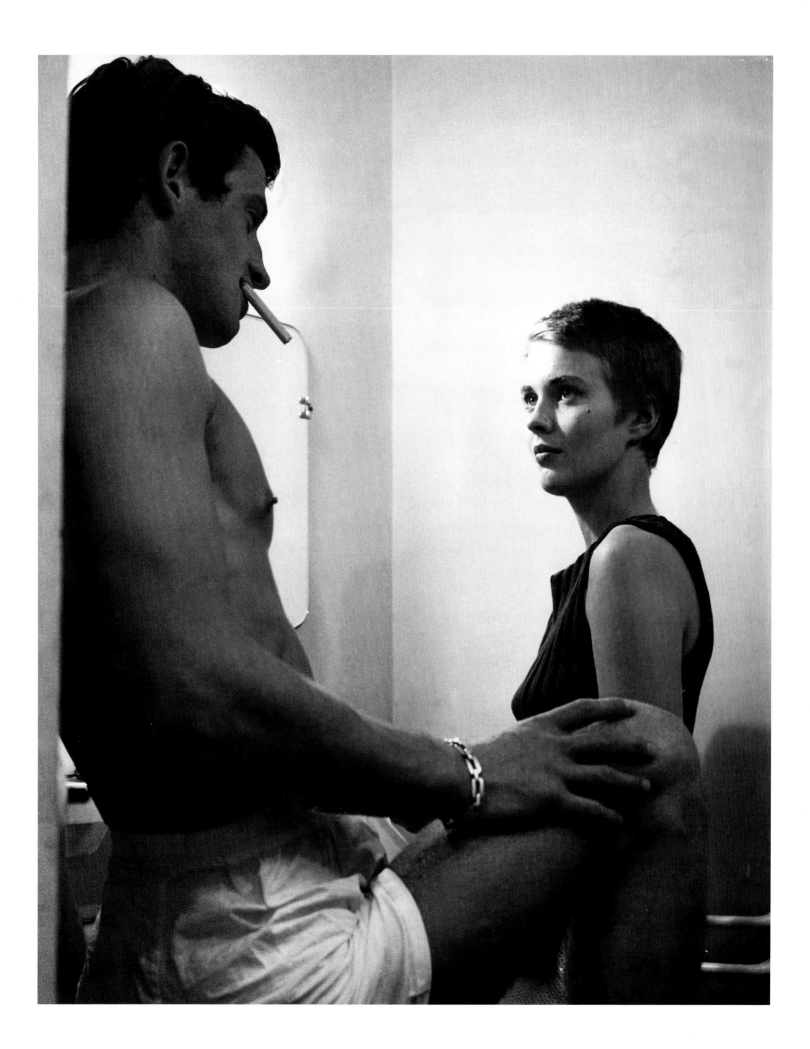

Ben Hur

USA, 1959
Running time: 213 minutes
Directed by William Wyler; *written by* Karl
Tunberg, *based on the novel of the same name
by* Lewis Wallace; *cinematographer,* Robert
Surtees; *music by* Miklos Rozsa; *edited by*
Ralph E. Winters *and* John Dunning
With: Charlton Heston (Ben Hur), Stephen
Boyd (Messala), Jack Hawkins (Quintus
Arrius), Haya Harareet (Esther), Hugh Griffith
(Scheich Ilderim)

The original poster (USA), 1959

As the winner of the chariot race, Ben Hur is presented
with a crown of laurels

William Wyler's monumental adaptation of
Lewis Wallace's religious epic, published in 1880,
was a film of many "firsts." It was the most expensive production of its day, at approximately
fifteen million dollars, and it featured more
extras and had more crew than any other film
before it (22,000 extras were transported daily to
Cinnecitta for shooting the famous chariot race
alone). It took a year to construct a replica of a
Roman circus, and more than 100,000 costumes
had to be made. *Ben Hur* also earned record
sums at the box office worldwide, and it was
the first film ever to receive eleven awards at
the Oscars in 1960.

In unequalled, brilliant Technicolor, the
three-and-a-half hour, wide-screen epic tells the
story of Jewish nobleman Ben Hur (Charlton
Heston), a contemporary of Jesus, who was enslaved by the Roman tribune Messala, a friend
from his youth, because he refuses to join in a
pact against Jewish rebels. Years later, Ben Hur
returns as the adoptive son of Roman consul
Arrius whose life he saved during a battle at
sea and for which deed he was granted his
freedom. Driven by a strong desire for revenge,
Hur beats his old foe, Messala, in a chariot race,
during which the tribune is horribly injured and
dies—but not before revealing to Ben Hur that
his mother and sister have been condemned to
live among lepers. Ben Hur is consumed by rage
and hatred, but, after seeing Jesus on his way
to Golgotha, has a transforming experience.
He understands that forgiveness, not blind
revenge, can change the characters and fates
of people.

Wyler's adaptation of the classic was a remake of the 1924 silent film by director Fred
Niblo, which in turn had been based on a fif-
teen-minute film treatment of the material by
Sidney Olcott. Although the chariot race was
the highlight even in Niblo's earlier version,
Wyler's powerful rendition of it made the
others pale by comparison, as he captured
the struggle between the quadriga with un-
surpassed energy and speed. All other crowd
scenes in the film pale against this spectacle
in the Roman circus, even the battle at sea
and Hur's pompous, triumphant progress
through Rome on his patron's chariot (though
the latter is especially splendid in all its technicolor glory). Wyler's *Ben Hur* is unique among
biblical epics in that it succeeds in creating
psychological coherence even though the pace
and the score are sometimes too gaudy and
pompous for modern tastes. From the perspective of film as historic document one cannot
ignore certain anti-Semitic undertones—only
some of which originate in the novel—even
though they are swept aside by the melodramatic exuberance of the on-screen action. *J.L.*

>>> William Wyler, *The Big Country,* and Biography,
see p. 74

Deadly duel: Ben Hur (Charlton Heston) pushes ahead
of Messala (Stephen Boyd, left)

Brilliantly choreographed crowd scenes: the chariot race in the film lasts twenty minutes

USA, 1959
Running time: 120 minutes
Black and white
Directed by Billy Wilder; *written by* Billy
Wilder *and* I. A. L. Diamond, *based on a story
by* R. Thoeren *and* M. Logan; *cinematographer,*
Charles Lang, Jr.; *music by* Adolph Deutsch;
edited by Arthur Schmidt
With: Jack Lemmon (Jerry Daphne), Tony
Curtis (Joe Josephine), Marilyn Monroe
("Sugar Kane"), George Raft ("Spats"
Colombo), Pat O'Brien (Mulligan), Joe E.
Brown (Osgood E. Fielding III), Nehemiah
Persoff (Little Bonaparte)

Smitten tango dancer: Joe E. Brown (left) as Osgood
E. Fielding III and Jack Lemmon as Daphne

"I was the prettiest girl ever as a man!"
Tony Curtis commenting on his superb performance in drag

>>> Billy Wilder, *Sunset Boulevard,* and Biography,
see p. 54
>>> Jack Lemmon in *Short Cuts,* see p. 162

"Endless re-takes were necessary"—Marilyn Monroe as "Sugar Kane" with her lady's band

Tony Curtis and Jack Lemmon in drag, running
from the Mob? The hilarious story became a
box office hit and established Curtis as a star.
The comedy is just as funny now as it was then:
the way Curtis and Lemmon squeeze themselves into women's clothing as Josephine and
Daphne and struggle with all the challenges of
womanhood—"You tore off my breasts!"—is
Hollywood at its best. Rarely were dialogues so
witty and gags so timeless.

Director Billy Wilder handled the comedic
stereotype of "men in women's clothing" with
style and aplomb. He avoided dirty jokes and
seedy insinuations and shot his film in black
and white so that the heavy make-up wouldn't
look grotesque. "The result, in my humble
opinion, is the greatest film comedy of all
times. Billy Wilder was an absolute genius,"
Jack Lemmon reminisced enthusiastically
about the over-the-top flick.

But the path to the finished product was
rocky. "I had no idea that we were in mid-flight
with a crazy woman on board," Wilder later
commented about work on the set. What was
the problem? Marilyn Monroe. Monroe was
unable to remember her lines, and it took

forty-seven takes before she managed to say:
"It's me, Sugar." Some of her variations were
"Sugar, it's me" and "It's Sugar." After the
thirtieth take, Wilder wrote the line onto a
chalkboard. Tony Curtis later commented that
"The strangest thing about the endless repeti-
tions was that all she had to do was a single
line. But at other times she would deliver an
entire scene in one perfect take. The only
reliable thing about her was her unreliability."
Jack Lemmon's assessment of the situation
was a bit different: "I don't think it was caprice.
It was pure egotism."

Regardless of Monroe's behavior, Wilder
finished the film and it was worth it. What we
see on the screen is the irresistible Monroe in a
breathtaking dress singing "I Wanna Be Loved
By You," practicing her kisses on Curtis, or
accepting a priceless bracelet with the words:
"Oh, diamonds! They must be almost as valu-
able as gold." One thing is certain, audiences
would have regretted it if Mitzi Gaynor had
played Sugar, as was initially intended.   *S.R.*

"A comedy like a firework display"—
Marilyn Monroe as "Sugar Kane" and
Tony Curtis as Josephine

Secret rendezvous in the train: Jack Lemon and Marilyn Monroe

Psycho

USA, 1960

Running time: 110 minutes

Black and white

Directed by Alfred Hitchcock; *written by* Joseph Stefano, *based on a novel by* Robert Bloch; *cinematographer,* John L. Russell; *music by* Bernard Herrmann; *edited by* George Tomasini

With: Anthony Perkins (Norman Bates), Janet Leigh (Marion Crane), Vera Miles (Lila Crane), John Gavin (Sam Loomis), John McIntire (Al Chambers), Martin Balsam (Milton Arbogast), Lurene Tuttle (Mrs. Chambers), Simon Oakland (Dr. Richmond)

Alfred Hitchcock

1899 Born on August 13 in London. Studied engineering and worked as a technician.

1920 Started his career in the movie industry.

1925 Movie debut with *The Pleasure Garden*

1926 His first thriller: *The Lodger*

1935 *The 39 Steps*

1938 *The Lady Vanishes* ended his so-called British period and he moved to Hollywood.

1940 His first US movie, *Rebecca*, received an Oscar for best film.

His Masterpieces:

1946 *Notorious*

1951 *Strangers on a Train*

1954 *Dial M for Murder* and *Rear Window*

1955 *The Trouble With Harry* and *To Catch a Thief*

1958 *Vertigo*

1959 *North by Northwest*

1960 *Psycho*

1963 *The Birds*

1971 *Frenzy*

1976 *Family Plot* was his last movie

1979 One year before his death, Hitchcock received the Life Achievement Award of the American Film Institute.

1980 Alfred Hitchcock died in Hollywood.

"He tried to be his mother—and now he is."

Dr. Richmond (Simon Oakland) explaining what's happened to Norman Bates (Anthony Perkins)

Anthony Perkins as psychopath Norman Bates

Psycho was a remarkable project for director Alfred Hitchcock in many ways. Throughout the 1950s, the "master of suspense" had celebrated one success after another with a string of elegant suspense films and a cast of stars: *Dial M for Murder*, *Rear Window*, and *To Catch a Thief*, among others. Then he discovered a horror novel by Robert Bloch, for which he could find no financial backers. In the end, Hitchcock financed and produced *Psycho* on his own—inexpensively, at 800,000 dollars— by working with a television crew. "I think the only thing I liked, and which made me decide to make the film, was the unexpected murder in the shower," Hitchcock told French director François Truffaut during an interview in 1966.

It is one of the most disturbing shower scenes of all times, one in which a young woman, Marion Crane (Janet Leigh), is killed in a sinister motel, to the accompaniment of a screeching violin. Hitchcock carefully planned the scene—which was outrageous for its time —with a full storyboard. Out of four weeks of shooting time, he devoted seven full days to the shower scene and spliced together more than seventy camera angles, none of which show the actual murder. This manner of depiction was so cunning that the scene has been permanently imprinted in viewers' memories. Even actress Janet Leigh confesses that she is afraid in the shower to this day.

For Anthony Perkins, too, things were never the same after *Psycho*. Professionally, we was never able to shake the Norman Bates character, which he had embodied so flawlessly. His performance was so successful that he was permanently typecast, viewers wanting to see

him only in the role of a murdering psychopath. In fact, there were three sequels to *Psycho*, none of which was directed by Hitchcock.

The achievement of the actors aside, the thriller bears the unmistakable mark of Hitchcock's genius. His manner of repeatedly sending viewers down false paths, allowing them to sympathize with murderers and thieves, has lost none of its fascination after forty years. Countless references to *Psycho* have been made in other director's films, and, in 1998, Gus Van Sant even remade the movie.

With *Psycho*, Hitchcock went beyond the usual shock elements of the horror genre by experimenting with symbolism. Stuffed birds are used as metaphors of death throughout the film, while mirrors and criss-crossing graphic lines represent the schizophrenic nature of the characters. As critic Hellmuth Karasek wrote: "Hitchcock extrapolate[d] horror from the nice next-door neighbor and a threatening atmosphere from a climate of daily neuroses, frustrations, and disappointments." In so doing, he crafted a captivating and brilliantly told thriller in which the audience is superbly manipulated.

In 1968, Hitchcock received an honorary Oscar for lifetime achievement after "the film academy had judged him as a brilliant, but unimportant entertainer for nearly thirty years and ignored his art as a director." Today, Hitchcock is considered "the most famous director in the history of film."   *S.R.*

"No horror on the screen can be as awful as that in the mind of the viewer,"
said Alfred Hitchcock. Pictured above is the legendary house of horrors

Neuroses and frustration: Janet Leigh as
Marion Crane and John Gavin as Sam Loomis

Breakfast at Tiffany's

USA, 1960
Running time: 115 minutes
Directed by Blake Edwards; *written by* George
Axelrod, *based on a short story by* Truman
Capote; *cinematographer,* Franz Planer; *music
by* Henry Mancini; *edited by* Howard Smith
With: Audrey Hepburn (Holly Golightly),
George Peppard (Paul Varjak), Patricia Neal
(2-E), Mickey Rooney (Mr. Yunioshi), Buddy
Ebsen (Doc Golightly), Martin Balsam
(O. J. Berman)

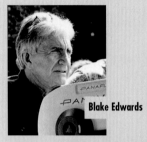

Blake Edwards

1922 Born on July 26 as William Blake McEdwards in Tulsa,
 Oklahoma. Both his father and grandfather had worked
 as directors in the movie business. Edwards started his
 movie career as an actor in 1942. Made a name for
 himself as a scriptwriter, developed successful TV series
 such as *Peter Gunn.*
1955 *Bring Your Smile Along* (Edwards' first movie)
1959 Box office success with the comedy *Operation Petticoat*
1961 *Breakfast at Tiffany's,* based on the novel by Truman
 Capote, was a worldwide success
1962 *Days of Wine and Roses*
1963 *The Pink Panther* criminal comedy was followed by
 a whole series of PinkPanther movies, including *The
 Return of the Pink Panther* (1974), *The Pink Panther
 Strikes Again* (1976), *The Trail of the Pink Panther*
 (1982)
1969 *Darling Lili* (with Julie Andrews, whom he married
 the same year)
1978 *10*
1981 *S.O.B.*
1982 *Victor/Victoria* (Oscar for Julie Andrews)
1987 *Blind Date*
1991 *Switch*
1993 *Son of the Pink Panther* (with Roberto Benigni). After
 the unsuccessful attempt to revive the *Pink Panther*
 series, Blake Edwards directed no more movies.

After her breakthrough in *Roman Holiday* (William Wyler,
1953), Audrey Hepburn (1929–93) appeared in films
such as *Sabrina, War and Peace, Funny Face, The Nun's
Story, Breakfast at Tiffany's, Charade, My Fair Lady,*
and *Wait Until Dark.*

Holly (Audrey Hepburn): the seductress of many a man

This was perhaps Audrey Hepburn's best role.
As New York call girl Holly Golightly, she combined waywardness, fragility, and childlike
innocence in such an inimitable way, that it
is difficult to imagine that Marilyn Monroe
was first asked to play the part. Strangely,
Monroe declined because she felt the role was
too risqué. Her refusal was a stroke of luck for
Hepburn, for whom the role seemed to have
been written. Only she could have interpreted
the character from Truman Capote's novel in
such a sensual and naive way, creating a bitter-
sweet love story full of mischievous humor
and wonderful feelings served up in grand,
cinematic style.

In the beginning, Hepburn also had mis-
givings. After all, her character, Holly Golightly,
jumps from one man to the next, has a pimp,
and falls in love with an attractive writer
(George Peppard) who is kept by an older
woman. Later, though, Hepburn saw an opportunity to break with her innocent image.
In the end, she decided to interpret the role
to suit her own sense of morality—as a scared

little mouse who never actually did "anything." Hepburn even commented that she
had "lived in circumstances myself that were
quite similar to Holly's."

Blake Edwards, then a young, up-and-
coming director—his *Pink Panther* was still
to come—transformed the story of a nineteen-
year-old girl (played by a thirty-year-old
Hepburn), who flirts with rich men in search
of true love, into a tender love story with the
right blend of tragedy and comedy.

At first, critics felt that Hepburn had
been miscast. How could such an aristocratic
European play an American country girl turned
New York model? But Hepburn created a
whole new type of girl with Holly Golightly, a
bohemian who takes her breakfast at, or,
rather, in front of, Tiffany's. The way she hails
a cab, calls everyone Darling, gracefully wields
a long cigarette holder, and keeps her shoes
in a fruit bowl is unforgettable. Hepburn's
wardrobe, designed by Givenchy and intended
to resemble ready-to-wear clothing in its sim-
plicity, launched a fashion trend that is still

Beguiling and naive: Audrey Hepburn in front of the window at Tiffany's

popular today. Following her role in *Sabrina* (1954), Heburn employed Givenchy for both her work and personal wardrobe. "Givenchy's creations have always given me a feeling of security and self assurance," she reminisced. "It made work easier knowing that my appearance was absolutely perfect."

The song "Moon River," composed by Henry Mancini especially for *Breakfast at Tiffany's* received an Oscar and became a classic. The appeal of the tearjerker, sung by Hepburn as she strums a guitar, is eternal—at least for the romantics among us.   *S.Al.*

A girl looking for happiness:
Holly (Audrey Hepburn) with Paul (George Peppard, right)

Lawrence of Arabia

USA, 1962

Running time: 222 (187) minutes
Directed by David Lean; *written by* Robert Bolt
and Michael Wilson, *based on* The Seven
Pillars of Wisdom *by* T. E. Lawrence;
cinematographer, Freddie Young; *music by*
Maurice Jarre; *edited by* Anne V. Coates
With: Peter O'Toole (T. E. Lawrence), Alec
Guinness (Prince Feisal), Anthony Quinn
(Auda Abu Tayi), Jack Hawkins (General
Allenby), José Ferrer (Turkish Bey), Anthony
Quayle (Colonel Harry Brighton), Claude
Rains (Mr. Dryden), Arthur Kennedy
(Jackson Bentley), Omar Sharif (Sherif Ali
Ibn El Kharisch)

David Lean

1908 Born on March 25 in Croydon, England.
1927 Started in the movie business. Worked his way up from
errand boy to cutter.
1942 Directing debut with the war drama *In Which We Serve,*
which he produced together with Noel Coward.
1944 *Blithe Spirit*
1946 *Great Expectations*
1948 *Oliver Twist*
1957 International recognition for *The Bridge on the River
Kwai* (seven Oscars). With this and the following three
productions, Lean founded his reputation as the master
of monumental epics.
1962 *Lawrence of Arabia* (seven Oscars)
1965 *Doctor Zhivago* (five Oscars)
1969/1970 After the failure of *Ryan's Daughter*, had a
comeback after 14 years.
1984 *A Passage to India* (his last movie). Lean was knighted.
1990 Life Achievement Award of the American Film Institute.
1991 David Lean died in London at the age of 83.

"It's clean..."
Peter O'Toole as T. E. Lawrence, on what attracts
him to the desert.

It was only in 1989 that David Lean could see his film on the
screen in the way that he had imagined it. In the years
following its release, the film had been trimmed from 222
minutes to 187. After numerous restoration attempts, and
insertions of the original material, the film reappeared in the
movie theaters 27 years later.

above and opposite page: Peter O'Toole (right) as T. E. Lawrence and his counterpart,
Omar Sharif (left) as Sherif Ali Ibn El Kharisch

When *Lawrence of Arabia*—a larger than life,
spectacular, psycho-thriller/adventure film set
in colonial Britain—hit the cinemas, the three-
hour epic on the giant screen was a welcome
antidote to flat television images. (Today, whenever the film is shown in re-runs on television,
it is robbed of half of its power.)

In Superpanavision, director David Lean
combined landscape, Oriental folklore, war,
insanity, psychology, and politics into a
"men's film" that could easily be criticized
for its celebration of pathos if its portrayal of
the contradictory nature of an individual's
development weren't so artful. The making
of *Lawrence of Arabia* required both vision
and hubris, which is why it is truly inspired
cinema.

After his international success with *The
Bridge on the River Kwai*, David Lean could afford
the outrageously expensive *Lawrence of Arabia*.
With the help of a wonderful cast, including

Peter O'Toole, Alec Guinness, Antony Quinn,
Jack Hawkins, and Omar Sharif, he succeeded in
magically recreating a myth in all its treacher-
ous complexity.

The character of Lawrence of Arabia, who
was deeply involved in the World War I fight
against the Turks—and whose eccentric ideals
conflicted with British interests—is depicted
in a dubious light. We see a man who has
a dangerous fixation on pushing the limits,
a fascination with the idea of the *übermensch*
and a tendency to constantly challenge his
own strength and intelligence. He comes very
close to excessive arrogance. Lawrence is a
spartan masochist, venerated as a demigod
by the bedouins, who fails in the end when it
becomes clear that he is no longer the master
over himself. Rather, he is dominated by his
own nature.

The film subtly follows a fanatic who uses
his blue eyes, British fads, steely endurance of

pain, Oxford education, Oxford arrogance, and his suggestive power over others. Battle is intoxicating to him, the desert a test of will and imagination.

The beauty of this elegy to the desert, emotionally sustained and poetically heightened by Maurice Jarre's melancholy, sentimental musical (the film score of the century!), is its timeless magic as historic war spectacle and psychoanalytical melodrama: genius and madness on the road from Oxford to Damascus.

Po.

Goldfinger

England, 1964
Running time: 106 minutes
Directed by Guy Hamilton; *written by* Richard
Maibaum *and* Paul Dehn, *based on a novel by*
Ian Fleming; *cinematographer,* Ted Moore;
music by John Barry; *edited by* Peter Hunt
With: Sean Connery (James Bond), Gert Fröbe
(Goldfinger), Shirley Eaton (Jill Masterson),
Bernard Lee ("M"), Honor Blackman (Pussy
Galore), Lois Maxwell (Miss Monneypenny),
Desmond Llewelyn ("Q")

Guy Hamilton

1922 Born to British parents in Paris.
1940 Served in the British marines during World War II;
subsequently assistant director in London for productions
including *The Third Man* and *The African Queen.*
1952 Directing debut with *The Ringer*
1957 *Manuela/Stowaway Girl*
1959 *The Devil's Disciple*
1964 *Goldfinger* was his first James-Bond movie, followed
by three more 007 adventures:
1971 *Diamonds Are Forever*
1973 *Live and Let Die*
1974 *The Man With the Golden Gun*
1978 *Force 10 From Navarone*
1980 *The Mirror Crack'd* (based on Agatha Christie)
1981 *Evil Under the Sun* (based on Agatha Christie)
1985 *Remo Williams: The Adventure Begins*
1989 After the French production *Try This One for Size,* action
specialist Hamilton retired from the movie business.

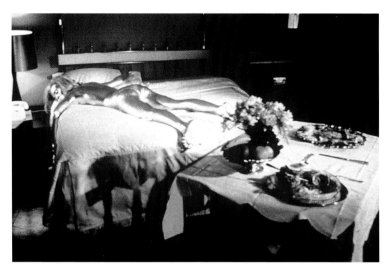

All that glitters is not gold:
Shirley Eaton as the
Bond girl

Some bands drag themselves onto the stage
dressed in rags, reel off their set in a self-
important way, and then wrap up by sighing
into the microphone: "Oh, yeah, and by the
way, children are starving in Angola." Then
there are bands whose costumes are as perfect
as their sound, who burst with energy and
keep their audiences spellbound to the last
note. In this second sense, James Bond is the
funk singer James Brown of cinema. He's sex
appeal and style.

Her Majesty's playboy has been playing the
field for over forty years. He survived the ideo-
logical changes of the last decade, four casting
changes, and the competition of action flicks
such as *Die Hard.* He is the most famous and
most enduring trademark product in the history
of film. Q may die, but Bond lives forever. Just
as every forward needs a good pass to score in
soccer, so the universal success of the Bond films
would be unthinkable without the machismo
of the original 007, Sean Connery. In *Goldfinger*
(1964), he laid the foundation for the Bond
legend. Following on the heels of *Doctor No*
(1960) and *From Russia with Love* (1963), 007's
third assignment was the first "event movie"
in cinematic history, earning record sums at
the box office within a short period of time.
Ever since, hits of this magnitude have been
called "blockbusters" in reference to the line-
up of hopeful cinema fans stretching past
several city blocks.

Guy Hamilton's *Goldfinger* was the last true
spy thriller of the series. In the next sequel,
Thunderball (1965), the rugged Mickey Spillane-
inspired Bond was sacrificed to fireworks, gags,
and special effects. *Goldfinger* was more of a

balance between Eddie Constantine and
Rocketman. Yet, this was not the only one
reason it became a cult film. *Goldfinger* has
style! The Korean character, Odd Job, was a
killer of unusual talents and in Gerd Fröbe
there was a bad guy of substance. Shirley
Bassey's title song became the quasi hymn
of the entire series.

Above all, there are stunning visuals that
stay with us. At a time when pyjama parties
were the epitome of socially acceptable sexu-
ality, the nearly naked, gold-painted corpse
of Goldfinger's escort, played by Shirley Eaton,
must have awakened erotic fantasies in the
viewing public. Likewise, the scene in which
Goldfinger tortures Bond with a laser beam
stirred a deep unease in every row of every
cinema. Incidentally, this was the first time
that the brand-new laser technology was
shown in a film, making the uncomfortable
feeling of the scene all the more potent.

The multimillion dollar James Bond enterprise grew out of this tension between lascivious
eroticism and high-powered action. Later Bond
films were more like high-tech extravaganzas.
The original formula deteriorated, first with the
lightweight insouciance of Roger Moore, then
the Ramboesque interpretation of Timothy
Dalton, and finally the "pretty boy" facade
of Pierce Brosnan. There's only one Bond.
But that's telling Sean Connery something
he already knows.   *H.R.*

Shirley Eaton:
"My name is Pussy Galore."
James Bond:
"I must be dreaming..."

Bond never dies: Sean Connery as the agent who always
survives...

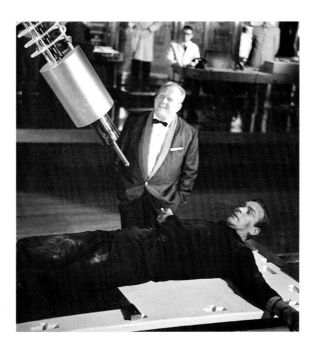

...even if it sometimes seems impossible! Goldfinger (Gerd Fröbe)
trying to laser 007 to death. Bond asks: "Do you expect me to talk?"
Goldfinger answers: "No, Mr. Bond, I expect you to die!"

The Fearless Vampire Killers

or Pardon Me, Your Teeth Are in My Neck
England/USA, 1967
Running time: 108 minutes (orig. 118)
Directed by Roman Polanski; *written by* Roman
Polanski *and* Gérard Brach; *cinematographer,*
Douglas Slocombe; *music by* Krzysztof
Komeda; *edited by* Alastair McIntyre
With: Jack MacGowran (Professor Abronsius),
Roman Polanski (Alfred, his assistent),
Sharon Tate (Sarah), Ferdy Mayne (Count
von Krolock), Ian Quarrier (Herbert von
Krolock), Terry Downes (Koukol)

Roman Polanski

1933 Born on August 18 to Polish parents in Paris.
1936 Family returned to Kraków. During World War II, his
      parents were deported to a concentration camp, where
      his mother died. Polanski survived in the underground
      after his escape from the Kraków ghetto.
1954–59 Studied at the Lodz Film School. Directed highly
      acknowledged short films such as *Two Men and a
      Wardrobe* (1958)
1961 Debuted with *Knife in the Water*
1962 Polanski moved to Paris and worked in the West
1964 *Repulsion* (Silver Berlin Bear)
1965 *Cul-de-Sac* (Golden Berlin Bear)
1967 *Dance of the Vampires/The Fearless Vampire Killers*
      (with Sharon Tate)
1968 *Rosemary's Baby*
1969 Sharon Tate, married to Polanski since 1968, was killed
      by the Manson gang.
1971 *Macbeth*
1974 *Chinatown*
1976 *The Tenant*
1979 *Tess*
1986 *Pirates*
      Directed three movies with the actress Emmanuelle
      Seigner, whom he married in 1989:
1987 *Frantic*
1992 *Bitter Moon*
1999 *The Ninth Gate*
      In between, he directed *Death and the Maiden* (with
      Sigourney Weaver and Ben Kingsley) in 1994
1997 Polanski produced a musical version of *Dance of the
      Vampires* in Vienna

Sinking his teeth into the bible: Count von Krolock's homosexual son (Ian Quarrier, left) and Alfred (Roman Polanski)

Polanski's vampire satire is only one of a number of
movies along the same line. Since Murnau's *Nosferatu*,
the "undead" have populated the screen: Bela Lugosi,
Lon Chaney, John Carradine, Christopher Lee, Klaus Kinski
(in Herzog's *Nosferatu* remake) and Gary Oldman in
Coppola's vampire version of 1992.

The MGM lion roars, mutates into a grotesque
vampire face, blood drips from its mouth and
runs down the screen. Even in the opening
sequence, Roman Polanski sets the mood for
The Fearless Vampire Killers, originally shot to
be 118 minutes running time. Originally is
the operative word, because in Europe this film
—an amusing comedy of horrors—is usually
screened in a version cut by ten minutes. By
contrast, it was cut down to 91 minutes in the
States, making it incomprehensible and, as
a consequence, a box office flop. In Europe,
the tale of the bloodsuckers enchanted both
the critics and public. Like other film directors
before him, Polanski opposed these ruthless
cuts to *The Fearless Vampire Killers* vehemently,
but his protests were in vain. Yet, in his interpretation of the Dracula legend, Polanski toys in
an intelligent and stylistically brilliant manner
with the content and form of the genre.

In their search for vampires, the famous
bat researcher, Professor Abronsius, (Jack
MacGowran), and his simpleton helper, Alfred
(Roman Polanski), set off through a Transylvania
covered in deep layers of snow (the externals
were all shot on location in the Dolomites).
In a country inn they are surprised to find
huge amounts of garlic, crosses, and wooden
stakes—classic anti-vampire tools. During the
night, the innkeeper's beautiful daughter,
Sarah (Sharon Tate), is abducted by the dark
Count Krolock (Ferdy Mayne) and taken to his
gloomy castle. Professor Abronsius and Alfred
follow the count to embark on, and survive,
a series of spine-tingling and yet hilarious

adventures. Among others, they are pursued
by the count's gay son, Herbert (Ian Quarrier),
before they succeed in liberating the delightful Sarah during a midnight vampire ball.
Gloriously happy, Abronsius steers his horse-
drawn sleigh away from the castle, blissfully
unaware that Alfred is being bitten by Sarah
—who has already turned into a vampire—
and "[is] taking the Evil which he had hoped
to wipe out forever, with him," as a voice-
over informs us as the film ends. The fearless
vampire killer inadvertently becomes Count
Krolock's helper. This turn of events, which
seems to confirm Polanski's pessimistic view
of the world, was the director's way of turning
the classic vampire scheme upside down. Sadly,
this otherwise delightfully subversive comedy
was overshadowed in 1969 by the tragic murder
of Polanski's pregnant wife, Sharon Tate, by
members of the Manson cult. But in 1997, *The
Fearless Vampire Killers* experienced a cheerful
revival as a musical in Vienna directed by
Polanski himself.   *B.A.*

Bloodsucking done differently: scenes with Sharon Tate as Sarah, and Roman Polanski, as the shy assistant Alfred

In the Heat of the Night

USA, 1966

Running time: 110 minutes
Directed by Norman Jewison; *written by*
Stirling Silliphant; *based on the novel by* John
Ball; *cinematographer,* Haskell Wexler; *music
by* Quincy Jones; *edited by* Hal Ashby
With: Sidney Poitier (Virgil Tibbs), Rod
Steiger (Bill Gillespie), Warren Oates (Sam
Wood), Lee Grant (Leslie Colbert), James
Patterson (Purdy)

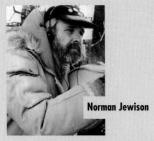

Norman Jewison

1926 Born Norman Frederick Jewison on July 21 in Toronto.
     After studying at the University of Toronto he gained
     experience as a TV director in England, Canada, and the
     US. Became known in the US mostly for CBS music
     shows (with stars like Judy Garland and Harry
     Belafonte).
1962 Movie debut with *40 Pounds of Trouble*
1963 *The Thrill of It All* (with Dorris Day)
1964 *Send Me No Flowers* (with Dorris Day)
1965 *The Cincinnati Kid*
1967 *In the Heat of the Night* (five Oscars)
1968 *The Thomas Crown Affair*
1973 *Jesus Christ Superstar*
1986 Founded the Canadian Center for Advanced Film Studies
     in Toronto.
1987 *Moonstruck* (Silver Berlin Bear for Jewison)
1991 *Other People's Money*
1994 *Only You*
1996 *Bogus*
1999 *The Hurricane*

Relaxed and in control: Sidney Poitier
as Mr. Tibbs and Rod Steiger as sheriff
Gillespie

"They call me MISTER Tibbs." This calm,
self-assured line from *In the Heat of the Night*
caused quite a stir in 1960s America. Civil
rights and racial discrimination were at the
forefront of American politics, and the idea that
a black man should be addressed as Mister,
on film or in real life, was controversial.

The film begins as a standard detective story.
When a powerful industrialist is killed in the
small town of Sparta, Mississippi, the local,
gum chewing, arrogant sheriff Gillespie (Rod
Steiger) doesn't waste time looking for a culprit.
He picks up a stranger, who happens to be
black, near the train station. The case seems
cut and dry, but then comes the sobering and
embarrassing truth. The well-dressed man,
played elegantly by Sidney Poitier, turns out to
be a colleague. Virgil Tibbs, a police detective
from Philadelphia, is just passing through
town.

Tibbs volunteers to help solve the crime,
and Gillespie grudgingly accepts his offer.
The stage is now set for two worlds to collide.
Filled with prejudice, Gillespie has difficulties
interacting with a "negro" whose superiority
he feels all too keenly. The unfolding relationship between the two men becomes more
gripping than the crime story. Gradually,
they draw closer together, in an atmosphere

loaded with hatred and mistrust, ultimately
solving the case. When the two investigators
bid each other goodbye, they do so with deep
mutual respect.

Director Norman Jewison brilliantly combined suspense and human drama in this
masterful work. Despite its hot political topic,
the film turned out to be a commercial and
artistic success, receiving five Oscars, out of
seven nominations. Steiger won the coveted
prize, but Poitier came away empty-handed
—a fact that did not go unnoticed by African
Americans.

Today, it is almost impossible to express,
especially to audiences outside of the US,
how much Poitier boosted the confidence of
the black community. For decades, he was the
only African American superstar in Hollywood.
He became the first to receive an Oscar—for
Lilies of the Field (1963)—and the first to act
out a romance with a white woman on screen.
As one US film critic wrote, Poitier didn't
"make films, he made milestones."   *P.W.E.*

"From beginning to end, *In the Heat of the Night* is carefully directed by Jewison who eschews sentimentality and
all the racial clichés that could have so easily crept into
almost every scene."
The Motion Picture Guide

Criminal tension and racial problems: Sidney Poitier stars in this literary-based film

Hate and mistrust in Mississippi

Le Samourai (The Godson)

**Le Samouraï/Frank Costello faccia d'angelo
France/Italy, 1967**
Running time: 98 minutes (orig. 103)
Directed by Jean-Pierre Melville; *written by*
Jean-Pierre Melville, *based on the novel* The
Ronin *by* Goan McLeod; *cinematographer,*
Henri Decaë; *music by* François de Roubaix;
edited by Monique Bonnot amd Yolande
Maurette
With: Alain Delon (Joseph "Jeff" Costello),
Nathalie Delon (Jeanne Lagrange), François
Périer (Detective Superintendent), Cathy
Rosier (Valérie), Catherine Jourdan
(cloakroom attendant)

Jean-Pierre Melville

1917 Born Jean-Pierre Grumbach on October 20 in Paris.
1937–1945 Army duty
1945 Founded his own production company.
1946 First (and only) short film: *Vingt-quatre heures de la vie d'un clown*
1947 Movie debut with *Le Silence de la Mer*
1949 *The Strange Ones* (based on a novel by Cocteau)
1956 *Bob the Gambler* (Melville's first gangster movie which has stylistic and thematic elements of his later movies)
195 *Deux hommes dans Manhattan*
1960 Melville had a small role in Godard's *Breathless*
1961 *Leon Morin, Priest*
1963 *Magnet of Doom; Doulos the Finger Man*
1966 *Second Breath*
1967 *The Godson*
1969 *The Shadow Army*
1970 *The Red Circle*
1972 *Dirty Money*
1973 Jean-Pierre Melville died in Paris.

The archetypal gangster: Alain Delon as 'Samurai' in a lonely world

Sparse, cool, calculated, rigorous, and aesthetic. *Le Samourai,* by director Jean-Pierre Melville, is a classic of the genre and created the foundation for the myth of a star. Alain Delon plays professional killer Jeff Costello, a man who handles his contracts without emotion and with clockwork precision, an artful figure acting in a world of loneliness, isolation, and alienation.

"There is no greater loneliness than the loneliness of the samurai, aside from the loneliness of the tiger in the jungle." This quotation at the film's opening is supposedly taken from the samurai code of conduct, the *Bushido,* but, in reality, it was written by Melville himself (a fact that went unnoticed even in Japan). Costello is both the samurai who plies his trade according to fixed rules and ritualized gestures and a tiger being chased through the urban jungle. There is no psychological study of his behavior, nor do his past or social environment play a role. The camera simply records how he exercises his profession.

Retained by a gangster syndicate, Jeff Costello shoots and kills a night club owner. Since he has a foolproof alibi in his girlfriend, Jeanne (Nathalie Delon), the police are unable to pin anything on him, but they keep him under observation. Thus, he becomes a liability to his clients. Hunted by policemen and gangsters, he accepts one last contract for the sole purpose of getting close to, and killing, the syndicate boss. He points his gun so demonstratively at his victim (Cathy Rosier) that the police shoot and kill him instead. Ironically, Costello's gun wasn't loaded in the first place. Thus, what Jeff has done is commit hara-kiri, setting the scene of his own

death and directing and planning it as perfectly as he would any of his other jobs. This is his final triumph because, as the protagonist in this film with so little dialogue remarks, "I never lose, not really."

The inevitability of these events is reminiscent of a Greek tragedy. Alain Delon plays his part in this "requiem for a killer" with minimal gestures and expressions. For the director, whose real name was Grumbach but who called himself Melville in homage to the famous author, the collaboration with Delon was a key factor: "The most important element in creating *Le Samourai* was undoubtedly the idea I had formed of Alain Delon's behavior, not his behavior in life, but his behavior on screen in a film I would direct....A great actor, a star, is always the co-author of a film. He is... inspiring."

B.A.

Jeff Costello (Alain Delon, above, and right with hat) is
a calculating professional killer who is on the run from
would-be assassins and in the end provokes his own death

Bonnie and Clyde

USA, 1967
Running time: 111 minutes
Directed by Arthur Penn; *written by* David
Newman, Robert Benton; *cinematographer,*
Burnett Guffey; *music by* Charles Strouse;
edited by Dede Allen
With: Warren Beatty (Clyde Barrow), Faye
Dunaway (Bonnie Parker), Gene Hackman
(Buck Barrow), Estelle Parsons (Blanche),
Michael J. Pollard (C. W. Moss), Denver Pyle
(Frank Hamer), Gene Wilder (Eugene
Grizzard)

Arthur Penn

1922 Born on September 27 in Philadelphia. Interested in the
   theater at an early age.
1951 Started to work for TV stations as an author and
   director of television plays.
1958 was the decisive year for his career. First Broadway
   production *Two for the Seesaw* and first feature movie
   The Left-Handed Gun (with Paul Newman)
1962 *The Miracle Worker* (the movie adaptation of his
   successful Broadway production)
1967 *Bonnie and Clyde* (nominated for eight Oscars and
   awarded two)
1969 *Alice's Restaurant*
1970 *Little Big Man*
1975 *Night Moves*
1976 *The Missouri Breaks*
1981 *Four Friends*
1985 *Target*
1989 *Penn & Teller Get Killed*
1996 *Inside*

The bloody ending to a thrilling gangster movie

**The sociopsychological thriller was awarded two Oscars and
nominated for six more. It started a 1930s fashion revival
and catapulted Faye Dunaway and Warren Beatty into the
first line of movie stars.**

A bloody ballade
with great actors:
Faye Dunaway and
Warren Beatty

When Arthur Penn's *Bonnie and Clyde* hit the
cinemas, no one was prepared for a gangster
film of its kind. Ferocious violence and emotional detachment pervade the movie, culminating in the ambush of Bonnie Parker (Fay
Dunaway) and Clyde Barrow (Warren Beatty)
by Texas rangers. Even though the protagonists'
lives end in a bloodbath, Penn's direction dis-
courages viewers from developing compassion
for them.

The movie is based on the real-life story of
Depression-era bankrobbers, Bonnie and
Clyde. In the movie, Bonnie is a world-weary
waitress who hooks up with Clyde, an ex-con-
vict. Like-minded drifters, the two form a
gang and embark on a series of bank robberies
which make them famous. The pair become folk
heroes at a time when credit institutions are
driving indebted farmers to ruin. Confident and
cocky, they make no attempt at dissemblance,
giving interviews and boldly stating: "We rob
banks!" Morever, they gain the sympathy of
the "little man." Cast as forerunners of modern
media stars, they bask in the glow of self-made
publicity which they perpetuate with poems
that praise their escapades. Penn depicts both
characters as quintessential desperados: living
on the edge, free of ties, and accountable to
no one. In real life and on the screen, country
folks sympathized with the gang because they
had no ties to organized crime. Thus, the gang
could be celebrated as embodiments of the
American myth of the free spirit.

Penn's adaptation of the Bonnie and Clyde
legend was influenced by 1960s, European
cinema, particularly the French New Wave.
In fact, François Truffaut had initially been
chosen as the film's director. It has also been
suggested that Penn's depiction of the bitter
struggle between outlaws and state power
—and vice versa—reflected struggles in America
at the time in which the movie was mad. These
include the Vietnam war and student protests.
Bonnie and Clyde do resemble peaceful hippies,
who become ruthless outlaws. In view of the
power and inventiveness at work in this film,
it is difficult to understand why Penn, who
created other cult classics such as *Alice's
Restaurant* and *Little Big Man*, is often excluded
from the ranks of innovative, independent,
American filmmakers.   *H.M.*

Two disillusioned people as gangsters:
Bonnie and Clyde become heroes

England, 1965–68
Running time: 149 minutes (orig. 160)
Directed by Stanley Kubrick; *written by* Stanley Kubrick *and* Arthur C. Clarke, *based on a short story by* Arthur C. Clarke; *cinematographer,* Geoffrey Unsworth, John Alcott; *music by* Aram Khatschaturian, Richard Strauss, Johann Strauß, and György Ligeti; *edited by* Ray Lovejoy
With: Keir Dullea (David Bowman), Gary Lockwood (Frank Poole), William Sylvester (Dr. Heywood Floyd), Leonard Rossiter (Smyslov), Daniel Richter (Moonwatcher)

Stanley Kubrick

1928 Born on July 26 in New York.
1945–50 Worked as a photographer for *Look* magazine after the end of World War II.
Subsequently gained movie experience with short films and documentaries.
Kubrick financed his first two movies with money borrowed from friends and relatives
1953 *Fear and Desire*
1955 *Killer's Kiss*
1956 *The Killing* was Kubrick's first professional movie after he founded his own production company with producer James B. Harris. A small oeuvre of milestone productions came into being.
1957 *Paths of Glory* (the beginning of Kubrick's fame)
1959 *Spartacus*
1960 Moved to England, last US production
1961 *Lolita*
1963 *Dr. Strangelove or How I Learned to Stop Worrying and Love the Bomb*
1965–1968 *2001: A Space Odyssey*
1970–1971 *A Clockwork Orange*
1973–1975 *Barry Lyndon* (costume drama)
1980 *The Shining* (based on Stephen King)
1987 *Full Metal Jacket* (Vietnam movie)
1999 *Eyes Wide Shut* was Kubrick's legacy. The director died on March 7 in England. The movie premiere took place at the Venice Film Festival in September.

>>> Another icon in science fiction movie making: *Star Wars* (1977), see p. 122

The premiere was a disaster. "Monumental lack of imagination," was the biting commentary of famous critic Pauline Kael in *Harper's*. *The New York Times* called it "unbelievably boring." Stanley Kubrick's film *2001: A Space Odyssey* nearly drowned in an onslaught of negative reviews. Today, we know better: *2001*, undoubtedly the masterpiece of the inspired director who died shortly after completing his last work, *Eyes Wide Shut*, is one of the greatest achievements in the history of film.

To begin with, there is its visionary genius. At the end of the sixties, Kubrick and his screen writer, Arthur C. Clarke, cast merciless eyes on how the computer-driven world was developing. In doing so, they created a scenario of relationships between humans and machines that are both fantastic and realistic.

The theme itself wasn't really new. Its science fiction take moves, as in almost all of Kubrick's films, within conventional stereotypes. Yet, despite the film's smooth, scientific precision, the director manages to disclose images and mysteries, metaphors and statements that far surpass the genre. Some are still not fully deciphered, such as the role of the black monolith or the embryo floating in space, whose eyes seem to presage the evil look of Alex DeLarge (Malcolm McDowell) in *Clockwork Orange* (1971), Kubrick's subsequent work.

In this sense, *2001* is an insider film on a large scale, wrested from the clichés of the industry, and marked by the obsessions of a highly educated, self-taught filmmaker. Kubrick describes human consciousness in scenes of breakdown, irrationality, and progress through murder. The only character—and here is the grotesque twist—still capable of authentic feelings in the end, is the computer. "Dave, I'm afraid. My brain is growing empty...." moans Hal 9000, when astronaut Bowman starts deleting his memory. Then we hear a plaintive nursery song sung by the machine in a dying voice. This could very well come across as flat or funny, artificial or superfluous. Instead, Kubrick succeeds in transforming superficial effects into dismayed astonishment. A bone as an ape's killing tool in the opening sequence of *2001* turns into a space station rotating on its own axis to the tune of a Viennese waltz. These are perfect, surprising, and moving images such as only the cinema can offer. *2001: A Space Odyssey* is a wonderful imposition. *M.R.*

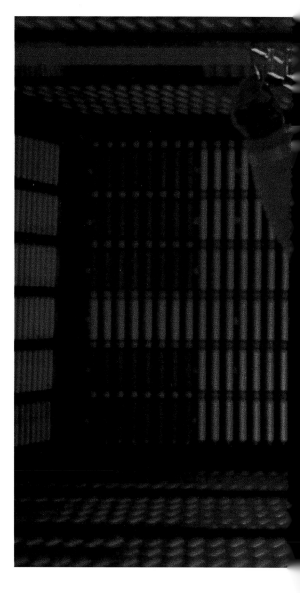

Fantastic trick sequences with
a philosophical touch—poster and
scene from Kubrick's *opus magnum*

Once Upon a Time in the West

**C'era una volta il West
Italy/USA, 1968**

Running time: 164 minutes (orig. 176)
Directed by Sergio Leone; *written by* Sergio
Donati *and* Sergio Leone, *based on a story by*
Dario Argento, Bernardo Bertolucci, Sergio
Leone; *cinematographer,* Tonino Delli Colli;
music by Ennio Morricone; *edited by* Nino
Baragli
With: Claudia Cardinale (Jill MacBain), Henry
Fonda (Frank), Charles Bronson (Harmonica),
Jason Robards (Cheyenne), Gabriele Ferzetti
(Morton), Frank Wolff (Brett MacBain), Keenan
Wynn (Sheriff), Paolo Stoppa (Sam), Lionel
Stander (Barman), Woody Strode (Stony), Jack
Elam (Knuckles), Marco Zuanelli (Wobbles),
John Frederick (member of Frank's Gang),
Enzo Santianello (Timmy), Dino Mele
(Harmonica as a boy)

A gruesome discovery: Jill MacBain (Claudia Cardinale) has just discovered the corpse of her husband and his children

Jill (Claudia Cardinale)

Without Ennio Morricone's haunting soundtrack, with its world-famous harmonica melody
to blend in with the rich images of *C'era una
volta il West* (original title), the western epic
would be unthinkable. "For me," said director
Sergio Leone, "the score is the true dialogue of
the film. In that sense Ennio is my best scriptwriter." In contrast to standard procedure,
Morricone composed a theme for each protagonist before shooting began. The scenes
were then filmed together with the music
—similar to an opera.

Director Leone makes high demands on
his audience. For 164 minutes, he tells a classic
western story of the struggle between good
and evil at an agonizingly slow pace. The
opening sequence in a train station takes half
an hour. Three men wait for a train. Water drips.
A fly buzzes. Faces are shown in close-up. No
one speaks. Nothing happens. Nothing. The
audience grows restless. Still nothing. Then,
a train pulls into the station, and a man with
a harmonica steps down. A brief gunfight
ensues. Then, again, nothing.

The movie was a box office flop, but it did
become a cult film—and not only because of
the music. Sergio Leone knew how to unleash
visual power on the screen like no one else.
Cameraman Tonino Delli Colli captured the
tense atmosphere with pure genius; his close-
ups and unusual dolly shots captivate the
viewer.

Then there's the cast. Rarely was a bad guy
as mean as Henry Fonda, in his role as the hero,
or a woman on the Western frontier as confident as the beautiful Claudia Cardinale.
Because Fonda was the top star, he was allowed

to choose his role, and he decided to play the
bad guy. "The film was a pure joy to make.
I enjoyed every minute. Leone is an incredible
character," Fonda said after the shoot was
finished. The role of the harmonica player was
given to relative newcomer Charles Bronson,
for whom Leone had to fight hard with the
producers at Paramount.

Leone was already regarded as an expert of
the Italian Western genre. He catapulted Clint
Eastwood to stardom as the taciturn lead of his
A Fistful of Dollars series that initiated a wave
of spaghetti westerns. The Paramount money
enabled him to realize his biggest project and
to develop the trademark style that marks *Once
Upon a Time in America.* Leone was a director
who took the time to develop his characters
—a virtue that is perhaps lacking in many
filmmakers today.   S.R.

102 | 103   >>> **Sergio Leone, *Once Upon a Time in America,* and
Biography, see p. 138**

above: The song of death and the scene that noone forgets

right: Harmonica (Charles Bronson) and his mouth organ

Easy Rider

USA, 1969

Running time: 95 minutes
Directed by Dennis Hopper; *written by* Peter
Fonda, Dennis Hopper, *and* Terry Southern;
cinematographer, Laszlo Kovacs; *edited by*
Donn Cambern
With: Peter Fonda (Wyatt), Dennis Hopper
(Billy), Jack Nicholson (George Hanson),
Robert Walker, Jr. (Jack), Luana Anders (Lisa),
Antonio Mendoza (Jesus), Phil Spector
(Connection), Mac Mashourian (Bodyguard),
Warren Finnerty (Rancher), Karen Black
(Karen)

Jack Nicholson (left) as
attorny George Hanson
and Peter Fonda as Wyatt

Dennis Hopper

1936 Born on May 17 in Dodge City, Kansas.
Actor in Hollywood since the mid-1950s; soon acquired
the reputation of being a difficult and angry young man.
Smaller parts next to the admired James Dean in *Rebel
Without a Cause* (1955) and *Giant* (1956).
1969 Hopper's directing debut, *Easy Rider,* became the cult
movie of a whole generation.
1971 *The Last Movie* had little success.
Hopper "drops out," moves to New Mexico, but
continues to work as an actor (*The American Friend* and
Apocalypse Now).
1980 Comeback as director with *Out of the Blue*
1988 *Colors*
1993 *The Chasers* (his last movie as a director for the time
being)
Continues to be active as an actor, with over 100 roles
in movie, TV, and video productions. Highlights include
Blue Velvet (1985) and *Speed* (1994).
Latest movies:
1998 *Straight Shooter* (a German production with Katja Flint
and Heino Ferch)
1999 *Edtv*
2000 *Jason and the Argonauts*

George Hanson:
"They'll talk to ya and talk to ya and talk to ya about
individual freedom. But they see a free individual,
it's gonna scare 'em."

It seems natural that *Easy Rider* was made in the
year of Woodstock. However, the film breaks
with the love and peace mood of the legendary
rock concert and is by no means a hymn to
a generation. Instead, it is a brutal reckoning
with a country that no longer represents the
values it once promoted.

In his debut, director, author, and lead
actor Dennis Hopper created a work of superlatives: "ultimate cult film of the hippie era"
(Peter Engelmeier in *The Book on Film*); quintessential road movie; and, at a cost of only
400,000 dollars, followed by box office revenues
of over 50 million dollars, one of the most
commercially successful movies of its day. All
this, although director Dennis Hopper had set
out to make a modern cowboy film: "To me
Easy Rider was a western with two guys riding
motorcycles instead of horses."

Two spaced-out dropouts (Hopper and
Peter Fonda, who co-authored the script) sell
dope in Los Angeles, jump onto their Harley
Davidsons, and set off on a trip to New Orleans.
At first, the untouched landscape and infinite
horizon, combined with the folk-rock sound
of the era such as Steppenwolf's "Born to be
Wild" and the Byrds' "I Wasn't Born to
Follow," convey a sense of limitless freedom.
But the dream has long since been shattered.
The people who inhabit this landscape are
narrow-minded and disillusioned. The further
south the two, longhaired tramps travel,
the harder they are hit by the blatant hatred
of "normal" citizens. Alcoholic lawyer
George Hanson, played by the inimitable
Jack Nicholson, lends a helping hand in the
beginning, bailing them out of jail and joining them on their road trip. But the journey
soon turns into a nightmare that ends in
a bloodbath.

Easy Rider not only established Hopper in
the film industry, but his dream of a "completely different type of movie" set into motion

what would be called "New Hollywood."
A line-up of unbelievably young "wonder
boys" set out to conquer Hollywood and
then the world. Among them were Peter
Bogdanovich, Martin Scorsese, and the senior
of the group, Francis Ford Coppola. Like no
other film *Easy Rider* mirrors the sensibility
of an era; and that is precisely what makes it
a cult film. Even the great Luchino Visconti
uttered the following, if somewhat surprised,
praise: "These young people really did have
something to say. And they did so in an extraordinarily beautiful way!"   *S.Al.*

Crazy drop-outs: Robert Walker, Jr. (left)
and Peter Fonda

The two easy riders on the journey into a nightmare. As Billy and Wyatt, Dennis Hopper (left) and Peter Fonda come face to face with the hatred of "normal" people

The Garden of the Finzi-Continis

Il Giordino dei Finzi Contini
Germany/Italy, 1971
Running time: 95 minutes
Directed by Vittorio De Sica; *produced by* Gianni Hecht Lucari, Arthur Cohn, *and* Artur Brauner; *written by* Ugo Pirrom, Vittorio Bonicelli, *and* Vittorio De Sica; *based on the novel by* Giorgio Bassani; *cinematographer,* Ennio Guarnieri; *music by* Manuel De Sica; *edited by* Adriana Novelli
With: Lino Capolicchio (Giorgio), Dominique Sanda (Micol), Fabio Testi (Bruno Malnate), Romolo Valli (Giorgios Vater), Helmut Berger (Alberto)

Vittorio De Sica

1902 Born on July 7 in Sora, Italy. Grew up in Naples. Trained as auditor in Rome. First film role at 16, but also a successful theater actor who soon founded his own drama troupe.
In the 1930s, De Sica acted in numerous light film comedies and (as youthful lover and Casanova) became Italy's most popular actor.
In parallel with his directing activity, he later continued to stand in front of the camera, frequently in his own movies (as with Gina Lollobrigida in *Bread Love and Dreams*)—in part to finance ambitious directing projects.
1940 Directing debut with *Rose Scarlatte*
1941 *Doctor Beware*
1946 *Shoeshine* (Oscar)
1948 *The Bicycle Thief/Bicycle Thieves*, made in collaboration with scriptwriter Cesare Zavattini, was a key work of Italian Neo-Realism; awarded an Oscar for best foreign film.
1950 *Miracle in Milan*
1951 *Umberto D*
1960 *Two Women*
1962 *The Condemned of Altona* (based on Sartre)
1963 *Yesterday Today and Tomorrow* (third Oscar)
1964 *Marriage Italian Style*
1970 *The Garden of the Finzi-Continis* (Oscar number four, Golden Berlin Bear)
1973 *The Voyage*, De Sica's last film.
1974 Vittorio De Sica died in Neuilly-sur-Seine, near Paris.

"The movie is a gorgeous visual treat with wistful and tragic shadings."
San Francisco Chronicle

The beginning of the end: the Jewish citizens of Ferrara are rounded up

Describing, in a poetic way, how evil invades innocent lives is a great challenge to any author and even harder than telling a love story. Giorgio Bassani (1916–2000) mastered this literary terrain with an ease that had many admirers; his masterpiece, *The Garden of the Finzi-Continis*, was beautifully adapted to film in 1970 by Vittorio De Sica.

Readers and cineastes also have Bassani to thank for introducing them to Tomasi di Lampedusa whose book, *The Leopard*, was adapted to film in 1963 by Luchino Visconti. In *The Leopard*, as in his polished parable of murder, *The Damned*, Visconti created variations on the same theme: lives that are destroyed when evil corrupts the wholesome and happy world of large families.

With Monet-like images, De Sica introduces us to the Italian town of Ferrara in 1938. The quixotic dreams of its young people, dressed in impeccable summer whites for outings to the tennis courts and other amusements, are gradually overshadowed by darkening clouds. Mussollini's corrupt Italy grows more ferocious in its persecution of Jews, and even artistocrats, such as the Finzi-Continis, are no longer safe. Their overgrown garden, once a paradisiacal oasis for Ferrara's upper class, no longer offers any refuge, only mournful nostalgia.

Subtly intertwined love stories—Dominique Sanda, Helmut Berger, Fabio Testi, and Lino Capolicchio watch as the harsh shadow of Fascism darkens their place in the sun—elegant dialogues and innocent characters come together in a poignant story in which despair leaves no one untouched. De Sica didn't produce scenes of violence to achieve this goal;

he was a virtuoso of the gentle touch. His reply to criticism that he played down the horror of the Holocaust was definitive: "Beauty and style cannot destroy tragedy...."

Film producer Arthur Cohn remembers that no one would distribute *The Garden of the Finzi-Continis* in Europe at the beginning of the decade—not until it received the Oscar for best foreign film in 1971 and twenty-seven other awards. As Cohn surmised: "Only films that are understood by the American public are received with interest in Europe....To be successful you have to think with your heart."

P.W.E

The intensity of despair: Dominique Sanda and Fabio Testi as
Micol and Bruno

The dreams of the younger generation
in Ferrara will never come true

The Godfather

USA, 1971
Running time: 176 minutes
Directed by Francis Ford Coppola; *written by*
Mario Puzo *and* Francis Ford Coppola, *based
on the novel by* Mario Puzo; *cinematographer,*
Gordon Willis; *music by* Nino Rota; *edited by*
William H. Reynolds, Peter Zinner, Marc Laub,
and Murray Solomon
With: Marlon Brando (Don Corleone),
Al Pacino (Michael), James Caan (Sonny),
Robert Duvall (Tom Hagen), Richard
Castellano (Clemenza), Sterling Hayden
(Capt. MacCluskey), John Marley (Jack
Woltz), Diane Keaton (Kay Adams), Talia
Shire (Connie), John Cazale (Fredo)

The contemplative *Cosa-Nostra* lifestyle: Don Vito (Marlon Brando, right) with his son Michael (Al Pacino)

A Sicilian wedding: the groom, Michael Corleone
(Al Pacino), will not be happy for long

108 | 109   >>> Francis Ford Coppola, *Apocalypse Now,* and Biography,
see p. 130

While his daughter celebrates her wedding in
the shimmering heat of a garden, Don Vito
Corleone (Marlon Brando) holds audience in
his shaded study. There he receives petitioners
and promises to help with all kinds of problems,
securing the loyalty of his large clan. Yet, the
family over which Corleone believes himself to
be presiding has long since begun to fall apart.
In the 1950s, the comfortable *Cosa-Nostra* lifestyle of the Mafia clan is threatened by criminal
activities of the modern kind. Drug trade is the
business of the day, and old patriarch Don Vito
is hesitant to react. After being assassinated, his
son, Michael (Al Pacino), becomes his unlikely
successor. Michael has been a decent American
citizen, wanting nothing to do with the family
dealings. Now he joins in with brutal determination, liquidating adversaries with his own
hands and handing out contracts for murder,
even for family members.

Francis Ford Coppola's 1971 film, followed
by two sequels, destroyed any lingering myth
of the Mafia as an "honorable society." Beyond
the confines of the genre, the filmmaker tells the
story of unstoppable disintegration in a family
whose credo is implacable persistence. The inevitability with which the Corleone family slides
towards its own downfall links Coppola's film
trilogy to the tragedies of Antiquity, mirroring
the breakdown of the family ideal and the
simultaneous rise of societal structures characteristic of capitalism.

This development is especially evident in
the second part of the trilogy, which focuses
on Don Vito's youth and rise to power—the
young clan leader is played by Robert De Niro
—as well as on Michael's efforts to fortify his
power in the 1960s. The combination of these
two story lines creates a structural problem in
the narrative, since the film is forced into re-
peated forward and backward flashes. On
the other hand, the treatment does reveal
differences in power structures. While Don
Vito strives to prove himself to the family,
Michael is caught in a web of political intrigue.
The surface veneer of the "empire" is stripped
away, laying bare just how fundamentally
unhealthy Michael's character is; at the same
time, it becomes visible as an economic force.

In the third part of the trilogy, Michael
Corleone discovers the limitations of power.
He "gets clean" and invests his money in the
state and the church. Turning his back on the
familiar criminal environment, he comes face
to face with new enemies and discovers that
they are far more ruthless than he is, more
adept at political violence. A vicious cycle
ensues, with his helplessness serving only

No honorable company: the Godfather, Don Vito (Marlon Brando), decides over life and death

to augment the potential for violence. While the first part of the trilogy is dominated by acts of private vengeance which escalate into executions in the second part, the third features what amount to acts of ethnic cleansing. The trilogy is a brilliant swan song that bridges eight decades of the twentieth century and demonstrates, in the final analysis, the individual's impotence against established societal structures.   *H.M.*

Cabaret

USA, 1972

Running time: 117 minutes
Directed by Bob Fosse; *written by* Jay Presson
Allen, *based on the play of the same name by*
Joe Masteroff, I am a Camera *by* John van
Druten, *and stories by* Christopher Isherwood;
cinematographer, Geoffrey Unsworth; *music
by* John Kander; *edited by* David Bretherton
With: Liza Minnelli (Sally Bowles), Michael
York (Brian Roberts), Joel Grey (Compère),
Helmut Griem (Maximilian von Heune), Fritz
Wepper (Fritz Wendel)

Bob Fosse

1927 Born on June 23 as the son of a vaudeville entertainer
in Chicago. Began stage acting in boyhood. Performed
with both his first wife, Mary-Ann Niles, and his
second, Joan McCracken. Fosse appeared as dancer and
actor in various movies, including *Kiss Me Kate*, 1953.
1954 *The Pajama Game*, his Broadway debut as choreographer,
won the Tony Award.
1959 First own Broadway production, *Red Head* (third wife,
Gwen Verdon, in the starring role)
1968 Feature film directing debut with *Sweet Charity*
1972 *Cabaret* (Oscar, best direction)
1974 *Lenny*
1979 *All That Jazz*
1983 *Star 80*
1987 While working on a stage remake of *Sweet Charity*,
Bob Fosse died at the age of 60.

A divinely
decadent
experience!

COME TO THE

CABARET

Filmposter (USA), 1972

"This was the first major American cooperation with a
German Studio—the Bavaria in Munich. And it has produced
a film of remarkable quality. Even more important, it has
deepened the Americans' understanding for the German
passion and filmmaking . . ."
Peter E. Strauss, Head of Production *Cabaret*

"Life is a Cabaret"

Director Bob Fosse's *Cabaret* is a fascinating look
at changing events in Berlin in the early 1930s.
The film is set in the seedy Kit Kat Klub, whose
macabre, white-faced MC (Joel Grey) greets
audiences with the words, "Welcome, will-
kommen, bienvenue." Every night, American
Sally Bowles (Liza Minelli) dances and sings
on stage. All of the club-goers appear to be
having fun, but, outside in the streets, the
Nazis have begun to ply their despicable trade.
In the end, even the club performers don't get
away unscathed.

With his milestone musical, Fosse—himself a dancer and choreographer—put an end
to the lightheartedness and gormless humor
associated with the genre. Irony is wielded like
a weapon, such as when the club MC rhetori-
cally asks: "Where are your troubles now?
Forgotten. I told you so. We have no troubles
here. Here life is beautiful. Even the orchestra
is beautiful...." Words that mark the beginning of the end in Germany.

The story is centered on Sally, a singer who
is hungry for life and full of ambition. When
a na ve student named Brian (Michael York)
rents a room in her building, they become
lovers. In turn, they both have affairs with
a decadent, worldly baron, Heune (Helmut
Griem). Shocked by her boyfriend's bisexuality,

Sally, who has become pregnant, decides to
have an abortion.

Political events of the era form the background of these personal tales. Sally's friend
Natalia (Marisa Berenson), the daughter of
a Jewish merchant, and her boyfriend Fritz
(Fritz Wepper) are persecuted by the Nazis.
As Sally begins to lose the ground under her
feet, Brian returns to England and Heune
leaves Germany. Yet, Sally remains in Berlin
—no longer a place for happiness—and de-
fiantly belts out her song to anyone who will
listen: "Life is a cabaret."

Liza Minelli couldn't have distanced herself
more from the classic, high-gloss musicals that
were the trademarks of both her father, director
Vincente Minelli, and mother, singer-actress
Judy Garland. The role of Sally catapulted
Minelli to international fame, and she received
one of the eight Oscars that were awarded to
the film shot in Munich's Bavaria Studios.

It is worth noting that Fosse's film treatment
of the rising Nazi terror is much sharper and
edgier than the original Broadway version
on which it was based. The brilliantly choreographed cabaret scenes are by no means escapist
interludes; instead, they mirror the harsh reality
beyond the walls of the club—which could
not be hidden by even the most outrageous
theatrical glitter.   *P.W.E.*

A wild demonstration of human weakness:
Michael York and Liza Minnelli

Lisa Minnelli as the exuberant singer Sally Bowles

Day for Night

La nuit americaine
France/Italy, 1972
Running time: 116 minutes
Directed by François Truffaut; *written by*
François Truffaut, Jean-Louis Richard, *and*
Suzanne Schiffman; *cinematographer,* Pierre-
William Glenn; *music by* Georges Delerue;
edited by Yann Dedet
With: Jacqueline Bisset (Julie Baker "Pamela"),
Valentina Cortese (Séverine), Jean-Pierre
Aumont (Alexandre), Jean-Pierre Léaud
(Alphonse), Alexandra Stewart (Stacey),
François Truffaut (director Ferrand), Nathalie
Baye (Joëlle), Jean Champion (Bertrand)

A melodrama unfolds:
Jacqueline Bisset and
Jean-Pierre Aumont (right)

François Truffaut

1932   Born on February 6th in Paris, as the son of a technical draftsman. Unhappy childhood and youth; found escape and consolation in the movies. Film critic of *Cahiers du Cinéma;* advocate and precursor of the "Nouvelle Vague" and author cinema.

1959   *The 400 Blows* (directing award in Cannes) formed the first of a fictitious biographical series devoted to the film anti-hero Antoine Doinel (played by Jean-Pierre Léaud). This continued with *Love at Twenty* (1961) and the feature films *Stolen Kisses* (1968), *Bed and Board* (1970), and *Love on the Run* (1979).

1961   *Jules and Jim*
1966   *Fahrenheit 451*
1967   *The Bride Wore Black*
1972   *Day for Night* (1973 Oscar for best foreign film)
1975   *The Story of Adèle H.*
1980   *The Last Metro*
       Truffaut's longtime partner Fanny Ardant was the main protagonist in his last two films:
1981   *The Woman Next Door*
1982   *Confidentially Yours*
1984   François Truffaut died in Neuilly-sur-Seine, near Paris.

A crowd scene being staged: a film within a film with François Truffaut as the film director Ferrand

His entire life was a love affair with film, which is why François Truffaut's *Day for Night* (original title) is such a beautiful declaration of love for the medium. Ever since movies have been made, filmmakers have made films about how movies are made. One recent effort was Finnish director Mika Kaurismäki's *LA Without a Map* (1999), a black comedy studded with young stars like Johnny Depp and seasoned ones like Anouk Aimée, who goes to see her own retrospective. In this film, the young ingenues are blinded by ambition, ready to do whatever it takes to succeed.

The casting couch is less blatant in Truffaut's movie, and his personal homage to the world of filmmaking may even seem a bit conservative and old-fashioned. Nevertheless, the problems of the producer, director, actors, and filmcrew in his film are much the same as they are today. Yet, this wholehearted celebration of French cinema in the seventies is not without a touch of "poison," similar to that in Buñuel's *The Discreet Charm of the Bourgeoisie.*

In *Day for Night*, Truffaut opens our eyes to the illusion of the camera, aiming its lens at the psychological carnival of lies and deception behind the scenes. In fact, the film's French title, *La nuit américaine*, is the expression used in the industry to describe the process of shooting footage through filters during the day to make scenes appear as though filmed at night. But for Truffaut, film has always been more than a game of tricks and deceptions. This film, es-pecially, helped him to clarify his process and come to terms with himself: "it simply shows how I live." As Truffaut said, he wanted to "invite a dialogue on filmmaking" and "to tell the truth about cinema, but not the whole truth....to speak of cinema how it has been up until now."

Accordingly, we become eyewitnesses to the filming of an old-fashioned love story, a film-within-the-film entitled *Meet Pamela*, in which Truffaut plays a director named Ferrand.

Jacqueline Bisset plays actress Julie Baker, the lead in *Pamela*. Although newly wed to Alphonse (Jean-Pierre Léaud), Pamela runs off with her father-in-law, Alexandre (Jean-Pierre Aumont), and is killed in a car accident. In a rage, Alphonse kills his father. As this melodrama unfolds, Truffaut shows us the technical apparatus of filmmaking—how dialogues are recorded, how dolly shots are set up, and how the movements of crowd scenes are choreographed. On top of this, he depicts the insanity on set, with nervous actors and a worried producer. After a series of mishaps and minor disasters, the real tragedy hits: the "actor" Alexandre is killed in an accident. When morning, and new hope, dawn in *Day for Night*, the *Pamela* film is also completed.

"Making a film is like a coach ride through the Wild West. In the beginning, you still have hopes for a nice trip. But soon you ask yourself whether you'll ever arrive at the destination," says Ferrand. With *Day for Night*, Truffaut arrived at *his* and his public's destination —making this film his greatest success since *Jules et Jim* in 1961.   P.W.E.

Everthing seems fake: Jacqueline Bisset (Julie) consoles
Jean-Pierre Léaud (Alphonse)

The producer isn't having an easy time:
Jean Champion (at front) as Bertand,
trying to keep Ferrand's troupe together

The Discreet Charm of the Bourgeoisie

Le charme discret de la bourgeoisie
France, 1972
Running time: 101 minutes
Directed by Luis Buñuel; *written by* Luis Buñuel *and* Jean-Claude Carrière; *cinematographer,* Edmond Richard; *music by* Guy Villette; *edited by* Hélène Plemiannikov
With: Fernando Rey (Rafaele Costa), Delphine Seyrig (Simone Thévenot), Stéphane Audran (Alice Sénéchal), Bulle Ogier (Florence), Jean-Pierre Cassel (Henri Sénéchal)

Luis Buñuel

1900 Born on February 22 in Calanda, Spain. Jesuit schooling. Attended University in Madrid. During this time met Federico García Lorca and Salvador Dalí.
1925 Began studies at the Académie du Cinéma in Paris.
1928 *An Andalusian Dog,* Buñuel's first short film, made in collaboration with Dalí, became a key work of cinematic Surrealism
1930 *The Golden Age,* his first long feature film
In the mid 1930s, dubbed American films; during the Spanish Civil War made propaganda films against Franco. After Franco came to power, Buñuel found a position at the Museum of Modern Art, New York.
From the end of the 1940s, worked in Mexico.
1950 *The Young and the Damned* (director's award, Cannes)
1952 *The Brute*
1956 *Death in the Garden*
1959 *Nazarin*
1961 *Viridiana* (Golden Palm, Cannes; the film, produced by permission of the Spanish government, was banned there)
1962 *The Exterminating Angel*
1964 *Diary of a Chambermaid*
1967 *Belle de Jour* (with Catherine Deneuve; Golden Lion, Venice)
1970 *Tristana*
1972 *The Discreet Charm of the Bourgeoisie* (Oscar, best foreign film)
1977 *That Obscure Object of Desire*
After this project Buñuel retired to private life.
1983 Luis Buñuel died in Mexico City.

"In addition to being extraordinarily funny and perfectly acted, *The Discreet Charm of the Bourgeoisie* moves with the breathtaking speed and self-assurance that only a man of Buñuel's experience can achieve without resorting to awkward ellipses."
The New York Times, October 14, 1972

The good and the bad: Julien Bertheau as the Bishop

Luis Buñuel, was a great cinematic provocateur and surrealist, who, like Bergman and Fellini, challenged hypocrisy and religious restrictions. His satirical rendition of *The Discreet Charm of the Bourgeoisie* evinces the love-hate attitude of a couturier forced to create a made-to-measure suit for a celebrity he dislikes but who has a fabulous figure.

Although he shared the same background, Buñuel despised the bourgeoisie—perhaps because he knew it so well—and he loved to undermine its foundations: religion, the military, and family. In this film he celebrates the elegance and charm of a group of well-raised, educated marauders as they navigate through a maze of immoral and unethical behavior as if they were walking through brocaded salons.

The film is ironic and biting because it drips with good manners. No matter how heinous the deeds of Monsieur or Madame, of the Ambassador from Latin America or the mild-mannered Bishop, they are always done with the casual attitude and self-confident small talk that are the marks a good upbringing. Buñuel's characters may behave like sewer rats, but they're eating in style. Coarseness is revealed only in their vulgar dreams (and they dream often). Otherwise, all we see is composure, discretion, and reigned-in passion. One must have taste, after all.

Certain scenes, such as that depicting an ill-fated dinner, are reminiscent of sequences in Buñuel's nightmarish *El Angel Exterminador* (The Exterminating Angel), from 1962, in which a small upper-class gathering finds itself suddenly unable to leave a room. *The Discreet Charm of the Bourgeoisie* is a surreal, intuitive, even nasty film that serves up a murderous dish of toadstool à la Buñuel for the discerning palate. Even its lead actors (Fernando Rey, Stephane Audran, Delphine Seyrig) act as if they were born to play snobs. A swan song for a dying class or proof of their immortality?

Po.

Surviving bewildering circumstances magnificently: Buñuel's swan song to the upper middle-class

The breathless nightmare of the overfed: Jean-Pierre Cassel (lying on the bed) suffering in silence

The Way We Were

USA, 1973

Running time: 118 minutes
Directed by Sydney Pollack; *written by* Arthur
Laurents; *cinematographer,* Harry Stradling, Jr.;
music by Marvin Hamlisch; *edited by* Margaret
Booth
With: Barbra Streisand (Katie Morosky),
Robert Redford (Hubbell Gardiner), Bradford
Dillman (J. J.), Lois Chiles (Carol Ann),
Patrick O'Neal (Georg Bissinger), Viveca
Linfors (Paula Reisner)

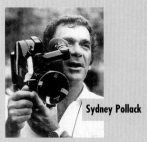

Sydney Pollack

1934 Born on July 1 as the son of Russian-Jewish immigrants
in Lafayette, Indiana.
1952 Pollack went to New York; actor's training at the
Neighbourhood Playhouse; actor and director of
television series
1965 Directed his first feature film, *The Slender Thread*
1968 *Castle Keep*
1969 *They Shoot Horses Don't They?*
1971 *Jeremiah Johnson*, the first in a sequence of films made
with Pollack's favorite actor, Robert Redford:
1973 *The Way We Were*
1974 *Three Days of the Condor*
1978 *The Electric Horseman*
1985 *Out of Africa* (seven Oscars)
1990 *Havana*
1982 *Tootsie* (starring Dustin Hoffman)
1993 *The Firm*
1995 *Sabrina*
1999 *Random Hearts.* That same year appeared as an actor
in Stanley Kubrick's last film, *Eyes Wide Shut.*

Katie (Barbra Streisand) is indignant about fascism in Europe

The sentimental song, "Memories," earned composer Marvin Hamlisch an Oscar and singer Barbra Streisand popularity. But if you haven't seen the movie for which the song was written—and which was nominated for six Academy Awards—you've missed a great deal. *The Way We Were* is one of the most unforgettable love stories in American film, especially since it is an unhappy one.

As with Scarlett O'Hara and Rhett Butler in *Gone with the Wind*, unrequited love remains a thorn in the public's side and requests persisted for years. Couldn't Katie Morosky (Barbra Streisand), a Jewish communist passionately opposed to fascism in Europe, and Hubbell Gardner (Robert Redford), a carefree all-American with a to-die-for smile reunite in a sequel and live happily ever after?

No, they couldn't, and luckily director Sydney Pollack resisted the temptation. Gardner and Morosky simply don't suit each other. He isn't the romantic she believed him to be, and she isn't the good little wife of a California scriptwriter.

Set in Hollywood during the McCarthy era, the film chronicles the difficult relationship between Gardner and Morosky. When Morosky rallies to support the "Hollywood Ten," the improbable marriage falls apart, even though she is a woman who never gives up. All that's left for the couple after the cold war is a peaceful coexistence.

When the film was released, women, in particular, identified with the character of Morosky, catapulting Streisand to cult status among intellectuals, lesbians, and homosexuals.

Sydney Pollack has been criticized for not developing the movie's political theme more fully, which may be a valid point. Still, he did address this dark period in the history of American democracy, even if only as the background for this wonderfully sentimental, but never insincere, love story.   *A.K.*

>>> Sydney Pollack, *Out of Africa,*
see p. 140

All American boy meets intellectual idol:
Robert Redford and Barbra Streisand

One Flew over the Cuckoo's Nest

USA, 1975

Running time: 134 minutes
Directed by Milos Forman; *written by* Lawrence
Hauben *and* Bo Goldman, *based on a novel of
the same name by* Ken Kesey *and a play by*
Dale Wasserman; *cinematographers,* Haskell
Wexler, William A. Fraker *and* Bill Butler;
music by Jack Nitzsche; *edited by* Richard
Chew, Lynzee Klingman, Sheldon Kahn
With: Jack Nicholson (Randle Patrick
McMurphy), Louise Fletcher (Schwester
Mildred Ratched), William Redfield (Harding),
Brad Dourif (Billy Bibbit), Will Sampson
(Häuptling Bromden), Michael Berryman
(Ellis), Danny DeVito (Martini)

"Chief" (Will Sampson, left) and Randle Patrick McMurphy (Jack Nicholson), the "troublemaker," in a psychiatric asylum

Milos Forman

1932 Born on February 18 in Cáslaw, Czechoslovakia. During
World War II, his parents were murdered by the Nazis.
After the war Forman attended film college in Prague.
Worked as a director's assistant, made documentaries
and shorts.

1963 Feature film debut with *Black Peter/Peter and Pavla*
(First Prize, Locarno Film Festival).

1965 *Loves of a Blonde/A Blonde in Love*

1967 *The Fireman's Ball/Like a House on Fire* received an
Oscar nomination and opened the door to Hollywood.

1969 Moved to the U.S.

1970 Successful U.S. debut with *Taking Off*

1975 *One Flew Over the Cuckoo's Nest* (five Oscars)

1979 Adaptation of hippie stage musical *Hair*

1981 *Ragtime*

1984 *Amadeus* (eight Oscars)

1990 *Valmont*

1996 *The People vs. Larry Flynt* (Golden Berlin Bear)

1999 *Man on the Moon,* a biography of the comedian Andy
Kaufman awarded the Golden Globe and the Silver
Berlin Bear for best direction.
Concerning his further plans, Forman says he is still in
love with *Man on the Moon* and that at his age it makes
no sense to take on a pile of work he can't handle.

Casting genius Milos Forman: the gigantic Indian painter
Will Sampson, as the chief Bromden, performed unforget-
tably. Tim McCall, the former governor of Oregon, appeared
as a news commentator—and for Brad Dourif, who debuted
here, it was the start of a remarkable movie career.
Ragtime, Mississippi Burning

One might think that this acclaimed, five-Oscar
film would have received unanimous praise
from critics. Far from it. In his autobiography,
director Milos Forman remembers that when
his film adaptation of the bestselling book
opened, "the critics weren't falling over each
other with enthusiasm." One newspaper described it as a "pamphlet of social criticism"
and another called it a "rowdy romp." Even
the film's distributors were wary of its psychological subject and projected box office revenues
of 15 million dollars. Instead, the film classic
brought in 280 million dollars worldwide.

It took a long time before Ken Kesey's auto-
biographical novel found its way onto the
big screen. The book appeared in 1962, and
Hollywood star Kirk Douglas quickly bought
the rights. But all of the major movie studios
shared the opinion that "a film about the insane [would] never [make] any money." After
some time, Douglas senior grew tired of the
rejections and gave the rights to his son
Michael, still unknown in those days. In
his search for an inexpensive director, the
junior Douglas hired Czech immigrant Milos
Forman, who was immediately intrigued by
the material.

The rest is history. Jack Nicholson was cast
in the role of rebellious Patrick McMurphy,
who chooses to be institutionalized rather
than undergo forced labour. The established
order of the asylum into which he is interned
begins to unravel as more and more patients
side with him and insist upon their rights. In
the end, the troublemaker McMurphy loses
the battle. Yet, thanks to an act of mercy killing
by his fellow inmate, "Chief," McMurphy isn't
condemned to a lobotomy. The ending is bitter
but, in the context of the film, logical.

The care Forman took in casting the supporting roles was amply repaid in the dynamic
performances of Nicholson's co-stars. Forman
worked hard to create characters who would
come across as unique figures in the group
therapy scenes, ultimately casting Danny de
Vito (Martini), Brad Dourif (Billy Bibbit), and
Will Sampson (Chief). Most of the smaller
supporting roles were performed by extras
recruited from a psychiatric hospital, giving
the film authenticity.

A courageous outsider drama, *One Flew over
the Cuckoo's Nest* was an extraordinary success
that fully deserved the five Oscars it received.
Only Frank Capra's comedy *It Happened One
Night* had achieved the same. Capra acknowl-
edged this parallel in a telegram he sent to
Forman after the Oscars: "Welcome to the
club!"   S.R.

Jack Nicholson as the rebellious patient Randle

Unmistakable characters: Jack
Nicholson surrounded by patients
(front right Danny DeVito) and Will
Sampson (background)

Taxi Driver

USA, 1975

Running time: 114 minutes
Directed by Martin Scorsese; *written by* Paul
Schrader; *cinematographer,* Michael Chapman;
music by Bernard Herrmann; *edited by* Marcia
Lucas
With: Robert De Niro (Travis Bickle), Peter
Boyle (Wizard), Cybill Shepherd (Betsy),
Jodie Foster (Iris), Harvey Keitel (Matthew
("Sport"), Martin Scorsese (passenger), Steven
Prince (Andy the gun salesman), Diahnne
Abbott (candy seller), Victor Argo (Melio)

Martin Scorsese

1942 Born as the son of Italian immigrants in Flushing, Long
Island. Grew up in Manhattan's Little Italy. Spent a
year in a priests' seminary, then studied cinema
sciences at New York University. Took on a teaching
post after graduating in 1966. Award-winning short
films.
1968 First feature film, *Who's That Knocking at My Door?*
1973 *Mean Streets* (a critical if not commercial success)
1974 *Alice Doesn't Live Here Anymore*
1975 *Taxi Driver* (Golden Palm, Cannes)
1977 *New York, New York*
1979 *Raging Bull*
1982 *The King of Comedy*
1986 *The Color of Money*
1988 *The Last Temptation of Christ,* a film on the life of Jesus,
triggered a scandal.
1990 *Good Fellas* (Silver Lion, Venice)
1991 *Cape Fear*
1995 *Casino*
1997 Life Achievement Award of the American Film Institute
1998 The Tibet film *Kundun* is accompanied by a documentary,
In Search of Kundun—With Martin Scorsese, screened
the same year.
1999 *Bringing Out the Dead*
At present Scorsese is working on the projects *The Gangs
of New York* (with Leonardo DiCaprio) and *Dino* (a Dean
Martin biography with Tom Hanks).

Cab dispatcher:
"How's your driving record? Clean?"
Travis Bickle:
"Clean. Just like my conscience."

After a decade of war in Vietnam and the 1973
Watergate fiasco, which ended in President
Richard Nixon's resignation, Americans yearned
for a new beginning. They voted peanut farmer
Jimmy Carter into the White House, but bombs
were still ticking in many heads.

Martin Scorsese's fourth film, *Taxi Driver*
(1976), is a portrait of a divided America, in
which a different kind of jungle war rages in
the mean streets of its big cities. Scorsese's
antihero is Vietnam veteran, Travis Bickle
(Robert de Niro), who drives a taxi through
New York's dirtiest slums in the dark hours of
the night. A lonesome cowboy and a disturbed
man, Bickle suffers from self-hatred and hallu-
cinates about a great "cleansing." "Someday
a real rain will come and wash all the scum
off the streets," he muses as his eyes travel
contemptuously over the whores, pimps, and
drug dealers on the sidewalks. Out of love for
a child prostitute, played by twelve-year-old
Jodie Foster, Bickles shaves his head into a
mohawk to bring this "rain" on the city
himself.

Taxi Driver doesn't take a moral standpoint,
nor is it a theory about social justice. However,
the film is radical and relentless as it penetrates
the psyche of a loner whose pseudo religious,
neurotic worldview brutally propels towards
violence. Evil isn't held in check, it is unleashed. From out of the depressing, urban,
concrete jungle inconspicuous "nobodies"
emerge—like John Hinckley Junior, who shot
Ronald Reagan five years later after seeing the
film. (Hinckley claimed that he was influenced
by the film and wanted to attract the attention
of Jodie Foster, with whom he was obsessed.)

Scorsese's outsider drama is one of the
most ambivalent films of the seventies, along
with *Apocalypse Now* and *The Deer Hunter.*
Its detached, pessimistic ending reflects the
agony of the Watergate era and Americans'
disbelief in their society. A pathological killer
goes unpunished and is celebrated by the
silent majority for doing the dirty work of
others.

Taxi Driver was a milestone in American
cinema. It influenced Quentin Tarrantino's
Reservoir Dogs as much as it did Matthieu
Kassovitz's *Hatred,* Danny Boyle's *Trainspotting,*
and David Fincher's *Seven.* The character of
Travis Bickle is still out there somewhere
waiting for his hour to strike. Only in the
real world, his name has changed—perhaps

Robert De Niro as Travis Bickle, a Vietnam veteran and lonely
cowboy bent on revenge

to Dylan Klebold or Eric Harris, the shooters at
Littleton High School, or to Timothy McVeigh,
the Oklahoma bomber. The form he takes is
always in tomorrow's papers.   *H.R.*

Loner with a troubled psyche: taxi driver Robert de Niro

The twelve-year-old prostitute Iris (Jodie Foster)

The Star Wars Trilogy

USA, 1977
Running time: 121 minutes
(special version: 126)
Directed and written by George Lucas; *cinematographer,* Gilbert Taylor; *music by* John Williams; *edited by* Paul Hirsch, Marcia Lucas, Richard Chew
With: Mark Hamill (Luke Skywalker), Harrison Ford (Han Solo), Carrie Fisher (Princess Leia Organa), Peter Cushing (Moff Tarkin), Alec Guinness (Ben Kenobi), David Prowse (Darth Vader)

George Lucas

1944 Born on May 14 in Modesto, California. After a serious accident gave up his passion, motor racing. Studied film in Los Angeles.
1967 *THX 1138: 4EB,* done as part of his final examination. That same year, assistant during the making of Coppola's *Finian's Rainbow;* Coppola became his mentor.
1968 *Filmmaker* (a documentary)
1970 *THX 1138* (new long cinema version)
1973 Breakthrough with critics and audience with *American Graffiti*
1977 *Star Wars*
With his enormous earnings from *Star Wars,* Lucas established companies such as Industrial Light and Magic (special effects) and the production company Lucasfilm.
Relinquished direction of first two *Star Wars* sequels, *The Empire Strikes Back* (1979) and *The Return of the Jedi* (1982), to Irvin Kershner and Richard Marquand, respectively. (At this writing the trilogy has boxofficed approximately 500 million dollars.)
Lucas devoted himself primarily to producing and writing, for instance developing, in collaboration with Spielberg, the *Indiana Jones* trilogy.
In the early 1990s, entered the television business with the series *The Indiana Jones Chronicles.*
1999 Remake of the *Star Wars* trilogy with new computer and sound effects.
Star Wars: Episode I—The Phantom Menace
He plans to direct the forthcoming episodes II and III scheduled for 2002 and 2005.

"Star Wars...is the most elaborate, most expensive, most beautiful movie serial ever made... [It] is good enough to convince the most skeptical eight-year-old sci-fi buff, who is the toughest critic."
The New York Times, May 26, 1977

A special kind of empire: scene with Harrison Ford, Mark Hamill, and Carrie Fisher

The *Star Wars* trilogy established science fiction as a genre to an extent that had previously been unimaginable. In addition to watching Stanley Kubrick's *2001: A Space Odyssey* (see pp. 100–101), George Lucas had fed his imagination with comic strips, serials, and 1930s film series. He felt inspired to fuse legends of warriors, such as King Arthur, and stories about magic, such as Tolkien's *Lord of the Rings*, with the novels of Carlos Castaneda. Every aspect of the *Star Wars* trilogy makes reference to these literary models, bringing memories to life and revealing the familiar in a hyper-technological world among distant stars and planets—a monumental quarry of references and citations.

Star Wars takes us on a journey to "far, far away" galaxies, a turbulent adventure that is a hybrid of myth and fairy tale, virtual battle and trivial poetry. All three films are built around the principle of a serial, where viewers are offered a carefully apportioned ration in each installment, with a cliff-hanger ending that leaves them hungry for the sequel. *Star Wars* ends with victory of the rebels over the Death Star, the "dark knight of evil" and the escape of Darth Vader; in *The Empire Strikes Back*, Luke Skywalker, the last Jedi knight, learns that Darth Vader is his father; *The Return of the Jedi* ends with the destruction of the Death Star, the liberation of Darth Vader, and the death of the Emperor. These stories embrace more than one generation, most likely because

their simple plots are mythological in character. The public identified strongly with the characters—backed up by a huge marketing machinery—and seemed to appreciate them more than the slick special effects which simulated spaceflight at twice the speed of light. Skywalker's fate touches our hearts, and the stubborn little robot R2-D2 comes across as loveable and sympathetic. Even the spaceships develop a life of their own that is identifiable down to the last detail—so much so that the saga grew into an ever-expanding cosmos with a semantic all of its own. No matter how many ancient myths and legends it plundered, the trilogy established its own place as an original cinematic theme.

Alec Guinness in the role of Ben Kenobi

David Prowse as Darth Vader, Luke Skywalker's ancestor in the kingdom of the Jedi knights

From the start, Lucas had questioned and expanded the idea of the serial by introducing an interesting variation on the theme. His first film starts out with the caption: *Star Wars—Episode IV: New Hope* According to this heading, the two sequels would be episodes V and VI, with the first three episodes as yet untold. Lucas invented the term prequel in order to continue spinning the "story of all stories." Consequently, after *Star Wars Episode I* (1999), two more parts of a new trilogy await the public in the years to come.   *H.P.K.*   C3PO and R2D2

The Marriage of Maria Braun

Die Ehe der Maria Braun
Germany, 1978
Running time: 120 minutes
Directed by Rainer Werner Fassbinder; *written by* Peter Märthesheimer *and* Pea Fröhlich, *based on an idea by* Rainer Werner Fassbinder; *cinematographer,* Michael Ballhaus; *music by* Peer Raben; *edited by* Juliane Lorenz *and* Franz Walsch
With: Hanna Schygulla (Maria Braun), Klaus Löwitsch (Hermann Braun), Ivan Desny (Dr. Karl Oswald), Gottfried John (Willi), Gisela Uhlen (Maria's Mother)

Rainer Werner Fassbinder

1946 Born on May 31 in Bad Wörishofen, Germany. His father was a physician, his mother an interpreter. After their divorce he lived with his mother, who would later appear in many of her son's films under the name Lilo Pempeit or Liselotte Eder. Left school before graduating.
1967 Member of the Munich Action Theater
1968 Fassbinder founded the anti-theater in Munich
1969 Feature film debut with *Liebe ist kälter als der Tod;* that same year made *Katzelmacher* (based on his own stage play), *Gods of the Plague,* and *Why Does Herr R. Run Amok?*
1970 *Rio Das Mortes.* Married actress Ingrid Caven
1971 *The Merchant of Four Seasons*
1973 *Ali: Fear Eats the Soul / Ali*
1974 *Effie Briest* (successful filming of the eponymous novel by Fontane)
1976 *I Only Want You to Love Me*
A trilogy of postwar German history emerged with the films:
1978 *The Marriage of Maria Braun* (Silver Berlin Bear),
1981 *Lola* and *Veronika Voss*
In the meantime Fassbinder made
1980 *Lili Marleen,* a television series with 13 episodes, and an epilogue, *Berlin Alexanderplatz* (after the novel by Alfred Döblin).
1982 *Querelle* (based on a novel by Jean Genet) was his last film. Rainer Werner Fassbinder died on June 10 in Munich.

Rainer Werner Fassbinder, the great German film and production talent, made 42 films in 17 years, wrote the script for most of them, appeared in at least 40 movies, wrote theater and radio plays, made two TV series and often took over production and cutting jobs.

Rise and fall: Hanna Schygulla as Maria Braun

Maria Braun's marriage lasts only "half a day and a whole night." Then, her newly wedded husband, Private Hermann Braun, is sent off to the Eastern front. Regardless, the young woman sticks to her marriage vows, not only when her husband is declared missing at the end of the war, but also in the years that follow, when he languishes in prison because he has accepted responsibility for the death of her black GI lover.

In his award-winning, postwar drama, Rainer Werner Fassbinder explores how something that exists only in the imagination can become a reality that defines one's existence. With this portrait of a split personality, the filmmaker created a bitter commentary on the early days of the Federal Republic. Maria is a self-assured woman who knows how to get by in the years of hunger. With statements such as "I like you, but I only love my husband" she keeps temptation at bay as she slowly but steadily climbs the ladder to wealth and influence. She is hired by an industrial developer as a secretary, becomes his lover and eventually also the deputy of the business—half of which she ends up inheriting. At the height of her success however—within reach of her dreams and poised to begin a new life with her husband who has been released from prison—she becomes aware of her self-deceit, and the false structure she has constructed comes crashing down with a loud bang.

The Marriage of Maria Braun is a severe and, in its cinematic treatment, highly introspective film, with Hanna Schygulla as the perfect embodiment of its critical-descriptive stance. A vital and enigmatic woman, she moves through the postwar years of the "economic miracle" with determination but without full engagement. She's an "expert on the future," elegant, and assured in manner, but deep down she remains convinced that her actions are only a stepping stone, to that magical "Some Day"—her marriage and real life. To express the somnambulant state of his character and the society she reflects, Fassbinder ingeniously employed a soundtrack with many original devices that lend the film's events, spanning roughly one decade, an authenticity that is almost documentary in feeling. Over time, the search for missing persons on the radio becomes no more than background noise, no different than the ceaseless noise of pneumatic drills and shallow hit songs, or indeed Adenauer's contradictions about rearmament. People simply ignore all of it, the trivial and the serious. The growing loss of reality and the escape into beautiful appearances and prosperous normality finally come to a head in the famous broadcast of the world soccer championship in Bern in 1954. Its hysteric tones mark the ironic conclusion to Fassbinder's analysis of the era. In the film, the veil of illusion is pulled back, and the melodrama moves towards its inevitable conclusion. In real life, however, the illusion persists—right into Fassbinder's day. At least, that seems to be the message behind the decision to project portraits of the country's highest statesmen onto the screen as the credits roll.

J.L.

Maria Braun—an "expert on the future,"
waiting for the "real" life

Klaus Löwitsch plays Maria Braun's husband,
who is imprisoned because of her

Manhattan

USA, 1978

Running time: 96 minutes. Black and white
Directed by Woody Allen; *written by* Woody
Allen, Marshall Brickman; *cinematographer,*
Gordon Willis; *music by* George Gershwin;
edited by Susan E. Morse
With: Woody Allen (Isaac Davis), Diane
Keaton (Mary Wilke), Michael Murphy (Yale),
Mariel Hemingway (Tracy), Meryl Streep
(Jill), Anne Byrne (Emily), Karen Ludwig
(Connie), Michael O'Donoghue (Dennis)

Woody Allen

1935 Born on December 1 as Allen Stewart Konigsberg in
   Brooklyn, New York. Gag writer and author for newspapers and TV comedians; in the early 1960s began to
   work reluctantly but successfully as a stand-up comedian.
1964 First contact with cinema as author and actor in *What's
   New, Pussycat?*
1965 *What's Up, Tiger Lily?*, an ironic take off on a Japanese
   gangster film in which Allen is first billed as director.
1969 *Take the Money and Run* (his first independent movie
   as director, author, and actor in one)
1972 *Everything You Always Wanted to Know About Sex
   But Were Afraid to Ask*
1976 *Annie Hall* (with his then-partner Diane Keaton; four
   Oscar, for best film, direction, script and best actress)
1979 *Manhattan*
1980 *Stardust Memories*
1982 *A Midsummer Night's Sex Comedy* with Mia Farrow,
   who became his partner in life and subsequent films.
   The relationship ended with mudslinging in 1992, when
   Allen fell in love with Mia Farrow's adopted daughter,
   Soon-Yi, whom he would marry in 1997.
1982 *Zelig*
1984 *The Purple Rose of Cairo*
1985 *Hannah and Her Sisters* (Oscar for best script)
1987 *Radio Days*
1990 *Alice*
1992 *Husbands and Wives*
1995 *Bullets Over Broadway*
1997 *Everyone Says I Love You*
1998 *Celebrity*
1999 *Sweet and Lowdown*
2000 *Small Time Crooks*

Isaac Davis: "He was as tough and romantic as the
city he loved. ... New York was his town, and it always
would be."

"I am beautiful . . .": Woody Allen as Isaac and Diane Keaton as Mary

Manhattan is the archetypal Woody Allen film,
planting the seeds for subsequent successes
such as *Hannah and Her Sisters* and *Husbands
and Wives*. *Manhattan* is hysterical, comical,
and unbelievable. Unfortunately, it is also true.
This alone has earned *Manhattan* its place in
the pantheon of film and its top ranking among
all other Woody Allen comedies.

The Manhattan skyline, shot in black and
white, provides a static backdrop to the story
and a contrast to the chaotic lives of the characters. Woody Allen plays Isaac, an unattractive
television author who jilts his lover, a seventeen-
year-old acting student, to begin a half-hearted
affair with Mary (Diane Keaton), the lover of
his married friend.

Whenever the Manhattan panorama is
absent from the screen, viewers get dialogue
—lots of it—in an uninterrupted stream.
All the talk revolves around the characters'
emotional lives. Psychologists are quoted and
behavioral patterns sketched. Whenever the
characters are at a loss for words, they turn to
books. In fact, almost everyone in the film
wants to write a book, but only one character
actually does. Isaac's crazy ex-wife Jill (Meryl
Streep) takes advantage of the medium to air
her grievances about her supposedly perverted
marriage.

Everyone either talks obsessively or dashes
around frantically—whatever it takes to avoid
facing the truth. They wax superficially about
modern art and film and babble on about imagined feelings for one another, while thinking
only of themselves. All the quasi-intellectual

talk is a pretentious front that covers emotional chaos. This is the message of *Manhattan*—
and why watching it is both amusing and
frightening. Viewers recognize themselves in
Manhattan, and many will spot sentences
taken from their own repertoires.

One of the most-quoted lines from the film
is exclaimed by Mary, when she finds herself
cornered in an argument: "I am beautiful, I am
bright, and I deserve better!" Sadly, the mantra
doesn't work. In the end, intellect capitulates
to sentimentality and self-righteousness, and
everyone feels just as bad as they did in the
beginning—with one exception. Isaac feels
worse than he did in the beginning and wants
to get back together with his young lover. But
she's already on her way to London. As the
only one of the characters, who truly loved,
she is also the only one who comes through
it all unscathed. By the end of the story, she is
of legal age and, after offering a few words of
consolation to her ex-lover, rushes off to the
airport.   W.-C.F.

Woody Allen's favorite view: New York, the city of his black-and-white film world (here with Diane Keaton)

Either talking obsessively or dashing around frantically: TV scriptwriter Isaac Davis (Woody Allen) and Tracy (Marial Hemingway)

The Tin Drum

"Little Oskar" (David Bennent) joining in the protest

Volker Schlöndorff

Die Blechtrommel/Le tambour
Germany/France, 1978
Running time: 145 minutes
Directed by Volker Schlöndorff; *written by*
Jean-Claude Carrière, Volker Schlöndorff, *and*
Franz Seitz, *based on the novel of the same name*
by Günter Grass; *cinematographer,* Igor Luther;
music by Maurice Jarre, Friedrich Meyer; *edited*
by Suzanne Baron
With: David Bennent (Oskar Matzerath),
Angela Winkler (Agnes Matzerath), Mario
Adorf (Alfred Matzerath), Daniel Olbrychski
(Jan Bronski), Katharina Thalbach (Maria),
Heinz Bennent (Greff), Andréa Ferréol
(Lina Greff), Charles Aznavour (Sigismund
Markus), Mariella
Oliveri (Roswitha),
Ilse Pagé (Gretchen
Scheffler), Otto Sander
(Musiker Meyn)

1939 Born on May 31 in Wiesbaden, the son of a physician.
       Went to Paris as an exchange student in 1955 and
       stayed for 10 years.
       Studied political science; attended film college for one
       year.
1960 Short film *Wen kümmert's,* then assistant director with
       Melville, Resnais, Tavernier, and Malle
1965 Returned to Germany. Successful debut with *Young*
       Torless (based on Robert Musil).
1969 *Michael Kohlhaas—der Rebell* (based on the Kleist
       novella)
1970 *The Sudden Wealth of the Poor People of Kombach*
1971 Married director and actress Margarethe von Trotta,
       who collaborated on several of his films and remained
       his wife for 20 years.
1972 *A Free Woman/Summer Lightning*
1975 *The Lost Honor of Katharina Blum* (based on
       Heinrich Böll)
1978 *The Tin Drum* (based on Günter Grass; Oscar, best
       foreign film; Golden Palm, Cannes)
1981 *Circle of Deceit/False Witness*
1983 *Swann in Love* (after Marcel Proust)
1985 *Death of a Salesman* (based on the stage play by
       Arthur Miller)
1989 *The Handmaid's Tale* (based on Margaret Atwood)
1991 *Voyager* (based on Max Frisch)
1992 Schlöndorff assumed business management of the
       former East German Babelsberg Studios.
1996 *The Ogre* (based on Michel Tournier)
1998 *Palmetto* (after James Hadley Chase)
1999 *The Legends of Rita/Rita's Legends* (premiered at the
       Berlinale 2000)

Volker Schlöndorf: "This is my profession: filming books.
One learns to recognize one's self and one's borders. It's
a job like any other ... the books found me, they have
always suited a certain time in my life—these books
became my dialogue partners in life."

Mario Adorf as vegetable dealer Alfred Matzerath

By 1978, the scandal of Günther Grass's 1959
labyrinthine satire, *Die Blechtrommel* (The Tin
Drum), was long forgotten. Volker Schlöndorff's
adaptation was awarded the Palme d'Or at
Cannes and an Oscar in Hollywood for best
foreign film.

Twenty years separate the births of literary
character Oskar Mazerath and actor David
Bennent, who played the childlike dropout,
"Little Oskar," with a joyless expression in
his eyes. As Oskar, thirteen-year-old Bennent
terrorizes a Kashubian enclave with his un-
nerving drum rolls and ear-piercing voice.
Grass's grotesque antihero is interpreted as a
jealous Peter Pan who is unable to cope with
his mother's involvement with German green-
grocer Alfred Mazerath and Polish postman
Jan Bronksi. Escaping into a dystopian exile,

the taciturn boy makes a conscious decision, on
his third birthday, to stop growing. By the end
of World War II, he has become a monstrous
young man in a child's body who terrorizes the
world around him.

Grass's over-the-top, irreverent, and highly
experimental novel was considered an unlikely
subject for film because of its bizarre details,
changing styles, and rhapsodic structure. Yet,
Schlöndorff tamed the material by cutting out
part three of the novel—which covered the
postwar era—and forcing the stream-of-con-
sciousness flow into a chronological order via
flashbacks narrated by Oskar in a grating tone
of voice.

Schlöndorff's realistic fairy tale begins and
ends with long shots of harvested potato fields
bathed in a surreal autumn light. The poly-

The pale boy with the drum: David Bennent as the defiant Oskar Matzerath

phonous chorus of the literary original is maintained throughout the film via alternating narrative levels, such as off-screen commentary, flashbacks, archival footage, and subjective camera shots. At the same time, the film delves into the full spectrum of the novel's many themes: fascism, anti-Semitism, racism, and the petit bourgeoisie. In a forced, time-lapsed view of the era—from the Führer's barked orders ("As of 5:45 a.m. we will return fire!") to the advancing Red Army—events are condensed into a ghostly vision in front of Oskar's eyes. He rebelliously refuses to participate, exonerating himself from having to pay tribute. In a famous drum sequence, the pale boy in a Hitler-youth uniform mesmerizes columns of goose-stepping Nazis into a swaying waltz, his own childish body a protest against the constraints of the day.

In Schlöndorff's adaptation, the impotence of the observer, whose hysteric screams seem ridiculous in the face of tanks and bombers, is not so much a sarcastic indictment of the war generation than a distillation of all that the generation of '68 stood for. From today's perspective, one could also interpret it as a sobering commentary on a society, whose obsession with infantilism compels it to worship youth, a scenario that springs from a tragic loss of self.   *J.L.*

Apocalypse Now

USA, 1976-79
Running time: 153 minutes
Directed by Francis Ford Coppola; *written by*
Francis Ford Coppola *and* John Milius, *based
on a novel by* Joseph Conrad; *cinematographer,*
Vittorio Storaro; *music by* Carmine Coppola,
Francis Ford Coppola; *edited by* Richard
Marks
With: Martin Sheen (Willard), Marlon Brando
(Colonel Kurtz), Robert Duvall (Kilgore),
Dennis Hopper (Photographer), Frederic
Forrest (Boss), Samuel Bottoms (Lance),
Laurence Fishburne (Clean)

Francis Ford Coppola

1939 Born on April 7 in Detroit to Carmine Coppola, a musician,
and his wife, an actress. Studied theater in Hempstead,
N.Y., then film in Los Angeles. While still a student,
assisted director Roger Corman. Short films including
Tonight for Sure!, 1962
1963 Made *Dementia 13,* his first long feature
1968 *Finian's Rainbow*
Established his own production company, American
Zoetrope
1971 Coppola landed a huge success with *The Godfather*
(three Oscars)
1973 *The Conversation* (Golden Palm, Cannes)
1974 *The Godfather Part II* (six Oscars)
1976–1979 *Apocalypse Now* (the dramatic production
conditions of this Vietnam film were be recorded in
the documentary *Hearts of Darkness—A Filmmaker's
Apocalypse,* 1991)
1981 The flop of the melodrama *One From the Heart* brought
Coppola to the brink of financial ruin and forced him to
sell his studio.
1982 *The Outsiders*
1983 *Rumble Fish*
1984 *The Cotton Club*
1990 *The Godfather Part III*
1992 *Bram Stoker's Dracula*
1996 *Jack*
1997 *The Rainmaker*
1999 Co-producer of the horror tale *Sleepy Hollow*

>>> Francis Ford Coppola, *The Godfather,* see p. 108

The end of three insane years of filming: Kurtz's camp

In recalling the difficulty of filming *Apocalypse
Now* Francis Ford Coppola has stated that:
"During the shoot there were times when
I thought I would die—literally—as a result
of my inability to solve my problems. I went
to bed at four o'clock in the morning, bathed
in sweat. When it was all over, I realized that
I had arrived at a completely different place.
I no longer looked upon things as I had done
before. I stopped worrying whether I was
talented or not, whether I'd win an Oscar,
whether I'd be rich or poor."

It took three insane and grueling years,
from 1976 to 1979. Afterwards, everything
really had changed. Coppola had filmed the
definitive war movie, and he had done so by
creating a work that refuses to take sides, remaining in limbo between enlightenment
and mystification. Although the genre peaked
with this film, generations of filmmakers have
felt inspired to measure themselves against
this model.

In his epic, Coppola wanted, more than
anything else, to tell the story on an emotional
level. He compared *Apocalypse Now* to Kubrick's

2001—A Space Odyssey, explaining that his
film was less about Vietnam than about a kind
of odyssey: Captain Willard's journey upriver.
Willard, bent on drinking himself to death in
his hotel room in Saigon out of despair over
his alienation in both Vietnam and America,
is sent on a secret mission. His task is to find
Colonel Kurtz, a war hero, who has gone insane
and has established his own reign of terror
behind the front lines. Willard's brief is to
eliminate Kurtz.

The genesis of the project, which often
seemed doomed from the outset, is surrounded
by legends. Casting the main role nearly
drove the director to the brink of insanity.
Steve McQueen, Al Pacino, James Caan, Jack
Nicholson, and even Robert Redford were dis-
cussed as options. Harvey Keitel was eventually
cast as Willard but fired after three weeks. In
Coppola's words he played "too feverishly…
like a second-rate actor." Marlon Brando,
cast as Kurtz, failed to communicate for weeks
on end and finally showed up on set weighing
285 pounds. When a typhoon on the
Philippines destroyed two sets at once, filming
ground to a halt for several weeks.

The film makes no attempt to tell a realistic
story. Coppola is interested in myth, horror,
and emotion. His lead actor, Martin Sheen,
perfectly captures the subjectivity of horror,
forcing us to look at things through his eyes.
Directorily speaking, this is where Coppola
was in his element.

What began in March of 1976 with a budget
of 12 million dollars and an estimated schedule
of four months turned into 230 days on set and
30 million dollars over budget—more than

A journey upriver which
ends in horror

Myth, horror, emotion: the shattering helicopter attack, just a matter of minutes in the film, took seven weeks to produce

Coppola and his Zoetrope studio could afford, even after the success of *The Godfather*.

Stylistically perfect and theatrical in structure and design, the film was honoured with two Oscars for camerawork and sound, but the more important Oscars never materialized. Nevertheless, the film, based loosely on Joseph Conrad's novella *Heart of Darkness* (1899), depicted war more elaborately and effectively than any other production before or since. Kurtz's last words sum it up: "The horror, the horror."   *M.B.*

Gandhi

England/USA/India, 1981/82
Running time: 188 minutes
Directed by Richard Attenborough; *written by*
John Briley; *cinematographer,* Billy Williams,
Ronnie Taylor; *music by* Ravi Shankar, George
Fenton; *edited by* John Bloom
With: Ben Kingsley (Mahatma Gandhi),
Candice Bergen (Margaret Bourke-White),
Edward Fox (General Dyer), John Gielgud
(Lord Irwin), Trevor Howard (Judge
Broomfield)

Richard Attenborough

1923 Born on August 29 in Cambridge, England.
Attended the Royal Academy of Dramatic Art in London.
Worked initially as an actor.
1942 First film role in Noël Coward's war drama *In Which We Serve*
Even after turning to producing and directing,
Attenborough continued to be active as an actor. To
date he has played about 70 roles (most recently in
The Lost World: Jurassic Park, 1997 and in *Elizabeth,*
1998).
1959 Began producing and founded his own production firm
Beaver Films (which was dissolved in 1964)
1968 Film directing debut with *Oh What a Lovely War!*
1972 *Young Winston*
1976 *A Bridge Too Far*
1981/82 *Gandhi* (eight Oscars)
1985 *A Chorus Line*
1987 *Cry Freedom*
1992 *Chaplin* (film biography)
1993 *Shadowlands*
1996 *In Love and War*
1999 *Grey Owl*

"In an early scene in South Africa, Gandhi, long before he
adopted the loincloth as his only dress, beams proudly at
his small, immaculately tailored sons.
'I am so proud of them,' he says. 'Perfect little English
gentlemen!'"
The New York Times, December 8, 1982

A serious appraisal of history: Ben Kingsley as Gandhi

Richard Attenborough reminisced that:
"Filming Mahatma Gandhi's life became enor-
mously important to me personally—it was
a task I simply had to complete before I could
carry on in peace." For twenty long years he
pursued his plan. The actor and director
searched in vain for a studio that would support
his project and for investors who would back
it. The idea became an obsession; Attenborough
rejected forty acting roles and twelve directorial
projects in order to realize *Gandhi*. In the end,
India's Prime Minister Indira Gandhi (who,
incidentally, is not related to her legendary
namesake) provided the financial assistance that
made the difference. On November 26, 1980,
the clapper finally marked the first shot. After
five months of shooting and a budget of more
than twenty-two million dollars *Gandhi* was
completed.

Attenborough's persistence paid off in a
three-hour-long epic, brilliantly directed and
photographed, movingly told, and convincing-
ly performed by an excellent cast. His reward
was eight Oscars—among others for best film,
best director, and best actor (Ben Kingsley)—
a Golden Globe, five British Academy Awards
and two from India, Gandhi's homeland:
the Lotus Decoration Award and the Padma
Bushan Award.

Attenborough describes fifty-four years of
the life of India's great freedom fighter in 189
scenes shot mostly on location in India. The
film opens with the assassination of seventy-
nine-year old Mahatma Gandhi after leading
his nation to independence. Gandhi's life is
then told in chronological backflashes, focusing
on the passive resistance that became the trademark of his struggle for independence from
Britain.

British actor Ben Kingsley, little known until
then, was ideally cast for the part. He studied
Gandhi in photographs and documentaries
for months, starved himself down to Gandhi's
extremely low weight, and began to look
astonishingly like the Mahatma. Kingsley
managed the near impossible feat of conveying
the incredible aura which Gandhi is said to
have had. "From the opening scene onwards,
we are captivated by Gandhi's life and after
seeing the film, we wish we could have met
this man in person," was the effusive praise
in the *Motion Picture Guide*.

With *Gandhi*, Attenborough proved that
epics on the scale of *Ben Hur* were still possible
in the eighties, and that historical epics would
always have a place in cinema. Perhaps this is
because Attenborough placed more emphasis
on taking a serious look at history than his
predecessors had done.   *S.Al.*

Mahatma Gandhi, the upholder of a philosophy
of nonviolence, in the midst of his supporters

Blade Runner

USA, 1982
Running time: 117 minutes
Directed by Ridley Scott; *written by* Hampton Fancher *and* David Peoples, *based on the story* 'Do Androids Dream of Electric Sheep' *by* Philip K. Dick; *cinematographer,* Jordan Cronenweth; *music by* Vangelis; *edited by* Terry Rawlings
With: Harrison Ford (Deckard), Rutger Hauer (Batty), Sean Young (Rachael), Daryl Hannah (Pris), Edward James Olmos (Gaff), Emmet Walsh (Bryant), Joe Turkel (Tyrell), Brion James (Leon), William Sanderson (J. F. Sebastian)

Ridley Scott

1937 Born on November 30 in South Shields, England. Attended the Royal College of Art in London. Television director for the BBC; established his own production company and made highly successful advertising films.
1977 Feature film debut with *The Duellists* (Cannes prize, best first film)
1979 *Alien,* a science-fiction hit that catapulted Scott into the ranks of star directors
1982 *Blade Runner* cemented his cult status
1985 *Legend*
1989 *Black Rain*
1991 *Thelma & Louise*
1992 *1492: The Conquest of Paradise*
1995 *White Squall*
1997 *G. I. Jane*
2000 *Gladiator*
Planned for 2001 is *Hannibal,* in which Anthony Hopkins will again play psychopathic killer Hannibal Lecter.

One of the most dramatic and nerve-wracking sequences which boosted cinematographer Jordan Cronenweth to fame

>>> Ridley Scott, *Thelma and Louise,* see p. 158

Ridley Scott's melancholic and futuristic tale, *Blade Runner* (based on Philip K. Dick's novel *Do Androids Dream of Electric Sheep?*), was the most influential science fiction film of the 1980s and 1990s. Beyond cult status and its enormous stylistic influence, the visual force with which futuristic scenery, action, and philosophic reflections on the postmodern era fuse into a daring elegy remains fascinating to this day.

It is the year 2019. Former Blade Runner Deckard (Harrison Ford) is hired to search for replicates, robots on the prowl in a dystopic Los Angeles. The replicates are machines brought to life through gene technology and virtually indistinguishable from humans. Only a complicated procedure can reveal their artificial nature. As biotechnological gadgets, created as slaves to develop space, they are forbidden from living on Earth. For security reasons their life-spans are limited because their makers were uncertain as to the emotional reactions of their creatures. Indeed, the four Nexus models, which Deckard is asked to destroy, are driven by fear of their imminent death. With the courage of those who have nothing left to lose, they search for their creator in the hope that he will postpone their demise.

In contrast to other films of the genre, Ridley Scott's "gritty and gloomy counter image to Kubrick's *2001*" makes do with a minimum of action scenes and special effects. Instead of spectacle, viewers are captivated by the claustrophobic visuals, which—combined with a deliberately slow pace—create a highly suggestive, hypnotic atmosphere in which the psychology of the unscrupulous head-hunter is revealed. Just as a constant dampness corrodes the nocturnal and pluralistic architecture in the film, so a profound doubt in the ability of humans to understand themselves permeates the ghostly scenarios. Ridley Scott uses the eye motif, varied in multiple, almost kaleidoscopic, refractions, to ponder the age-old question of whether "truth" is possible—a question whose postmodern relativization throws the story into question.

In his 1991 director's cut, Scott revoked several concessions he had made in the interest of mass appeal, such as Deckard's voice-over narration and a positive ending. The perspective is made all the more radical because Deckard, too, is revealed to be an android. The central question of what is "artificial" and what is "natural" is unmasked as an elaborate McGuffin, since even human identity and memory can be artificial in nature. This, more than any other theme, gives the film a film noir quality, and opens the discourse on the humanity of man's future.

J.L.

With a minimum of action-packed scenes, *Blade Runner* succeeds in creating a maximum degree of tension thanks to its suggestive pictorial language

Half creature, half creator: Daryl Hannah (center) as Pris

Paris, Texas

Germany/France/England, 1984
Running time: 145 minutes
Directed by Wim Wenders; *produced by* Don Guest; *written by* Sam Shepard; *based on the novel by* L. M. Kit Carson; cinematography, Robby Müller; *music by* Ry Cooder; *edited by* Peter Przygodda
With: Harry Dean Stanton (Travis Clay Henderson), Nastassja Kinski (Jane), Dean Stockwell (Walt Henderson), Aurore Clément (Anne), Hunter Carson (Hunter), Bernhard Wicki (Dr. Ulmer), John Lurie (Slater) Jeni Vici (Strech)

Wim Wenders

1945 Born on August 14 as the son of a medical doctor in Düsseldorf.
1967–70 Attended the Hochschule für Fernsehen und Film (College of Television and Film) in Munich. Did short films and movie reviews.
1970 *Summer in the City,* his final examination and first long film.
1971 *The Anxiety of the Goalie at the Penalty Kick.* That same year, became founding member of the Filmverlag der Autoren, a production company run by film authors.
1974 *Wrong Move*
1975 *Kings of the Road*
1977 *The American Friend* brought Wenders to the U.S.
1978–82 Directed *Hammett* at Coppola's invitation
1981 *The State of Things* (Golden Lion, Venice)
1984 *Paris, Texas* (Golden Palm, Cannes)
1987 *Wings of Desire* (directing prize, Cannes)
1991 *Until the End of the World*
1995 *Lisbon Story*
1997 *The End of Violence*
1998 *Buena Vista Social Club* (Oscar nomination for best documentary)
1999 *The Million Dollar Hotel* (premiered at the Berlinale 2000; Silver Bear)

Harry Dean Stanton as Travis in Wim Wenders' 'guy movie,' based on the book by Sam Shepard

As *Paris, Texas* opens, we see its central character, Travis (Harry Dean Stanton), stumbling through the Texas desert, drinking his last drops of water, and wanting to forget everything. Once the obsessive and jealous husband of Jane (Nastassja Kinski), he may have good reason to be on the road.

This much is certain: Wim Wenders makes "guy movies." In the case of *Paris, Texas*, the subject matter is a sure give away. Before lonesome Travis goes back to a life on the road, he returns his seven-year-old son, Hunter, to his former wife—who had given the child to his aunt and uncle four years earlier. For Travis, the barren Western desert, punctuated by giant billboards, seems more wholesome than the reunion between mother and son. The "girl flick" begins in the minds of female viewers only after the credits have rolled.

Although the film lends itself to highbrow interpretations, it can also be enjoyed without the help of intellectual constructs. Travis ("Traveller") is one of Wenders' archetypal lone wanderers. Fleshed out by the plaintive music of Ry Cooder and the camerawork of Robby Müller, Travis's inner landscape is revealed. He resembles a man who has "fallen off the earth," and it is his son, a fan of outer space and extra terrestrials, who catches him and brings him back.

Travis's former wife, Jane, works in a peepshow. Yet, the symbolic mirrored glass of the show window that separates her from him never breaks. As Travis and Jane speak into microphones, painfully reminiscing on their destructive love, their faces overlap for a few seconds and merge into one. Then, their reflections separate once more, signaling that their relationship is over. Travis goes back on the road en route to Paris, Texas. The desert outpost with the alluring name has become his *idée fixe*, for he believes that this is where he was conceived.

The German-French co-production, which won the Palme d'Or, finally catapulted the German *auteur* filmmaker, with a knack for "the visual language of America," onto the international scene. Many of his other titles have also received worldwide attention: *The American Friend*, *Wings of Desire*, and *Far Away, So Close!* In 2000, Wim Wenders was nominated for an Oscar for another great "guy movie." His documentary film, *Buena Vista Social Club*, another collaboration with Ry Cooder, brought international fame to the old-time musicians of Havana, Cuba. *A.K.*

"For a long time films were a mirror of society. But at the end of the [20th] century, it seems as if that mirror is determining the direction more and more and dictating what we are to think. Movies have become a powerful weapon. This does not mean that the cinema is just exploitive. It can still reflect on the nature of life."
Wim Wenders, 1997

Captivating Nastassja Kinski as Travis' wife, Jane

Travis' dreamworld

Once Upon a Time in America

USA, 1982–84
Running time: 228 minutes
(short version: 167)
Directed by Sergio Leone; *written by* Sergio
Leone, Leonardo Benvenuti, Piero de Bernardi,
Enrico Medioli, Franco Arcalli, *and* Franco
Ferrini, *based on the novel* The Hoods *by* Harry
Grey; *cinematographer,* Tonino Delli Colli; *music
by* Ennio Morricone; *edited by* Nino Baragli
With: Robert De Niro (Noodles), James Woods
(Max), Elizabeth McGovern (Deborah), Larry
Rapp (Fat Moe), Tuesday Weld (Carol), Treat
Williams (Jimmy O'Donnell), Burt Young (Joe),
Danny Aiello (Chief Inspector), William
Forsythe (Cockeye)

Sergio Leone

1929 Born on January 3 in Rome as the son of silent film
    director Vincenzo Leone and actress Francesca Bertini.
1948–59 Assistant director (among others for Vittorio De
    Sica's *The Bicycle Thief* and for U.S. directors filming in
    Rome such as William Wyler, Raoul Walsh, Mervin
    LeRoy, and Robert Wise).
1959 Stepped in for director Mario Bonard during the
    shooting of *The Last Days of Pompeii*
1960 Official movie debut with *The Colossus of Rhodes*
1964 *A Fistful of Dollars* made Leone famous as the
    "inventor" of the spaghetti western, and lead actor
    Clint Eastwood a star. Two other movies from the
    "Dollar Trilogy" were internationally successful!
1965 *For a Few Dollars More* and
1966 *The Good, the Bad and the Ugly.*
1968 *Once Upon a Time in the West*
1973 *My Name is Nobody/Lonesome Gun*
1982–84 *Once Upon a Time in America* (his last movie)
1989 Sergio Leone died on April 30 in Rome, while involved
    in plans for a giant project about the German siege of
    St. Petersburg during World War II.

Rich and beautiful—but criminals: Robert De Niro as Noodles and Darlanne Fluegel as Eve

Once Upon a Time in America is set in the 1920s, the dry years of prohibition. Director Sergio Leone paints a memorable portrait of New York's backyards and back alleys, its gambling dens and slums, and its inhabitants caught in a brutal struggle for survival. These images are fascinatingly captured by cameraman Tonino delli Colli and accompanied by the music of Ennio Morricone, the master of emotive film scores. A sensitive gangster biography, the movie details the aesthetics of crime in blood-filled scenes that evince the fierce will to live.

The 228-minute drama is centered on Noodles (Robert de Niro) and Max (James Wood), members of the Backstreet Boys gang who promise each other lifelong friendship. But exactly what "lifelong" means in a world of sudden death is uncertain. To explore the concept, Leone developed a complex and highly artistic technique of flashbacks, which move viewers through the multilayered story. Changes in the two protagonists' characters, the process of aging, and cultural upheavals in New York between 1920 and 1968 are brought vividly to life in a tour de force of violence that is simultaneously moving and repulsive.

Sergio Leone's artistry is revealed in sensitive pauses between scenes of violent action. These quiet, beautiful, even poetic, passages are bathed in a bronze light and provide striking counterpoints to the wild manhunts shot in cold, blue-gray. There are also scenes full of devilish irony—beautifully choreographed and cunningly scored—such as when the friends punish a corrupt police chief by switching his baby son with a girl in the hospital.

The mafioso drama, which comes off like a stageplay when compared to gorefests like *The Godfather* (see p. 108), ends on a sad note. The promise of lifelong friendship is devoured by the ravenous jaws of a garbage truck as youngsters listen to *God Bless America* on a car radio. In the end, the movie is less a high-voltage epic and than it is a deeply distressing elegy. "A monument in the history of film," as one ad writer put it in 1984.   P.W.E.

Tuesday Weld (Carol)

>>> Sergio Leone, *Once Upon a Time in the West,*
see p. 102

An early scene in this gangster biography set in New York between the 1920s and 1960s

The murderous manhunt: Noodles
(Robert De Niro) caught in a volley of bullets

Out of Africa

USA, 1985

Running time: 161 minutes
Directed by Sydney Pollack; *written by* Kurt
Luedtke, *based on a book by* Karen (Tania)
Blixen; *cinematographer,* David Watkin; *music
by* John Barry; *edited by* Fredric Steinkamp,
William Steinkamp, Pembroke J. Herring,
Sheldon Kahn
With: Meryl Streep (Karen Blixen), Robert
Redford (Denys Finch Hatton), Klaus Maria
Brandauer (Bror Blixen), Michael Kitchen
(Berkeley Cole), Malick Bowens (Farah Aden),
Mike Bugara (Juma), Joseph Thiaka (Kamanta),
Michael Gough (Lord Delamere)

Pure emotion: Meryl Streep and Robert Redford at the foot of Mount Kilimanjaro

Meryl Streep as Karen Tania Blixen and Klaus Maria
Brandauer as her husband

"I had a farm in Africa, at the foot of the Ngong Mountains." This opening, narrated sentence sends shivers down our spines everytime we hear it, for one thing is certain. The seven-time Oscar-winning *Out of Africa* is a film we want to watch over and over again. It meets all of our expectations of a great film: an intelligent script, excellent direction, and a superb cast. Hang-ups, high emotions, and breathtaking visuals characterize this movie, bringing to life the spirit and *joie de vivre* of a writer who spent seventeen years on a coffee plantation in the high plains of Kenya.

The film is based on the autobiography of Karen Tania Blixen, who left her native Denmark in the glamorous first decade of the twentieth century to start a plantation with her husband, Bror, in the foothills of Kilimanjaro. Many years later, after she had lost everything in Africa and returned to Denmark, Blixen recorded her experiences under the pen name, Isak Dinesen. The panoramic scope and breath of her memoires permeate every scene in the film—her passion for Africa and its people, and the passions that course between three protagonists.

Even in his early work—*They Shoot Horses, Don't They?*, *They Way We Were*, and *The Electric Horseman*—Sydney Pollack proved himself to be a master of the languorous rhythm that is so effectively used in *Out of Africa*. He has always had a sure touch in the selection of his material, and, in this case, he leaves his favourite theme—the suppression of the individual by a group—behind to venture into the territory of romance, all the while remaining true to his excellent development of characters.

His compelling portrait of a time of upheavals in an exotic location received seven Oscars, including those in the most coveted categories of best film, director, cinematography, film score, and script. Kurt Luedtke performed the miracle of extracting a plot-driven script from five different sources, among them Blixen's introspective original work, her correspondence, and the autobiography of Denys Finch Hatton, played by Robert Redford. For a long time, Pollack felt that the project was "unfilmable"—too many emotions, too many observations, and too little action. Nevertheless, he achieved the impossible by translating Karen Blixen's exciting but difficult life—an unfaithful husband, an unfulfilled love affair, a ruined plantation, and myriad difficulties as a woman ahead of her time in a conservative society loyal to the Empire—into film.   *M.B.*

Meryl Streep was nominated for an Oscar for *Out of Africa,*
her third after *Kramer vs. Kramer* (1979) and *Sophie's
Choice* (1982)

>>> Sydney Pollack, *The Way We Were,* and Biography,
see p. 116

Meryl Streep plays the heroine in the Danish authoress' autobiography

For a long time, the Kenyan dreamworld
was considered unfilmable

Down by Law

USA, 1986
Running time: 106 minutes
Directed by Jim Jarmusch; *written by* Jim
Jarmusch; *cinematographer,* Robby Müller;
music by John Lurie *and* Tom Waits; *edited
by* Melody London
With: Tom Waits (Zack), John Lurie (Jack),
Roberto Benigni (Bob), Nicoletta Braschi,
Ellen Barkin, Billie Neal

Jim Jarmusch

1953   Born on January 22 in Akron, Ohio. Studied in New York
       and Paris.
1976–79 Attended NYU Film School and assisted Nicholas
       Ray.
1980   With Ray's support, Jarmusch made his directing debut
       in *Permanent Vacation,* done on a mini-budget of
       $12,000.
1984   *Stranger Than Paradise* (feature film version of the
       short *New World*) rapidly achieved cult film status and
       won best debut film award in Cannes.
1986   *Down by Law*
1989   *Mystery Train*
1991   *Night On Earth*
1995   *Dead Man*
1997   *Year of the Horse* (documentary on Neil Young and his
       band, Crazy Horse)
1999   *Ghost Dog: The Way of the Samurai*
       Jarmusch does not talk about his future plans, saying
       he is superstitious and wouldn't reveal an idea before
       its premiere.

"What I want to do is make films that ... tell stories, but
somehow in an new way, not in a predictable form, not in
the usual manipulative way that films seem to on their
audiences."
Jim Jarmusch, *Current Biography Yearbook,* 1990

Tom Waits (top), Roberto Benigni (bottom)

In a seedy part of New Orleans, an unemployed
DJ named Zack (Tom Waits) accepts the job of
driving a stolen car to the other side of town.
Unfortunately for him, someone has stuffed a
corpse into the trunk, and Zack lands in jail.

Zack's cellmate is Jack (John Lurie), a pimp
caught in a hotel room with a ten-year-old girl.
The twosome becomes a trio when an Italian
cardsharp called Bob (Roberto Benigni) joins
them—bringing life into the cell and the film.
His broken English is hilarious and at times
unforgettable, as in his conjugation exercise,
"I scream, you scream, we scream for ice-cream."
In a key scene, Bob tells Zack and Jack that he's
in jail because he has beaten a man to death
with a billiard ball: "the eighth ball, very good
ball, black!" After this astonishing revelation,
the three enter into a temporary friendship.

"It's a sad and beautiful world," says Bob,
stating the central theme of the film. The three
can escape from the narrow confines of prison
life because Bob remembers old American
movies. They manage to escape through an
underground tunnel—the kind that only exists in movies. Their movie escape leads them
straight into the swamps of Louisiana, where
they are chased by bloodhounds and survive
encounters with alligators, until they come
upon a snack bar in the middle of nowhere,
where Bob finds happiness in the shape of a
beautiful fellow countrywoman (played by
Nicoletta Braschi). The others carry on, but
at the next fork in the road they, too, go their
separate ways.

Director Jim Jarmusch's independent masterpiece is full of melancholy, humanity, and
comedy, all of which are conveyed by the outstanding performances of the lead actors and
the calm but addictive black-and-white images
of cameraman Robby Müller. *Down by Law*,
with singer Tom Waits, musician John Lurie,
and then-unknown Roberto Benigni (of *Life is
Beautiful* fame, see p. 174–75), marked Jarmusch
as one of the finest directors in America.

With films such as *Stranger Than Paradise*
(1984) and *Night on Earth* (1991), Jarmusch
established himself as a cult filmmaker, and
he continues to resist mainstream Hollywood.

His latest movie, *Ghost Dog* (2000), is a
meditation on gangster life that delivers proof
of his mastery. Inspired by *Le Samurai*
(see pp. 96–97) and Akira Kurosawa's samurai
movies, it tells the story of a professional
hitman who raises doves. The lead is played
by Forest Whitaker, Jarmusch's favorite actor
and for whom he wrote the script. Hollywood
has still not invented a cliché into which
Jarmusch might fit.   *P.W.E.*

Tom Waits, John Lurie, and Roberto Benigni
A strange start to a life on the run: The three
soon get caught up in the swamps of Louisiana

"It's a sad and beautiful world"—Tom Waits and Ellen Barkin in Jarmusch's masterpiece

The Last Emperor

England, 1986/87

Running time: 162 minutes (TV 225)
Directed by Bernardo Bertolucci; *written by*
Bernardo Bertolucci *and* Mark Peploe, *based
on the autobiography by* Pu Yi; *cinematographer,*
Vittorio Storaro; *music by* David Byrne, Su
Zong, Ryuichi Sakamoto; *edited by* Gabriella
Cristiani
With: John Lone (Pu Yi), Joan Chen (Wan
Jung), Peter O'Toole (Reginald Johnston),
Dennis Dun (Big Li), Victor Wong (Chen Pao
Shen), Maggie Han (Juwel des Ostens)

Bernardo Bertolucci

1940 Born on March 16 in Parma as the son of poet and film
critic Attilio Bertolucci. Began to study literature and
wrote and published poetry from a young age. Met Pier
Paolo Pasolini and in, 1961, assisted him on his first
film, *Accatone.* Decided to abandon his literature
studies.

1962 Directing debut with *The Grim Reaper* (based on a screenplay by Pasolini)

1964 *Before the Revolution*

1969 *The Spider's Strategem*

1970 *The Conformist*

1972 *Last Tango in Paris* (with Marlon Brando) caused a
scandal and became an international success

1976 *1900* (two-part, five-hour epic)

1979 *La Luna*

1986/87 *The Last Emperor* (nine Oscars)

1989/90 *The Sheltering Sky*

1993 *Little Buddha*

1996 *Stealing Beauty*

1998 *Besieged*

1999 *Paradiso e inferno*

"Combining the command of the historical epic he displayed
in 1900 with the political intrigue and melodrama of *The
Conformist*, Bertolucci has, in *The Last Emperor*, constructed
a beautiful film about the transformation of one man and
one country from monarchy to communism during the full
expanse of the 20th century."   *The Motion Picture Guide*

Peter O'Toole as Reginald Johnston

Bernardo Bertolucci's monumental epic
(the TV version is even sixty minutes longer),
was awarded eight Oscars. Produced at great
expense, it employed a huge cast of extras,
and was filmed entirely on location in China.
This alone was a sensation: Beijing's Forbidden
City was named thus for good reason well into
the eighties.

The film takes us into the life of Pu Yi, the
last emperor of the Qing dynasty. As a three-
year-old he ascends the throne as "Emperor
for 10,000 years," even though his empire
is instable and crumbling beyond the palace
walls.

Pu Yi experiences the vicissitudes of political fate firsthand when the Japanese storm
the palace and abduct him, taking him to
Manchukuo, where they set up a puppet
regime in an effort to oppose Communism.
Pu Yi, raised in an illusory world of ancient
traditions and staged opulence, is unable
to grasp the seriousness of his situation. He
becomes a toy in the hand of the new powers
and, ultimately, their victim. He ends up in
a Communist reeducation camp for ten years,
from which he gains an early release, and
returns to Beijing as a gardener.

The exoticism of the film is overwhelming.
It opens doors onto a world that is nearly incomprehensible to contemporary Westerners.
Eunuchs populate the palace, concubines offer
themselves, food tasters control the emperor's
nutrition, and doctors study his stool. Bertolucci
paints these large-format images with precision
and an aesthetic touch, all the while maintain-
ing a distance. Individual characters are carefully

hidden behind faces covered in stereotypical
make up. Pu Yi also remains a stranger, even
when he dances the Charleston or climbs into
bed with two women at the same time.

With *The Last Emperor*, Bertolucci created
a new film genre, that of the child-deity drama.
His successors were *Little Buddha*, *Seven Years in
Tibet*, and *Kundun*. These films are not only
similar in theme but also in production. In
each there is a bizarre discrepancy between
child and power, innocence and merciless
historic events. All of these children suffer
the fate of loneliness, and the drama is built
around liberating them from this. Europe, too,
has had its share of child-kings, but their stories
are too far in the past to touch us today.

The Last Emperor is a story without a happy
ending. While the child-deities in more recent
films fight for their liberation from exile—offering a glimmer of hope at least in the plot—Pu
Yi remains passive. At the end of his life, he is
reduced to a broken man in a Mao uniform.
Although tragic, one cannot help but feel that
somehow he is responsible for his own fate.

W.-C.F.

Joan Chen as Wan Jung

The little Pu Yi in a world of stage-managed magnificence

Dead Poets Society

USA, 1988

Running time: 128 minutes
Directed by Peter Weir; *written by* Tom
Schulman; *cinematographer,* John Seale;
music by Maurice Jarre; *edited by* William
M. Anderson
With: Robin Williams (John Keating), Robert
Sean Leonard (Neil Perry), Ethan Hawke
(Todd Anderson), Josh Charles (Knox
Overstreet), Gale Hansen (Charlie Dalton)

Peter Weir

1944 Born on August 21 as Peter Lindsay Weir in Sydney,
 Australia. Dropped his art and law studies in Sydney.
 European trip. After returning to Australia in 1967,
 made short films and worked for an Australian
 television station. Shot documentaries.
1974 Feature film debut with the horror comedy *The Cars
 That Ate Paris*
1975 *Picnic at Hanging Rock* (establishing Weir as top
 Australian director and bringing him an international
 reputation)
1977 *The Last Wave*
1982 *The Year of Living Dangerously*
1985 *Witness* (Weir's first Hollywood production)
1988 *Dead Poets Society*
1990 *Green Card*
1993 *Fearless*
1998 *The Truman Show*

Robert Sean Leonard and Ethan Hawke, members of the
Dead Poet's Society

To be read at the beginning of each meeting of the Dead
Poets Society: "I went to the woods because I wished to
live deliberately, / to front only the essential facts of life, /
and see if I could not learn what it had to teach, and not,
when / I came to die, discover that I had not lived."
Henry David Thoureau, *Where I Lived and What I Lived For*

The deceptive normality
of school sports: a scene
with Robin Williams as
teacher John Keating (left)

How can the comedian Robin Williams, the
extraterrestrial from *Mork & Mindy* and the
over-the-top DJ in *Good Morning, Vietnam*, be in
a serious role? This was difficult to imagine for
influential Hollywood magnates and for many
viewers in 1989. But with his work in *Dead Poets
Society*, Williams delivered one of the most impressive performances of his career.

New England, 1959: Tradition, honor, dis-
cipline, performance. These are the four pillars
on which the Welton Academy is founded.
Although the senior students make fun of the
school's motto ("Travesty, loathing, decadence,
lethargy"), these noble values are firmly en-
trenched in the minds of the future elite.
Everyday life at the boarding school is turned
upside down when John Keating (Robin
Williams) arrives as the new English teacher.
With powerful poetry and eccentric teaching
methods, he tries to shake up his students and
to encourage their individuality. The group, led
by highly talented Neil, is enthusiastic about
Keating's motto *Carpe Diem* (Seize the day!)
and resurrects the *Dead Poets Society*, a kind
of secret society. Yet, the more the students
clamour for self-determination, the stronger
they are resisted by the adults around them
—a catastrophe in the making.

Some critics decried the film as banal and
artificial, and it was ignored at Oscar time, with
the exception of an award for best script by
Tom Schulman. However, the public made its
own judgement. *Dead Poets Society* was a box
office success, bringing in almost 100 million
dollars in the US alone, and without a cast of
stars or special effects.

Director Peter Weir relied on the strength
of the story to make the film work, as he had
done previously with *The Witness* (1985). The
story has ample time to unfold as the viewer
is bathed in the glow of dreamy New England,
which functions as an allegory for the action.
For example, when the shy character, Knox,
startles a gaggle of geese as he stumbles around
in his awkward infatuation, his inner turmoil
is poetically brought to life in the image.

Weir succeeds in unpretentiously breathing
new life into the simple message of "follow
your own path." His young protagonists move
towards independence in an honest and moving
manner, supported by a brilliant Robin Williams,
whose character fails at the movie's conclusion
but ends up winning the heart of the public.

S.R.

Relaxed, casual, and unrestrained: Robin Williams uses
the power of poetry to capture his pupils' attention

Rain Man

USA, 1988

Running time: 133 minutes
Directed by Barry Levinson; *written by* Ronald
Bass, Barry Morrow; *cinematographer,* John
Seale; *music by* Hans Zimmer; *edited by* Stu
Linder
With: Dustin Hoffman (Raymond Babbitt),
Tom Cruise (Charlie Babbitt), Valeria Golino
(Susanna), Jerry Molen (Dr. Bruner), Jack
Murdock (John Mooney)

Barry Levinson

1942 Born on April 6 in Baltimore. Studied radio journalism in
Washington, D.C. and worked part-time at a local
television station. Went to Los Angeles, acted and
wrote television scripts, and co-authored the Mel
Brooks films *Silent Movie* (1976) and *High Anxiety*
(1977). With author and actress Valerie Curtin, his wife
from 1975 to 1982, wrote the screenplay for *And
Justice for All* (1979)
1982 Directing debut with *Diner*
1984 *The Natural*
1987 *Good Morning, Vietnam*
1988 *Rain Man* (four Oscars and Golden Berlin Bear)
1991 *Bugsy*
1992 *Toys*
1994 *Disclosure*
1996 *Sleepers*
1997 *Wag the Dog* (Silver Berlin Bear)
1998 *Sphere*
1999 *Liberty Heights*
2000 *An Everlasting Piece*
Levinson is currently working on the film *Outlaws.*

"The performance is a display of sustained virtuosity ... so
remarkable, in fact, that it overwhelms what is otherwise
a becomingly modest, decently thought-out, sometimes
funny film."
The New York Times on Dustin Hoffman,
December 16, 1988

Two brothers with their emotions under control

A story about an eccentric, autistic man is perhaps a hard sell in Hollywood. Before filming
began on *Rain Man*, the script had already been
through the hands of several writers, directors,
and stars, including Steven Spielberg and Jack
Nicholson, both of whom rejected it. It was
director Barry Levinson, who had established
his reputation with *Good Morning Vietnam*, who
ultimately took on the project. With Oscars for
best film, best director, best script, and best actor, *Rain Man* became his most successful film.

Actor Dustin Hoffman's tenacity is the reason
that the movie was realized at all. Hoffman's
credo was that "The public should remember
two of my roles—Ratso in *Asphalt Cowboy* and
Raymond." His wish came true with *Rain Man*.
Hoffman won an Oscar for his realistic interpretation of the autistic Raymond, and the film
was a box office hit that saved MGM/United
Artists from financial ruin.

Hoffman is legendary not only for his per-
fectionism but for his painstaking research.
For *Rain Man*, he carefully studied autistics in
order to copy their mannerisms, in a precise
and believable way, on screen. As Raymond,
Hoffman stares into space, insists on sticking
to daily routines ("On Tuesdays we have pan-
cakes"), and drives his brother, Charlie (Tom
Cruise), to the edge of insanity by repeating
sentences over and over again. His performance
was an unforgiving and relentless introduction
to the inner world of the autistic, one of the
reasons why the *Washington Post* raved that
"Hoffman [blew] co-star Cruise off the screen."

At the same time, it is unfair to reduce Tom
Cruise's role to that of mere catalyst in important scenes. Even though his performance
cannot compete with Hoffman's, his character
has some of the most moving moments in
the film. As an egotistical and materialistic
brother, Cruise's Charlie is both a counterpoint
to Raymond and his mirror image. For, like
Raymond, Charlie is incapable of showing his
feelings or entering into real relationships.
Yet, through his relationship with Raymond,
Charlie undergoes a transformation over the
course of the film—from an angry young man
obsessed with money to an adult who loves
the brother he never knew. In the end, he
changes from a crass egotist into an understanding friend, discovering his true self in
the process.   *S.R.*

Dustin Hoffman and Tom Cruise as Raymond and Charlie Babbitt:
on the way to becoming friends (above and right)

Pretty Woman

USA, 1989
Running time: 119 minutes
Directed by Garry Marshall; *written by* J. F.
Lawton; *cinematographer,* Charles Minsky;
music by James Newton Howard; *edited by*
Priscilla Nedd
With: Richard Gere (Edward Lewis), Julia
Roberts (Vivian), Ralph Bellamy (James
Morse), Laura San Giacomo (Kit De Luca),
Hector Elizondo (Hotelmanager), Jason
Alexander (Philip Stuckey), Alex Hyde-White
(David Morse), Amy Yasbeck (Elizabeth
Stuckey), Patrick Richwood (elevator boy)

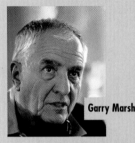

Garry Marshall

1934 Born on November 13 in New York City as Garry Kent
Masciarelli; his sister is actress and director Penny
Marshall *(Awakenings).* Studied journalism, followed by
work as a reporter, gag writer, and TV author.
Produced and directed successful television series such
as *The Odd Couple.* In 1968 produced his first cinema
film, *How Sweet It Is.*
1982 *Young Doctors in Love,* the first feature film directed by
Marshall
1984 *The Flamingo Kid*
1986 *Nothing in Common*
1987 *Overboard*
1989 *Pretty Woman*
1991 *Frankie and Johnny*
1994 *Exit to Eden*
1999 *The Other Sister*
Runaway Bride (with *Pretty Woman* team Julia Roberts
and Richard Gere)
2000 Marshall played a director in Sönke Wortmann's
Hollywood debut *The Hollywood Sign.*
A new comedy is scheduled for release in 2001.

Big bubbles: Julia Roberts as streetwalker Vivian, enjoying a stay in a
luxury hotel

Pretty Woman is a film about money and the
belief that it can buy anything. That was the
credo of the 1980s, and *Pretty Woman* is its
cinematic manifesto.

In this film, a streetwalker becomes a
millionaire's wife, not because of her sex
appeal but because of her charm and good
heart—qualities which redeem her from her
profession. The colorful collection of condoms
in her thigh-high boots are just a lark; they
might as well be candy.

Pretty Woman is a lifestyle variation on the
Cinderella story. As such, it is a fairy tale, pure
and simple. The story begins in a straight-
forward way: Richard Gere plays a millionaire
with puppy-dog eyes who is ready to pay for
his pleasure. Later on, we learn that he only
wants a female escort, but his search takes him
to LA's seedier side. From here, the fairy tale
begins. Julia Roberts enters the scene like an
innocent and quickly spots the soft core of her
benevolent suitor. The next thing we know,
she is staying at the luxurious Beverly Wilshire
Hotel. This is stark contrast to real-life Hollywood hookers who end up in the precinct jail.

In *Pretty Woman,* money triumphs, such as
when Roberts's character takes revenge on a
saleswoman who had refused to wait on her
when she was a lowly "prostitute." A great deal
of the action takes place on Rodeo Drive, so the
message is clear: money not only makes you
happy, it makes you powerful and, of course,
enchantingly beautiful.

"What's your dream?" Roberts's character
asks her friend. "Money!" we feel like shouting
at the screen, but the story of *Pretty Woman*
saves us from such humiliation. Just once in
a lifetime, we would all like to splash around
in a bathtub for two or fly to San Francisco for
a night at the opera. *Pretty Woman* allows all of
us to vicariously experience how beautiful life
is when you've got the right credit card. When
the film was released, this dream lifestyle
seemed romantic and somehow inspiring.
Today, we're all a few years older.   *W.-C.F.*

"... It's Roberts's memorably comic performance that is the
most distinguishing aspect of the movie. As the gawky
professional companion, she's ticklishly appealing ..."
The Washington Post

In the rags to riches story, Richard Gere plays the heartthrob businessman at Julia Roberts' side.

Do the Right Thing

USA, 1989

Running time: 119 minutes
Directed, produced and written by Spike Lee;
cinematographer, Ernest Dickerson; *music by*
Bill Lee; *edited by* Barry Alexander Brown
With: Danny Aiello (Sal), Spike Lee (Mookie),
Richard Edson (Vito), Ossie Davis (Da Mayor),
John Turturro (Pino), Bill Nunn (Radio
Raheem), Giancarlo Esposito (Buggin' Out),
Robin Harris (Sweet Dick Willie), Samuel
L. Jackson (Senor Love Daddy), Rosie Perez
(Tina)

Spike Lee

1957 Born on March 20 as Shelton Jackson Lee in Atlanta,
Georgia. Son of jazz bassist Bill Lee. Grew up in
Brooklyn, New York and studied film at New York
University.
1986 Feature film debut with *She's Gotta Have It* (in which,
as in all of his subsequent films, except for *He Got
Game,* Lee also appeared as an actor)
1989 *Do the Right Thing*
1990 *Mo' Better Blues* (with his father's music)
1992 *Malcolm X* (three-hour biography of the Muslim leader
Malcolm X)
1994 *Crooklyn*
1995 *Clockers*
1996 *Girl 6*
1998 *He Got Game*
1999 *Summer of Sam* (premiered in Cannes; with John
Leguizamo and Mia Sorvino)
2000 *Bamboozled*

Spike Lee (Mookie) with the yet to be discovered Rosie
Perez (Tina)

"Do the Right Thing **is living, breathing, riveting proof of
the arrival of an abundantly gifted new talent... it is one
terrific movie. Mr. Lee emerges as the most distinctive
American multi-threat man since Woody Allen."**
The New York Times

Racial tension in Brooklyn

"What's the difference between Hollywood
characters and my characters?" Spike Lee once
asked a journalist. "Mine are real."

That's not to say that he makes naturalistic
films. In his third feature *Do the Right Thing,*
the simmering tensions building in the Bedford-
Stuyvesant district of Brooklyn are played out on
a stage as formal and restricted as any theater.
One street, from Sal's Famous Pizzeria to the
local radio station WE-LOVE, serves as the
claustrophobic setting for the events that take
place on the hottest day of the year. While
characters sometimes seem impossibly loaded
with symbolic significance, the dialogue is
fresh off the street and Lee goes where no-one
had gone before; exploring the racial tension
between African Americans, Italian Americans
and the Korean storekeepers who are the latest
arrivals in the neighborhood. For this alone
the film is a landmark.

"Waaake Up!" The film opens with a close-
up of Senor Love Daddy (Samuel L. Jackson),
local DJ for WE-LOVE, observer of and commentator on life on the street, holding a ring-
ing alarm clock to the microphone. His words,
of course, are aimed as much at us, the audience,
as the figures on screen, struggling to raise
themselves from their beds. "I have today's
forecast for you: HOT!"

One by one we are introduced to the characters that will play their part in the drama.
Da Mayor (Ossie Davis), the local drunk and
unofficial leader of the community, who holds
court from the sidewalk. Mookie, the pizza
delivery boy, played by Spike Lee. Sal (Danny
Aiello), Italian and proud of it, father of two
dysfunctional sons and supplier of pizza to

the neighborhood for as long as anyone can
remember. Radio Raheem (Bill Nunn) a vast,
elemental figure in a Bed-Stuy T-shirt, who
somehow *is* the neighborhood. Raheem rarely
speaks but his beat-box pounds out the Public
Enemy theme that dominates the sound track.

This is an affectionate portrait of a mixed
community somehow rubbing along together,
until the unbearable heat of the New York
summer brings tensions to the boil. The issue at
the center of the film is one of identity. Three
elderly men who sit on the sidewalk acting as
a kind of Greek chorus discuss the fact that
Koreans who "haven't been off the boat for a
year" have opened a store in their neighborhood, while no new black-owned businesses
are opening. "Either those Korean mother-f-ers
are geniuses or your black asses are just plain
dumb" one tells his friends bitterly. "It's because we're black," another states, before the
most voluble, Sweet Willie Dixon (Robin Harris),
tells them "I'm tired of that old excuse!" and
marches across the road to patronize the store
by ordering another beer.

Meanwhile a local hothead, Buggin' Out
(Giancarlo Esposito), has noticed that the
photos in the Hall of Fame on the wall of Sal's
Famous Pizzeria are all of Italians: Sinatra,
Stallone, Perry Como. He demands that some
Brothers (African Americans) be put on the
wall. Sal responds angrily that his restaurant is
an Italian American one; if Buggin' Out wants
black heroes on the wall he should start his
own place. This is the beginning of an argument that ends in a riot and a tragic death.
Mookie is torn by opposing loyalties: to Sal,
who regards him as a son. To Buggin' Out,

Director and lead actor: Spike Lee as Mookie

who admonishes him to "stay black." To Da Mayor, who tells him "always do the right thing." Lee doesn't provide any easy answers, but has the courage to allow his characters to voice the hopes, fears and prejudices that inhabit the American inner city. Saturated in the color, sound and street wisdom of the Big Apple, *Do the Right Thing* made Lee into a major player and changed the face of American cinema for ever.   J.A.

Dances with Wolves

USA, 1990

Running time: 183 minutes
Directed by Kevin Costner; *written by* Michael Blake, *based on his own novel; cinematographer,* Dean Semler; *music by* John Barry; *edited by* Neil Travis
With: Kevin Costner (John J. Dunbar), Mary McDonnell (Stands with a Fist), Graham Greene (Kicking Bird), Rodney A. Grant (Wind in His Hair), Floyd Red Crow Westerman (Ten Bears), Tantoo Cardinal (Black Shawl), Robert Pastorelli (Timmons), Charles Rocket (Lt. Elgin), Maury Chaykin (Major Fambrough), Jimmy Herman (Stone Calf)

Kevin Costner

1955 Born on January 18 in Lynnwood, California. Obtained marketing degree, then decided to become an actor. Difficult beginnings; first successes with *Fandango* (1984) and *Silverado* (1985). International breakthrough in Brian de Palma's *The Untouchables* (1986). To date Costner has appeared in about 40 films (including *Robin Hood—Prince of Thieves,* 1991, *The Bodyguard,* 1992, *A Perfect World,* 1993, *Tin Cup,* 1996), but has directed only three (with himself in the starring role).

1990 His sensational debut *Dances With Wolves* (seven Oscars);

1995 the box-office disaster *Waterworld;* and

1997 *The Postman.*

His most recent acting appearances were in

1999 *Message in a Bottle* and *For Love of the Game*

Kevin Costner, the director and lead actor

One man, one movie. Kevin Costner fought for the material, contributed as co-producer, made his debut as a director, played the lead, and gave away two of his five million dollar fee to help pay for it. Thus, the grandiose western epic, *Dances With Wolves,* is largely Costner's achievement. His efforts were rewarded with seven Oscars, three Golden Globes, Berlin's Silver Bear, and box office returns of over 300 million dollars.

Yet, things didn't look promising at the outset. After Michael Cimino's megaflop *Heaven's Gate* (1980), Hollywood had given up on westerns. But the genre was about to make an unprecedented and unexpected comeback with Costner's film. The triumph was all the more surprising because Costner worked hard to achieve authenticity. He revised the Wild West cliché of the savage Indian and went to great lengths to show how closely the lives and culture of Native Americans were linked to nature. Long passages of dialogue are spoken in Lakota, the Sioux language, with English subtitles. In recognition of his efforts, Costner was elected honorary member of the Sioux nation.

Costner played the role of disillusioned Civil War lieutenant John Dunbar whose Indian name, "Dances with Wolves," provides the title for the film. The opening sequence shows Dunbar engaged in a suicide mission. Heavily wounded in his right leg, the Union officer rides into battle fully expecting to be shot—preferring death to amputation—but instead emerges a victorious hero.

Following this episode, Dunbar requests to be transferred to an outpost in Dakota, on the edge of civilization and surrounded by endless stretches of prairie. The fort there has been abandoned, but Dunbar doesn't mind. He's got his horse and the trust of a lonely wolf. Gradually, he develops a friendship with Indians in the area, and begins an affair with a white woman, "Stands with a Fist," (Mary McDonnell) who lives among the Sioux. When reinforcements unexpectedly arrive at the fort, his peaceful days come to an abrupt end—the soldiers turn out to be brutal intruders. To avoid putting the Sioux tribe at risk, Dunbar and his wife depart for an uncertain future.

Breathtaking panoramic views of the Western landscape characterize this film. Every now and then the calm flow of images is interrupted by dramatic action scenes which make *Dances with Wolves* so spectacular and which catapulted Kevin Costner to super-stardom in Hollywood.   *P.W.E.*

Kevin Costner revises the cliché of the Wild West

Scenes with Lieutenant Dunbar (Kevin Costner) and Kicking Bird (Graham Greene)

The Silence of the Lambs

USA, 1990

Running time: 118 minutes
Directed by Jonathan Demme; *written by* Ted
Tally, *based on a novel by* Thomas Harris;
cinematographer, Tak Fujimoto; *music by*
Howard Shore; *edited by* Craig McKay
With: Jodie Foster (Clarice Starling), Anthony
Hopkins (Dr. Hannibal Lecter), Scott Glenn
(Jack Crawford), Ted Levine (Jame Gumb),
Anthony Heald (Dr. Frederick Chilton)

Jonathan Demme

1944 Born on February 22 in Baldwin, New York. Film
reviewer, advertising copywriter, employed by various
movie companies. Screenplays for Roger Corman, who
encouraged Demme's directing debut:
1974 *Caged Heat/Renegade Girls.*
1975 *Crazy Mama*
1979 The comedy *Melvin and Howard* established Demme's
international reputation.
1984 *Stop Making Sense*
1986 *Something Wild*
1988 *Married to the Mob*
1990 *The Silence of the Lambs* (five Oscars), his greatest
artistic and financial success to date.
1992 *Philadelphia* (Oscar for leading man Tom Hanks)
1998 *Beloved*

Ten years after its appearance, the long awaited sequel,
Hannibal, will reach the movie theaters in 2001. Anthony
Hopkins will once again fill the role of the psychopathic
murderer, Dr. Hannibal Lecter. Jodie Foster will be replaced
by Julianne Moore (*Magnolia*), and Ridley Scott (*Blade
Runner, Thelma and Louise*) will direct.

Pure horror and the chilling presence of evil: Anthony Hopkins and Jodie Foster

Alfred Hitchcock knew that real horror isn't
on the screen but inside the viewer's head. The
film adaptation of Thomas Harris's bestseller
is based on the same concept.

Few thrillers get under your skin like
Jonathan Demme's perfectly directed masterpiece. What makes viewers' blood run cold
isn't overt brutality. In fact, the violent scenes
in this film are more reminiscent of religious
paintings than of real action. What instills
horror in viewers is the quiet malice that lurks
in the steel-blue eyes of the protagonist. "It
has been a long time since I've felt the presence of evil as directly as I did when Anthony
Hopkins first appears on the screen in *The
Silence of the Lambs,*" Roger Ebert wrote in the
Chicago Sun.

"Quid pro quo" are the words the highly
intelligent psychopath, Dr. Hannibal, uses to
challenge the young, rising, FBI agent, Clarice
Starling, to a game of cat and mouse. Clarice
—and with her, the viewer—agrees to participate in this dangerous dance, falling victim to
his cruel whims. In exchange for each piece of
information Hannibal provides Clarice about
sought-after serial killer, "Buffalo Bill," she
must bare her soul and expose herself to the
razor sharp intellect of the madman. Although
"Hannibal the Cannibal" appears on screen for
only about twenty minutes, his evil presence
dominates the film.

The role seemed custom-made for British
actor Anthony Hopkins, who achieved superstar
status at the age of fifty-four for his performance
as Dr. Lecter, setting new standards for how to

Scott Glenn as Jack Crawford and Jodie Foster as FBI agent
Clarice Starling

Setting new standards in how the deranged are seen: Anthony Hopkins as Dr. Hannibal Lecter with his counterpart, Dr. Frederick Chilton, played by Anthony Heald

act the role of a psychopath. Cool and relaxed, confident and acutely intelligent, Hopkin's Lecter provides a new perspective on insanity. Hopkin's brilliant co-star was Jodie Foster —young, intelligent, dedicated, and vulnerable. Foster, who has been considered a serious actor since her appearance in *The Accused*, gives a perfect performance as an ambitious female agent in a world dominated by men.

The disturbing relationship between Lector and Clarice—alternating between killer/agent, father/daughter, and psychologist/patient— gives the film its unique edge. This horrifying version of *The Beauty and the Beast* fascinated both the critics and the public alike. It even won over the film academy, usually highly skeptical of anything in the horror genre. After seven Oscar nominations, the film came out on top by winning the five most coveted awards: best film, best scrip, best director, best actor, and best actress.   *S.R.*

Thelma & Louise

USA, 1991
Running time: 129 minutes
Directed by Ridley Scott; *written by* Callie
Khouri; *cinematographers,* Adrian Biddle
and David B. Nowell; *music by* Hans Zimmer,
div. songs; edited by Thom Noble
With: Susan Sarandon (Louise), Geena Davis
(Thelma), Harvey Keitel (Hal), Michael Madsen
(Jimmy), Christopher McDonald (Darryl),
Stephen Tobolowsky (Max), Brad Pitt (J. D.)

"What kind of world do you think we live in?" Geena Davis as Thelma, slipping into the role of a murderess

Since Ridley Scott's road movie, *Thelma & Louise,*
racing through Utah's Monument Valley in a
T-bird like Geena Davis and Susan Sarandon, has
become the stuff of fantasy for many women.
The British director has always had a touch for
creating cult films; *Alien* set new standards for
the horror genre, and *Blade Runner* revolution-
alized science fiction. With *Thelma & Louise,*
Ridley created the first road movie for women,
with protagonists with whom the viewer identi-
fies. Callie Khouri deservedly won an Oscar for
the innovative script.

A weekend trip into the mountains turns
into a journey of no return for Thelma (Geena
Davis) and Louise (Susan Sarandon). In a parking lot, Louise shoots and kills Harlan, a slimy
character intent on raping Thelma. The trau-
matic event is the beginning of a complete break
with the women's humdrum and dissatisfying
everyday lives. The transformation of these two
characters during their flight to Mexico, from
suburban wives into feisty, cool outsiders, is
classy and smart. Their inner changes manifest
themselves externally: frilly dresses are replaced by jeans, lipsticks by guns, demure up-
dos by wild, flowing hair. The further south
the duo travels, the more we realize that this
story cannot have a Hollywood happy ending.
For Thelma and Louise are not willing to give
up their newly won freedom—no matter what
the price may be.

When the film was first released, some
labeled it as a high-gloss travelogue for America's Southwest with a plot devoid of logic
and male figures too stereotyped. It's true that
the two principle males—Thelma's husband,

Darryl, and the repulsive truck driver—are
only roughly sketched characters, but that's
not the point. The fact is that Thelma and
Louise are in a hostile land, a country that is
defined by the needs and desires of men, at
the cost of women.

We would be wrong, however, to write
off the film as a simple, feminist road movie.
Make no mistake, *Thelma & Louise* is great
cinema with stunning visuals, a perfect soundtrack, convincing leads—Susan Sarandon and
Geena Davis prove that action films are no
longer the domain of men—and a thrilling
story that delivers pure entertainment, even
to men.   *S.R.*

Thelma:

"My goodness, you're so gentlemanly about it!"
J.D.:
"Well now, I've always believed that if done properly,
armed robbery doesn't have to be a totally unpleasant
experience."

Thelma:
"I guess I've always been a little crazy, huh?"
Louise:
"You've always been crazy. This is just the first chance
you've ever had to really express yourself."

158 | 159 ⟫⟫ Ridley Scott, *Blade Runner,* and Biography,
see p. 134

Thelma and Louise (Susan Sarandon) chased by
the police, with only one way to go

Harvey Keitel as Hal,
the understanding policeman

Schindler's List

USA, 1993

Running time: 195 minutes
Black and white
Directed by Steven Spielberg; *written by* Steven
Zaillian, *based on a book by* Thomas Keneally;
cinematographer, Janusz Kaminski; *music by*
John Williams; *edited by* Michael Kahn
With: Liam Neeson (Oskar Schindler), Ben
Kingsley (Itzhak Stern), Ralph Fiennes (Amon
Goeth), Caroline Goodall (Emilie Schindler),
Jonathan Sagalle (Poldek Pfefferberg)

Steven Spielberg

1947 Born on December 18 in Cincinnati. In 1961 won an
amateur contest with his 40-minute war film *Escape
to Nowhere*. Studied cinema at California State College.
Directed episodes for TV series and TV movies such as
Duel (1971; later distributed to theaters).

1974 *The Sugarland Express* (his first feature film for theater
screening)

1975 *Jaws* (Spielberg's first box-office blockbuster, one of
seven of his productions on the list of all-time most
successful movies)

1977 *Close Encounters of the Third Kind*

1980 *Raiders of the Lost Ark* (first part of the popular
Indiana Jones trilogy with Harrison Ford)

1982 *E. T. The Extra-Terrestrial*

1986 *The Color Purple* (nominated for 11 Oscars but did not
win a single one)

1987 *Empire of the Sun*

1993 *Jurassic Park*

1993 *Schindler's List* (seven Oscars, three Golden Globes)

1995 Life Achievement Award of the American Film Institute

1997 *The Lost World: Jurassic Park*

1998 *Saving Private Ryan* (five Oscars)

1998 Spielberg awarded one of the highest honors Germany
has to give, the Bundesverdienstkreuz mit Stern.
Currently working on the films *A. I.* (based on material
on artificial intelligence taken over from Kubrick after his
death) and the sci-fi thriller *Minority Report* (with Tom
Cruise).

*"Schindler's List packs a punch all right, the overwhelming
wallop of six million Jews in general, and more than a
thousand so-called Schindler Jews in particular. Behind
that punch is director Steven Spielberg, for whom this
three-hour, black-and-white saga is a scorched-earth
proving ground."*
The Washington Post, December 17, 1993

Disturbing and authentic:
Liam Neeson and Martin
Semmelrogge (right)

"A masterpiece by a *Mensch*," was legendary director Billy Wilder's comment on *Schindler's List*. Indeed, Steven Spielberg's masterpiece is more than just a successful movie. With the real life story of Sudeten German Oskar Schindler, who saved 1,200 Jews from certain death in concentration camps, Spielberg brought the horrific story of the extermination of Jews by the Nazis onto the big screen. This provoked criticism from some, who felt that it is wrong to transform the horror into another Hollywood saga. Others praised the film for finally bringing the darkest chapter of Germany's history to the attention of younger generations. On the whole, the response was ecstatic. The *Frankfurter Allgemeine* hailed *Schindler's List* as "a film that is shockingly good in all aspects. A masterpiece of the craft, whose foremost outcome is a document to artistic truthfulness." The film was awarded, accordingly, with three Golden Globes and seven Oscars (among others for best film, best director, best script and best cinematography).

For a long time, it seemed that Spielberg, whose relatives had perished in the concentration camps in the Ukraine and in Poland, would never be able to realize the most important work of his life. Although he secured the film rights as early as 1982, when Thomas Kenneally's novel *Schindler's List* was published, another ten years passed before he was able to start filming. No one was willing to provide financial backing to the director best known for fantasy spectacles such as *E.T.* and *Jurassic Park*. They simply didn't feel confident that he was capable of coping with such difficult and serious material. In the end result convinced even the greatest sceptics. With a budget of twenty-three million dollars—fairly modest by Hollywood standards—Spielberg shot on

location, mostly with a handheld camera, in black and white, which gave the drama a documentary character. He invited "Schindler Jews," as those who were saved still call themselves today, onto the set as consultants. During casting, he decided to forego using any of the major American stars. Instead, little-known Irish actor, Liam Neeson, played the title role and Ralph Fiennes was cast as the sadistic camp officer Amon Goeth. Fiennes would later become a household name for his Oscar-winning role in *The English Patient* (1997). Ben Kingsley (*Gandhi*), who played Schindler's associate, Itzhak Stern, was the only member of the cast who was already a star.

The disturbingly authentic film, three-and-a-half hours in length, true to history and yet dramatically plotted, set new standards for the cinematic treatment of human drama. Today, *Schindler's List* is used in schools for teaching purposes, and in January 2000 it was voted "Best film of the 1990s" by the American Broadcast Film Critics Association.

Working on *Schindler's List* was a new experience for Spielberg: "Suddenly the camera, which I had used so often to hide from reality, was no longer a protective shield....The challenge was not to the power of my imagination but to the strength of my conscience. The film changed my life."
S.Al.

Liam Neeson (left) as Oskar Schindler, and Ben Kingsley as the
accountant Itzhak Stern

Ralph Fiennes (2nd from the left) as the sadistic officer Amon Goeth

USA, 1993

Running time: 188 minutes
Directed by Robert Altman; *written by* Robert Altman *and* Frank Barhydt, *based on short stories by* Raymond Carver; *cinematographer,* Walt Lloyd; *music by* Mark Isham; *edited by* Geraldine Peroni *and* Suzy Elmiger
With: Andie MacDowell (Ann Finnigan), Bruce Davison (Howard Finnigan), Jack Lemmon (Paul Finnigan), Julianne Moore (Marian Wyman), Matthew Modine (Dr. Ralph Wyman), Anne Archer (Claire Kane), Fred Ward (Stuart Kane), Madeleine Stowe (Sherri Shepard), Tom Waits (Earl Piggott), Lily Tomlin (Doreen Piggott), Jennifer Jason Leigh (Lois Kaiser), Christopher Penn (Jerry Kaiser), Lili Taylor (Honey Bush), Robert Downey jr. (Bill Bush), Tim Robbins (Gene Shepard), Frances McDormand (Betty Weathers), Peter Gallagher (Stormy Weathers), Annie Ross (Tess Trainer)

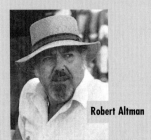

Robert Altman

1925 Born on February 20 in Kansas City, Missouri. Studied engineering. Served as bomber pilot in World War II. Wrote scripts, made industrial films.
1957 Feature film debut with *The Delinquents* Directed numerous episodes in TV series (such as "Bonanza")
1963 Founded own production company, Lion's Gate Films.
1968 *Countdown* (Altman's second feature, made ten years after his first)
1970 Great success with war-movie satire *M.A.S.H.* (Golden Palm in Cannes)
1971 *McCabe & Mrs. Miller*
1973 *The Long Goodbye*
1974 *Thieves Like Us*
1975 *Nashville*
1976 *Buffalo Bill and the Indians or Sitting Bull's History Lesson* (Golden Bear in Berlin) After several less commercially successful films, Altman came back in
1992 with *The Player,* a Hollywood satire
1993 *Short Cuts*
1994 *Prêt-à-porter—Ready to Wear*
1998 *The Gingerbread Man*
1998 *Cookie's Fortune*
2000 *Dr. T and the Women* (with Richard Gere) scheduled to appear; also planned is a film entitled *Another City, Not My Own.*

Great directors know that great gestures aren't what make a film memorable. Sometimes images do nothing more than set the mood. For example, in Robert Altman's *Short Cuts*, images of helicopters dumping insecticide onto Los Angeles set the tone of the film. The toxic mist falls on humans and animals, on houses and gardens, on streets and swimming pools, but life goes on as if nothing had happened. Thus, the "climate" of the film is poisoned from the very beginning, and, although this is not a movie about environmental damage, it *is* about emotional damage. The director uses the bird's-eye view to his best advantage. Curious, alert, and aloof, like a naturalist, he observes the antics of his characters.

Over the span of 189 minutes, Altman weaves the stories of twenty-two characters, only marginally connected, into a narrative without beginning or end. One could pick up the thread at any point and move from one story into the next. Everyone's fate intersects at some point, from parents who lose their child, to a drowned woman, from a pathologically jealous surgeon, to a housewife who makes her living from telephone sex. The mesh of this net is so finely spun, it sometimes succeeds in catching what we call life.

Robert Altman succeeded with this approach in his 1975 *Nashville*. This, after he had already revived different film genres with *M.A.S.H.*, *McCabe & Mrs. Miller*, and *The Long Goodbye*. And, although his early success was followed by a long descent into " TV land" and obscurity, he finally reemerged with *The Player*. Instead of seeking quick and easy success for his next project, he used his renewed market value to realize an oft-rejected idea: *Short Cuts*, a film based on Raymond Carver's short stories. In the end, *Short Cuts* became the novel that Carver never wrote.

What Altman has in common with the author of the original stories is that he recounts strange events without blinking an eye. Both blend the fatal with the banal, the obsessive with the inevitable. With *Short Cuts*, Altman paid homage to Carver while creating a film that is all his own, one that takes stock of modern life. In this sense, the film's title is ambiguous. For these are not only short cuts of Carver's stories but depictions of the short cuts people take to avoid expressing their true feelings. But sometimes, even detours lead to the goal.   *M.A.*

Lily Tomlin and Tom Waits: the secret ways of the human heart and the short cuts people take to get around their true feelings

Life goes on: four scenes from Robert Altman's film of tragicomic events (telephone sex, environmental pollution, jealousy, and other questions of fate) with Jennifer Jason Leigh, Josette Maccario; Robert Downey Jr., Lily Taylor; Frances McDormand, Tim Robbins; Andie MacDowell, Jack Lemmon (opposite page, from top to bottom)

Forrest Gump

USA, 1993

Running time: 142 minutes
Directed by Robert Zemeckis; *written by* Eric
Roth; *cinematographer,* Don Burgess; *music by*
Alan Silvestri; *edited by* Arthur Schmidt
With: Tom Hanks (Forrest Gump), Jenny
Curran (Robin Wright), Gary Sinise (Dan
Taylor), Sally Field (Mrs. Gump), Mykel
T. Williamson (Bubba Blue)

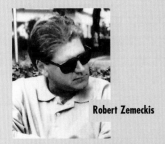

Robert Zemeckis

1952 Born on May 14 in Chicago. Film studies in Los Angeles.
Scripts for TV series (beginning of a long collaboration
with co-author Bob Gale). Short films, resulting in contact
with Steven Spielberg, who supported Zemeckis' feature
film debut in
1978 *I Wanna Hold Your Hand* and would subsequently
produce a number of his films.
1984 *Romancing the Stone,* a box-office hit that made
Zemeckis a star director
1985 *Back to the Future* (a time-travel movie expanded into
a trilogy with two sequels in 1989 und 1990)
1988 *Who Framed Roger Rabbit* (Oscar for best editing)
1992 *Death Becomes Her*
1993 *Forrest Gump* (six Oscars)
1997 *Contact*
2000 *Cast Away* and *What Lies Beneath*

Gary Sinise and Tom Hanks (right) in a scene from Robert Zemecki's story of a friendly village idiot

Forrest Gump is a patriotic incarnation of the
pure-hearted fool. Born into difficult circumstances—he has an IQ below 75 and shares his
name with a Ku-Klux-Klan founder—Gump
nevertheless copes with life and even achieves
national fame. This is because he has been
blessed with the ability to run quickly and
with a good heart—not just for running but
for performing many good deeds.

He tells the story of his life in a beautifully
broad, southern drawl to fellow travelers waiting at a bus stop, who roll their eyes with bore-
dom. "Life is like a box of chocolates. You never
know what you're gonna get." This gem of
wisdom, which Forrest spouts whenever possible, is one of his mother's sayings.

Forrest is a truly good person. In the jungle
of Vietnam he rescues injured army buddies.
He makes his war friend Buba's last wish come
true by starting up a lucrative shrimp factory. He
takes care of his former sergeant, now crippled,
and gives him new courage to live. And his
coast-to-coast marathon makes him a national
idol. The pure-hearted idiot with the simple
message saves the world.

In 1994, this jogging excursion through
thirty years of American history was awarded
six Oscars, among them "best film." This was
a big surprise to those who had pigeonholed
Robert Zemeckis as the eternal *Back to the
Future* director.

Forrest Gump is a lighthearted treatment of
serious events in recent history. Here is history
from an underexposed view, snapshot episodes
with a relentless tendency to end happily.
Everything seems to happen fortuitously, such

as when Forrest ends up in front of a microphone during a peace march in Washington.

Forrest Gump also operates on the episode
principle: the main character is a stereotype
who always acts and reacts in the same fashion
but is shown in different scenarios. The fact
that these cover nearly half a lifetime has the
advantage that we won't be subjected to a
Forrest Gump sequel for at least twenty years.

W.-C. F.

After his comedy success in *Sleepless in Seattle,* Tom Hanks
has taken on more serious roles. For his portrayal of the
lawyer with aids in *Philadelphia* in 1993, he received a
Golden Globe and an Oscar. *Forrest Gump,* in 1994, brought
him another Oscar.

Forrest Gump is a patriotic incarnation of the pure-hearted simpleton

M.C. Humphreys plays Gump as a young boy with
Hanna R. Hall as his playmate

Pulp Fiction

Tension that ends in laughter: Samuel L. Jackson as Killer Jules

USA, 1993

Running time: 154 minutes
Directed by Quentin Tarantino; *written by*
Quentin Tarantino *and* Roger Avary;
cinematographer, Andrzej Sekula; *music,*
various rock and pop songs; edited by Sally
Menke
With: John Travolta (Vincent), Bruce Willis
(Butch), Uma Thurman (Mia), Samuel
L. Jackson (Jules), Harvey Keitel (The Wolf),
Ving Rhames (Marsellus Wallace), Tim Roth
(Pumpkin), Amanda Plummer (Honey Bunny),
Rosanna Arquette (Jody), Christopher
Walken (Koons), Eric Stoltz (Lance), Quentin
Tarantino (Jimmie)

Quentin Tarantino

1963 Born on March 27 in Knoxville, Tennessee. Acting school. Job in a videotheque.
1992 Sensational film debut with *Reservoir Dogs* (as director, scriptwriter and actor)
1994 *Pulp Fiction* (Golden Palm in Cannes, Oscar for best screenplay)
1995 *Four Rooms* (to which Tarantino contributed one of four episodes). That same year he acted in *From Dusk Till Dawn,* based on his own screenplay.
1997 *Jackie Brown* (based on a novel by Elmore Leonard)
1998/99 Produced two sequels to *From Dusk Till Dawn,* which were marketed as videos.
2000 Tarantino played the role of a blind preacher in *Little Nicky*

"You don't merely enter a theater to see *Pulp Fiction;* you go down a rabbit hole." *The New York Times*

In 1994, the Palme d'Or went to the one entry for which there was no competition at the Cannes film festival, Quentin Tarantino's *Pulp Fiction*. This gangster burlesque was truly unique and remains so to this day. The success was all the more triumphant considering that this was only the second film by the young and rising thirty-one-year-old director, who made his more experienced colleagues look staid. His script was inspired by the legendary "pulp magazines" of the 1930s and 1940s, beautiful gangster trash such as *Black Mask*. As *Time Magazine* put it: "Tarantino has made a smart, deadly movie. It's *Die Hard* with a brain." (June 6, 1994)

The first scene takes place in a restaurant —as it did in his debut film *Reservoir Dogs*— where "lovebirds" Honey Bunny (Amanda Plummer) and Pumpkin (Tim Roth) have decided to rob the shop. The next scene opens with Samuel L. Jackson and John Travolta, elegant hitmen, black-clad like the killer gang in *Dogs*, en route to their next job and comparing the relative merits of American versus European fast food.

Through humorous dialogue and unpredictable action, Tarantino creates an ironic distance between his characters and their heinous deeds, taking the edge off their violence and releasing his viewers into liberating laughter.

After hitmen Vincent Vega and Jules have terminated a couple of kids who attempted to cheat their boss, Vega (Travolta) is given the dangerous, yet not unattractive task, of looking after his boss's wife, Mia (ultra cool Uma Thurman). The evening ends abruptly with Vincent saving Mia's life in a spectacular manner. Once again Tarantino winds up the tension only to release it into laughter. There's no cliché, no reference, Tarantino doesn't use to this end, including Harvey Keitel cast as the "clean-up man," the same role he played in *Codename Nina*.

The young genius, who went through a hiatus between the success of *Pulp Fiction* and his controversial *Jackie Brown* (1997), began his filmmaking career with a more limited plot in *Reservoir Dogs*, which he expanded into a much broader framework in *Pulp Fiction*. The story, divided into three parts, is multilayered and convoluted, with individual lines seeming to run independently of one another, only to link up again in a surprising way. It is an unmitigated pleasure to follow Tarantino's homage to American film history and to his own work. The film increased the existing fan club of the renegade director even further, who immortalized himself in the role of Jimmy in his greatest success. Without doubt, *Pulp Fiction* is a cult film with a style that quite a few filmmakers have since tried to emulate. Not surprisingly, Tarantino's gangster ballad has thus far escaped any attempts at cloning.

M.B.

Samuel L. Jackson and John Travolta (right) in
Quentin Tarantino's homage to American film history
and his own œuvre

"A smart fatal movie"—John Travolta as Vincent
and Uma Thurman as Mia

The English Patient

USA/England, 1996
Running time: 162 minutes
Directed by Anthony Minghella; *written by*
Anthony Minghella, *based on a novel by*
Michael Ondaatje; *cinematographer,* John
Seale; *music by* Gabriel Yared; *edited by* Walter
Murch
With: Ralph Fiennes (Count Laszlo Almásy),
Kristin Scott Thomas (Katharine Clifton),
Juliette Binoche (Hana), Naveen Andrews
(Kip), Willem Dafoe (Caravaggio), Colin Firth
(Geoffrey Clifton), Julian Wadham (Madox),
Jürgen Prochnow (Major Müller), Kevin
Whately (Hardy), Clive Merrison (Fenelon-
Barnes), Nino Castelnuovo (D'Agostino),
Hichem Rostom (Fouad Bey), Peter Rühring
(Bermann)

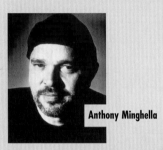

Anthony Minghella

1954 Born on January 6 in Ryde, Isle of Wight, England.
      Made a name for himself as a playwright, wrote award-
      winning stage plays, radio plays, and television
      screenplays. When he turned to cinema, continued to
      write his own films:
1990 Directing debut with *Truly, Madly, Deeply*
1996 *The English Patient* (nine Oscars)
1999 *The Talented Mr. Ripley*
2001 In preparation: *Cold Mountain*

Juliette Binoche as Hana, the English patient's nurse

Truly great emotional moments in film are
extremely rare. Most movies never get beyond
kitsch. What they offer is smouldering melodrama instead of a deeply moving story, trivial-
ized feelings instead of genuine ones. David
Lean's films belong into that rare second cate-
gory, where emotions are treated honestly and
straightforwardly. For instance, his *Out of
Africa* (see pp. 140–41) is deeply moving because it places the viewer into a suspenseful
state of empathy, in which love and death,
self-discovery and self-denial are defining
moments of human existence.

    The English Patient, too, dares to take an
honest and raw look at emotion, plumbing
the boundaries between love and death with
sensitivity and nuance, deep feeling and powerful imagery. Here is a film that washes over us
like a great wave. The opening scenes establish
the iconography of the film with a dream-like
beauty, a shimmering, infinite desert landscape
punctuated by carefully placed hieroglyphs
and ancient ruins. At first, these are as difficult
to decipher as it is to recognize that the figure
seated in front of Count Laszlo Almásy (Ralph
Fiennes), in his flight across the desert, is his
dead lover.

    An unexpected plane crash transforms Laszlo
into the disfigured English patient of the film's
title. Unable to move or to remember, his path
leads him from the African desert to a bombed
Tuscan monastery, where nurse Hana (Juliette
Binoche) looks after him at the end of World
War II. As the count gradually recalls his great,
though doomed, love affair, a second love story
unfolds between Hana and an Indian soldier
from the bomb-disposal squad.

Love, war, and death. The melodramatic
is always relativized by the omnipresence of
death, and each character must achieve out-
ward peace through a hard-fought inner peace,
reconciling physical and emotional suffering.
The English Patient is a cinematic epic that is
rich in nuance, and yet poetic in its rendition
of different locations and time periods. Director
Anthony Minghella has found a highly distinct
and independent approach to creating a film
adaptation of Michael Ondaatje's elegantly
crafted novel. "He registers everything as part
of a changing harmony," the author wrote in
an important section of the novel. "He sees
her at different hours and in different places,
which change her voice or her character, even
her beauty, just as the surf of the ocean favors
or condemns the fate of rescue boats."   *H.P.K.*

"This dreamlike, nonlinear tale moves in much the same
way, swooping gracefully from past to present, from one
set of lovers to another, from the contours of the body to
the topography of the desert sands."
The New York Times, November 15, 1996

Ralph Fiennes played the lead role in *Schindler's List,*
see p. 160

Endless desert in the border region between love and death: Ralph Fiennes as Laszlo Almásy

The power of feelings: Ralph Fiennes, as Count Laszlo Almásy,
and Kristin Scott Thomas, as Katharine Clifton

Broken Silence

Switzerland, 1996
Running time: 110 minutes
Directed and written by Wolfgang Panzer;
cinematographers, Wolfgang Panzer *and*
Edwin Horak; *music by* Filippo Trecca;
edited by Claudio di Mauro
With: Martin Huber (Fried Adelphi), Ameenah
Kaplan (Ashela), Michael Moriarty (Father
Mulligan), Colonel Kapoor (Director of
Immigration Office)

Thrown together by fate, an unlikely couple embarks on a long journey through Asia:
Ameenah Kaplan (left) and Martin Huber (center)

Wolfgang Panzer

1947 Born in Munich. Reporter for Swiss television;
cameraman and assistant director in Germany and
France. In 1977 began directing TV films and series
(such as *Matto regiert* or *Der König von Bärenbach*).
1985 Feature film debut with *Point Hope*
1996 Unexpected success with *Broken Silence*
1996–1999 Directed four films for the popular German TV
detective series 'Tatort'
1999 *Bill Diamond—Geschichte eines Augenblicks*
2000 *The Bookfair Murders* (TV film)

As character Blaise Pascal says in *Broken Silence:*
"All our problems come about because we
leave home." Although this sentiment runs
throughout the film, director, author, and producer, Wolfgang Panzer, was more interested
in journeys of the mind than in physical ones.
Ideas about transgressional thinking and experiential environments behind also crop up
in the movie.

Carthusian monk, Fried Adelphi, is the
hesitant narrator of the story. For twenty-five
years, he has lived in total isolation, committed
to a vow of silence. But when his monastery is
threatened by the expiration of its lease, Fried
is charged with the task of speaking to the
owner—who is "somewhere in Indonesia."
To do so, he is temporarily released from his
vow of silence.

The monk gives an account of his adven-
turous journey, in the form of flashbacks, from
a confessional in New York City. On the first leg
of his long journey to Asia, his fear of flying
forces him to leave the airplane at its first stop-
over in New Dehli. There he forgets his brief-
case, which is found by Ashela, a young African
American woman with no intention of returning it. After seeing the forlorn monk, lost and
confused in the airport, Ashela is moved to
help him—out of compassion and curiosity.
Because Fried will not board another plane,
she guides him halfway across Asia via rikshaw,
bus, car, train, and boat. The unworldly monk
has little knowledge of the practical things of
life, while the young woman has no experience
of the virtuous life. Over the course of their

journey, the two find the courage to learn
intimately from each other, despite their
differences.

Wolfgang Panzer traveled to India with
a minimal team—producer, sound engineer,
director, and two actors—and an unfinished
script. His plan was to bring his two-page out-
line alive on the screen within the framework
of whatever he found upon his arrival. With
simple technical means, a bare-bones budget
of 250,000 dollars, and three months of shooting, Panzer realized a gem that has received
several awards.

Panzer's unique film deals with the delicate
nature of human encounters and that which is
foreign or different. At its center is a story of
two people who are changed forever because
they take the risk of togetherness. Even though
it prompts difficult questions, it does not offer
easy, universally applicable solutions. Rarely in
the history of film has the relationship between
God and man been explored with such lighthearted and humorous grace.   *G.E.V.*

"One of the most beautiful 'little' films to vary the theme
of communication in a wonderful new way."
Peter W. Engelmeier

The nature of human encounter and the quest for God: Martin Huber as Fried, the monk unaccustomed to life in the real world, and Ameenah Kaplan as the Afro-American Ashela

Titanic

USA, 1997

Running time: 192 minutes
Directed and written by James Cameron;
cinematographer, Russell Carpenter; *music by*
James Horner; *edited by* Conrad Buff *and*
James Cameron
With: Kate Winslet (Rose DeWitt Bukater),
Leonardo DiCaprio (Jack Dawson), Billy Zane
(Cal Hockley), Kathy Bates (Molly Brown),
Bill Paxton (Brock Lovett), Bernard Hill
(Captain Smith), Jonathan Hyde (Bruce
Ismay), Victor Garber (Thomas Andrews)

James Cameron

1954 Born on August 16 in Kapuskasing, Ontario, Canada.
Studied physics in California. Wrote scripts, made a
short film. Entered motion pictures professionally as an
art director and miniature maker for Roger Corman.
1982 Directing debut with *Piranha II: the Spawning* (a rather
unexciting sequel to Joe Dante's *Piranha* of 1978)
1984 *The Terminator* (two Oscars) with Arnold Schwarzenegger
became a smash success and established Cameron's
reputation as a first-rate action-movie director.
1986 *Aliens*
1989 *The Abyss*
1991 *Terminator 2: Judgment Day* (four Oscars)
1994 *True Lies* (with Arnold Schwarzenegger)
1997 *Titanic* (eleven Oscars and four Golden Globes)
Scheduled for 2001: *True Lies 2* (again starring Arnold
Schwarzenegger) and an IMAX-Mars film.

"To be honest, I doubt Fox ever saw this as a particularly
commercial film. If they break even I think they will be
happy. As for me, I'm not making anything on it—essent-
ially it's been a three-year pro bono job. So nobody's
going to get rich. At this point Titanic is a gift—a gift to
the world."
James Cameron, prior to the release of the *Titanic*

"Ultimately a haunting tale of human nature; ... an
unforgettable vision of millennium-ready unease .... This
Titanic is too good to sink."
The New York Times, December 19, 1997

A condemned love story: Leonardo DiCaprio and Kate Winslet

James Cameron played at high stakes and won.
Throughout the long, worldwide, public rela-
tions campaign, everyone predicted yet another
Waterworld fiasco. But Cameron's optimism was
justified. Every single dollar of the 200 million
he invested in this most expensive movie in
the history of film was worth it. In the US alone,
Titanic brought in 29 million dollars at the
box office on the first weekend. In Germany,
it earned a sensational 14 million dollars. That
Titanic would then also earn eleven Oscars
seemed like a foregone conclusion; what did
surprise viewers, however, was that neither of
the lead actors won awards.

The director and scriptwriter's recipe for
success is simple enough. He followed the
pattern of most disaster films, fueling the
viewer's appetite for sensation for ninety
minutes. Together with the stars we explore
the ship, casually move around in the luxury
of first class, and dine elegantly from expensive
china with the finest of silver. We climb down
into the belly of the giant, where the coal fires
burn and the lower classes know how to cele-
brate life. All along there is the certainty that
all this will perish and sink, yet we feel no
regret for all the beautiful interiors.

The tragic accident would unfold without
a single tear dropping if it weren't for the ill-
fated lovers, classic accoutrements of disaster
films whose purpose it is to keep us on the
edge of our seats. Leonardo DiCaprio (Jack)
woos chubby Kate Winslet (Rose). The latter
shares her first-class ticket to the bottom of
the sea with a bitter mother and an insensitive
fiancé. Jack, on the other hand, is a steerage
passenger, who brings life into the bored atmosphere of the upper deck with his unbridled
charm. He feels like the "king of the world"
when he lets the sea breeze whip across his
face as he perches on the prow of the Titanic
in one of the film's most beautiful scenes. On
its own, the love story would be unbearably
banal. Luckily, there is the iceberg and, although
everyone knows the story of the Titanic, the
remainder of the film is incredibly gripping.

To shoot it, Cameron sank a 263-m-long
model of the steamer in a 64-million-liter
pool. All in real time. A cinematographic
stroke of genius, this allows us to follow the
tragic lovers through each dramatic stage of
the accident, always anticipating the next
phase in the fiasco.

Like the Hindenburg before it, the Titanic
has become a myth because unexpected, de-
vastating accidents undermine our twentieth-
century faith in technology. But that isn't really
the theme of this film. *Titanic* is first and foremost a fateful event staged on a grand scale
and served up in comfortable feature film
length.   *W.-C.F.*

263-m-long model of the steamer in a 64-million-liter pool

An underdog from below-deck joins the rich and the beautiful:
Leonardo DiCaprio, Kate Winslet and Billy Zane (right)

Life is Beautiful

La vita è bella
Italy, 1997

Running time: 122 minutes
Directed by Roberto Benigni; *written by*
Vincenzo Cerami, Roberto Benigni; *cine-matographer,* Tonino Delli Colli; *music by*
Nicola Piovani; *edited by* Simona Paggi
With: Roberto Benigni (Guido), Nicoletta
Braschi (Dora), Giorgio Cantarini (Giosuè),
Giustino Durano (Uncle), Sergio Bustric
(Ferruccio), Marisa Paredes (Dora's Mutter),
Horst Buchholz (Dr. Lessing)

Roberto Benigni

1952 Born on October 27 in Misericordia, near Arezzo, Italy.
In the early 1970s, began a stage career which would
soon make him the country's most popular comedian.
TV series star, first roles in Italian feature films.

1982 Directing debut with *Tu mi turbi,* in which the actor
Benigni was his own director and screenwriter for the
first time. His leading lady was Nicoletta Braschi,
whom he would wed in 1991.
International acting breakthrough in the Jim Jarmusch
films *Down by Law,* 1986, and *Night on Earth,* 1991.
Fellini, too, gave him a key role in his last film, *The
Voice of the Moon,* 1990.
As director, star, and writer in one Benigni made

1988 *The Little Devil* (with Walter Matthau),

1991 *Johnny Toothpick,*

1994 *The Monster* and

1997 *Life Is Beautiful* (three Oscars).

1999 As an actor only he appeared in *Asterix and Obelix vs.
Caesar/Asterix and Obelix Take On Caesar.*
Recently Benigni has begun to devote himself
increasingly to theater.

Through his clowning around Guido (Roberto Benigni, right) leads the Nazi régime to the brink of absurdity

"As soon as you say my name, I'm gone," quips
Dr. Lessing (Horst Buchholz), a cultured hotel
guest. The statement is really a riddle in dis-guise, as Lessing and Guido (Roberto Benigni),
the hotel waiter, exchange riddles on a frequent
basis. Each is more challenging than the one
before, and usually it is Guido who beats the
erudite doctor to the answer. The answer to
the riddle is so simple and yet the doctor can't
figure it out.

Life is Beautiful is the proclamatory and
provocative title of a film that attempts to
capture the horror of the holocaust by means
of comedy. Benigni's tender, cinematic poem
may never have been realized if Spielberg's
holocaust drama, *Schindler's List,* (see pp.
160–61) hadn't preceded it, proving that an
attempt to represent the genocide and the
simulated reality of the film medium need not
be mutually exclusive—in contrast to the sen-timental and shallow treatment of the material
in the 1978 US mini-series *Holocaust,* which
had only served to confirm such fears.

With the assurance of a sleepwalker, the
Italian comedian Roberto Benigni achieves the
impossible. By pushing the madness of the
Nazi regime to the point of absurdity via the
manners of a clown, he lets imagination and
hope triumph over the terror of marching
boots.

Sixty years after Charlie Chaplin's *The Great
Dictator,* Benigni again brings the phenome-non of fascism into a human context and poses
the question of human culpability. His night-marish parable consists of two "films" in one.
The first one takes place in 1939 and depicts
the life of Guido (Benigni), a Jewish man who
has "mastered the art of living" and fallen in
love with Dora, a beautiful teacher (played by

Benigni's muse and real-life wife Nicoletta
Braschi). A harlequin in the tradition of the
commedia dell'arte, Guido is pert, jumpy, at
times naïve, but with a heart of gold. Within
the frame of a single scene, the story jumps
five years ahead into the second "film." We
are suddenly transported from sun-drenched
Tuscany to a stone-gray concentration camp.

The camp, like the film, is a strange hybrid:
half-realistic construct, half Fellinesque stage
set. What was mere slapstick as an end in itself
in the first half, becomes a weapon and life-saver in the second half. To shield his young
son, Giosuè (Giorgio Cantarini), from the
horrors of the gas chamber, Guido distracts
him with a grand illusion, a pretence in which
the camp becomes the site of a game whose
first prize is a brand-new, armored tank. What
happens throughout the second half is a risky
balancing act, unthinkable without Benigni's
childlike innocence or the dignity and human-ity of his humor. In the end, all that remains
is that which is gone as soon as you say its
name: silence. *H.R.*

"The idea just suddenly occurred to me. Like Rossini once
said that he received his ideas and his creativity straight out
of the sky. The same thing happened to me. First I hesitated,
because it seemed too risky. But then I couldn't do other-wise: I had to make this film. I am in the fortunate position
to be able to make the films that I like. In Italy I am a little
like Steven Spielberg. Many warned me about this project.
But an artist must be ahead of his audience and not running
after them."
Roberto Benigni, 1998

When life was really still beautiful: Nicoletta Braschi and Roberto Benigni as Guido, who marries the lovely Dora

The Celebration

Festen
Denmark, 1998
Running time: 105 minutes
Directed by Thomas Vinterberg; *written by*
Thomas Vinterberg *and* Mogens Rukov;
cinematographer, Anthony Dod Mantle; *music
by* Morten Holm; *edited by* Valdís Óskarsdóttir
With: Ulrich Thomsen (Christian), Henning
Moritzen (Helge), Thomas Bo Larsen (Michael),
Paprika Stehen (Helene), Birthe Neumann
(Else), Trine Dyrholm (Pia)

Thomas Vinterberg

1969 Born on May 19 in Copenhagen, Denmark. Studied
directing at the Danish Film School. His final examination
film *Sidste omgang* won awards in 1993 at various
international student film festivals.
1994 *Drengen der gik baglæns (The Boy who Walked
Backwards)* (award-winning short film)
1996 Feature film debut with *De storste helte (The Biggest
Heroes)*
1998 *The Celebration* (special prize of the jury in Cannes)
2000 The episode *Niels Henning* in the interactive TV project
D-dag, made on New Year's Eve 2000
2000 *The Third Lie*

Attraction and sexual advances: Pia (Trine Dyrholm), an employee in the family-run hotel, and Christian (Ulrich Thomsen), the hotel manager's son

Those Scandinavians. Ibsen, Strindberg, Bergman—more than a century of family melodrama. If one includes Hamlet, Prince of Denmark, the tradition is even longer. Families living tortured lives in dollhouses, confined by the corset of respectability, abandoned to their own devices somewhere in a northern nowhere.

Thomas Vinterberg's *The Celebration* takes place in a rural setting. In the opening sequence, we see the protagonist, Christian (Ulrich Thomsen), walking to his father's sixtieth birthday party. The young man seems to stagger beneath the weight of his suitcase, but he isn't nearly as helpless and hopeless as he appears—at least not for long. All of a sudden, his mobile phone rings, and he's again very much in touch with the outside world. Christian returns to his childhood home for only a short time, but long enough to reveal a horrible truth. Nothing is as it seems, and ambiguity characterizes the entire film.

While filming in Copenhagen in 1995, Danish directors Thomas Vinterberg and Lars von Trier set forth purist rules for this intimate family subject. For example, they used a handheld camera—one of the *Dogma* rules—to make viewers feel as though they are watching a home video, eliminating the distance between them and the movie screen. When we are in the thick of the action, we ignore Christian's speech about how his father brutally raped him and his twin sister—just like the other characters in the film do. Like them, we carry on with his father's birthday celebration.

Like an ancient god of vengeance with Scandinavian blonde hair, Christian fights hard to break through the barrier of bourgeois complacency and stubborn silence. He perseveres so that the guilty will suffer hell on earth, and their victims will receive recompense. In the end, Christian does not work alone. With icy politeness, the other birthday guests join him in rejecting the defeated rapist—played sympathetically by Henning Moritzen—so that they may eat in peace.

Although contemporary, the film is classic in tone because of its Aristotelian unity of time, place, and action. This satisfies another *Dogma* rule: to film only on location and to show action only in the here and now. *The Celebration* (the first *Dogma* film), which was followed by *The Idiots* and *Mifune*, is deeply moving, haunting, and memorable. Whatever else *Dogma* may stand for artistically—irony or creative playfulness—it is an inspired marketing tool for worthwhile films from a small country.   *A.K.*

"Dogma 95: No genre stories or superficial action. No
special lighting or extra sound. No tarting up the location
with props; no optical tricks; no camera work that isn't
handheld. No black-and-white or flashbacks. '[The] supreme
goal is to force the truth out of [the] characters and
settings,' say the group's Vows of Chastity."
The New York Times, October 7, 1998

Ejected by an ancient god of vengeance: Christian (Ulrich Thomsen) is removed from the celebration by his own brother and two other guests, beaten up and tied to a tree

Breakfast after a dramatic night: Christian asks Pia whether she wants to accompany him to Paris

Shakespeare in Love

122 minutes of pure pleasure: Joseph Fiennes as William Shakespeare (center) and Ben Affleck as Ned Alleyn (right)

USA, 1998

Running time: 122 minutes
Directed by John Madden; *written by* Marc Norman, Tom Stoppard; *cinematographer,* Richard Greatrex; *music by* Stephen Warbeck; *edited by* David Gamble
With: Joseph Fiennes (William Shakespeare), Gwyneth Paltrow (Viola De Lesseps), Geoffrey Rush (Philip Henslowe), Judi Dench (Elizabeth I), Simon Callow (Tilney, Master of Revels), Colin Firth (Lord Wessex), Ben Affleck (Ned Alleyn)

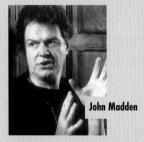

John Madden

1949 Born on April 8 in Portsmouth, England. Went in 1975 to the U.S., worked in radio and stage productions, taught at the Yale School of Drama. After returning to England, began in 1984 to devote himself to TV series and films (such as *The Return of Sherlock Holmes* and *The Widow Maker*).

1993 *Ethan Frome,* Madden's first feature film, with Liam Neeson

1994 *Golden Gate* (with Matt Dillon)

1997 Breakthrough with *Mrs. Brown/Her Majesty, Mrs. Brown*

1998 *Shakespeare in Love* (seven Oscars)
After this dazzling success, Madden says he wants to gain "a little distance." For

2001 he envisages filming *Captain Corelli's Mandolin,* a World War II romance (with Nicolas Cage)

Gwyneth Paltrow received an Oscar for her performance as Lady Viola

After a night of passion Viola De Lesseps (Gwyneth Paltrow) says: "I would not have thought it: there is something better than a play!"
Shakespeare (Joseph Fiennes): "There is."
De Lesseps: "Even your play."
Shakespeare: "Hmm?"

Shakespeare in Love—here's an idea that would have appealed to the poet. Romeo and Juliet have been the most famous lovers in the world for over 400 years. Finally, we get a glimpse behind the scenes of the unforgettable drama —on screen, that is. As successors to the incomparable bard, Tom Stoppard and Marc Norman have come up with an extraordinary script: cheeky, witty, clever, sparkling with irony, hilariously funny and full of feeling. In short, it is simply sensational. It all rings so true, though none of it is—because it's all a figment of the authors' imagination.

The story takes place in London in the year 1593. William Shakespeare (Joseph Fiennes), an ambitious young poet, broods over his new play entitled *Romeo and Ethel, the Pirate's Bride.* He's under pressure, the theater manager is pounding on the door and the impresario impatiently demands a final script. But no matter how desperately young Will chews on his quill, runs to his established competitor Christopher Marlow for advice or seeks the services of a soothsayer (where he flops down on a couch in a wonderful parody of the Freudian approach), nothing gets his imagination going. Until he meets the scintillating and enchanting Lady Viola (charm personified: Gwyneth Paltrow). The young genius catches fire, blissfully unaware that the beauty is mad about the theater and has been cast in the role of Romeo. She is disguised as a young man because women are not allowed to appear on the Elizabethan stage, but gradually the poet begins to see through the camouflage. In a turbulent comedy of errors Viola and Will end up as lovers. William over-comes his writer's block, art and love inspire each other, and the most beautiful verse flows from his quill for the new play now called *Romeo and Juliet.* But the beautiful and intelligent Viola has been promised to the detestable Lord Essex (Colin Firth), and William has a wife and children in distant Stratford-upon-Avon. The Queen herself steps in to set things straight. Elizabeth I (played by Judi Dench, who is wonderful, as always) ensures that the on-stage love drama receives its due fame— despite backstage intrigues and potential detractors—and that sweet Viola does indeed marry the old geezer to whom she has been promised.

Shakespeare in Love is a fabulous comedy, full of drama, action, and witty dialogue, a costume piece which gloriously depicts the Elizabethan era but remains nevertheless refreshingly contemporary in pace and style, never pretending that what you see is how it really happened with Shakespeare and *Romeo and Juliet.* Or as director John Madden praised the work: "It's a story that is all at once blasphemous, modern, and deeply romantic." The film received seven Oscars. But more importantly: the full-blooded production delivers 123 minutes of pure cinematic joy and audiences around the world have fallen in love with Shakespeare all over again.   *P.W.E.*

Shakespeare under pressure and still waiting for that stroke of genius: 'Joseph Fiennes in Love'

Romeo, Juliet, and the Queen in the audience: Judi Dench as Elizabeth I (center)

The Matrix

USA, 1999

Running time: 136 minutes
Directed and written by Larry Wachowski *and* Andy Wachowski; *cinematographer,* Bill Pope; *music by* Don Davis; *edited by* Zach Staenberg
With: Keanu Reeves (Thomas 'Neo' Anderson), Laurence Fishburne (Morpheus), Carrie-Anne Moss (Trinity), Hugo Weaving (Agent Smith), Gloria Foster (Oracle), Joe Pantoliano (Cypher)

Floating through the cyber-punk era: Keanu Reeves and Hugo Weaving (right)

Andy and Larry Wachowski

1965 Larry born on June 21; two years later, in 1967 his brother Andy born on December 29 in Chicago. "The Wachowski Brothers" have since become a byword in the film industry. Their joint oeuvre to date:

1995 Screenplay for *Assassins/Day of Reckoning* (directed by Richard Donner)

1995 Spectacular feature film debut with *Bound* (directing and screenplay)

1999 Sensational success with *The Matrix* (again screenplay and directing)
Planned for 2002 are sequels *The Matrix 2* and *The Matrix 3*.

Cascades of Japanese-like characters "drip" into columns of seemingly random combinations of numbers. The camera zooms in on one of the numbers and reveals the fine horizontal lines in the pixel resolution of each number. The camera takes us between these lines and into the world "behind," opening up a seemingly familiar cinematic reality to the viewer. We feel transported into a cop film or an action thriller, in which the police are just getting ready to make an arrest. The routine action becomes an orgy of fighting that overthrows the laws of gravity and the laws of human logic. The opening sequence of *The Matrix* toys with time in breathtaking virtuosity, stretching, expanding, and contracting it at will. It also manipulates space whose three-dimensional system of coordinates no longer offer a guide to orientation. A suspenseful chase ends with a woman being shot by a laser in a phone booth. "Is she dead?" a voice asks. Another answers, "She's gone."

Dead or gone? Life and death are no longer fixed coordinates in *The Matrix*, by far the most innovative science fiction film of the cyberpunk era, in which "reality" is depicted as a sequence of computer-simulated worlds. The not too distant future is revealed as a dark and threatening place that makes no allowances for individual desires. The boundaries between dream and reality have changed so dramatically as to be unrecognizable.

Immediately after the opening sequence described above, computer hacker, Neo (Keanu Reeves), is gently awakened by his computer. "Follow the white bunny," the green script instructs him, quoting Lewis Carroll's *Alice in Wonderland*. Indeed Neo, the "Chosen One," ends up in a frightening virtual wonderland where intelligent machines have usurped power over humans. Feeding on human brain energy, the machines insinuate images into people's

minds, which they experience as real, although they are in fact terrifying illusions. The struggle of a small group of rebels against this technocratic rule turns into a breathtaking action story full of mythical and religious allusions, drawing equally from the vocabulary of Hong Kong action films and of apocalyptic "End of Days" movies. *The Matrix* is stunning cinema on the discrepancy between being and seeming, founded on peoples' fear of a hypertechnological, soulless present.   *H.P.K.*

Life and death are not fixed points in the virtual wonderland: Keanu Reeves and Carrie-Anne Moss

In March 2000, *The Matrix* was awarded four Oscars for best editing, best effects (2) and best sound

American Beauty

USA, 1999
Running time: 136 minutes
Directed by Sam Mendes; *written by* Alan Ball;
cinematographer, Conrad L. Hall; *music by*
Thomas Newman; *edited by* Tariq Anwar *and*
Christopher Greenbury
With: Kevin Spacey (Lester Burnham),
Annette Bening (Carolyn Burnham), Thora
Birch (Jane Burnham), Wes Bentley (Ricky
Fitts), Mena Suvari (Angela Hayes), Peter
Gallagher (Buddy Kane)

Sam Mendes

1965 Born on August 1, 1965 in England
1987 Graduated from Cambridge University. Shooting star
      career in the theater. Awarded the Critics Prize as best
      newcomer for his stage production of *The Cherry
      Garden* with Judi Dench.
1990–93 Four productions for the Royal Shakespeare
      Company in London, including *Troilus and Cressida* with
      Ralph Fiennes in the title role.
Since 1992 Artistic director of the Donmar Warehouse in
      London. Awarded four Tony's for his *Cabaret* production
      (1993) staged in London and on Broadway, as was *The
      Blue Room* (1998).
1999 Cinema film debut with *American Beauty* (five Oscars
      and three Golden Globes)
2000 Awarded the Shakespeare Prize by the Alfred Toepfer
      Foundation in Hamburg for his work at the Donmar
      Warehouse.

Kevin Spacey as Lester Burnham:
"It's okay! I wouldn't remember me either."

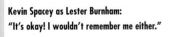

In March 2000, *American Beauty* was awarded five Oscars
for Best Actor, Best Cinematography, Best Director, Best
Picture, and Best Writing

Vacuuming with passion and compulsion: Annette Bening as
an uptight forty something

The project seemed doomed from the start.
There were many doubts in Hollywood when
producer Steven Spielberg gave Alan Ball's
sought-after script to British theater director,
Sam Mendes—who had never before directed
a film—over the likes of "star" directors such
as Robert Zemeckis and Mike Nichols. Likewise,
eyes rolled in an "I told you so" way when
Mendes called a halt to production after only
three days on the set and declared that he
wanted to start all over again. Spielberg agreed,
again, and was vindicated. For with *American
Beauty*, Mendes has succeeded in creating an
original, humorous, and ruthless satire of the
American Way of Life, hailed by viewers and
critics alike.

Yet, this film is not easy on viewers. On the
contrary, the hero and narrator of *American
Beauty*, Lester Burnham (Kevin Spacey), is boring
and ultra-conservative. Likewise, his wife,
Carolyn (Annette Bening), is forty-something
and bitter, so much so that the trade magazine
Variety stated: "She's scary!" The couple's teenage
daughter, Jane (Thora Birch), feels nothing but
embarrassment for her parents and, at the beginning of the film, has already asked her new
neighbor, Ricky Fitts (Wes Bentley), to kill her
father. Ricky is the one glimmer of hope in the
drama—an outsider in search of truth who
looks at the world through the lens of his camera. This prop was a stroke of genius on the
part of Mendes, as it enabled him to give the
audience a view of events from a different perspective. When Lester falls in love with Jane's
beautiful friend, Angela (Mena Suvari), he
makes a complete fool of himself, taking up
jogging, rediscovering Pink Floyd, and re-

opposite page: The American way of life or has someone
promised her a rose garden? Dream scene with the young
Angela (Mena Suvari)

belling against his life. This unleashes an
avalanche of events with catastrophic out-
comes.

With *American Beauty*, Mendes proved, again,
that foreigners often make good, typically
American, films. He is never shallow, although
he uses every cliché, and though his jokes may
come close to slapstick, the laughter sticks in
the viewer's throat. This is due in no small part
to the outstanding cast, led by Kevin Spacey
and Annette Bening, whose performances made
the film a hit with both the public and critics.
The satire went from being an insider's tip to
a surprise hit, earning over 70 million dollars,
in four months, in the US alone. The result of
the film's critical acclaim were three Golden
Globes (best drama, best director, best script)
and five Oscars—best film, best director, best
actor (Kevin Spacey), best original script, and
best cinematography (Conrad L. Hall). The secret behind the success of the tragi-comedy is
simple, according to Mendes: "It is a very human story without good and evil. Each main
character has his or her weaknesses, and yet
we can empathize with all the characters." *S.Al.*

It's not his day: Kevin Spacey as Lester Burnham

Michael Althen

How "The End" Disappeared from the Cinema Screen

Somewhere along the way, "The End" disappeared. And nobody knows when or why; one moment it was there and then it wasn't. In the past, "The End," "Fin," "Fine," or "Ende" appeared on the screen but that's no longer the case. Today a movie is simply over.

With this in mind, the history of film could be loosely divided into two eras: those with "The End" and those without. Instead of "The End" we now have lists of credits; the leads, the supporting actors, the bit players, the driver to the star, the driver's assistant, and the assistant's assistant. Then the music credits—listed at the very end so that everyone has to wait—followed by a statement to the effect that no animals were mistreated during the course of filming. Some movies no longer even have

opening credits which means that the scrolling names also list the director, cinematographer, and script writer, so that—technically speaking—they are films with neither a beginning nor an end.

The end of "The End", no doubt, evolved from years of careful research by the film industry. Test audiences probably found "The End" too negative a concept. After all, what does "The End" mean when the happy couple is just about to embark on a future together? Why "The End" when, in fact, it is just the beginning of a wonderful friendship? "The End" started losing favor sometime during the 1960s and '70s. Nobody knows exactly when. During this time there was a shift away from the tried and tested Hollywood recipe for storytelling in which "The End" reassured the audience that all was well with the world, that an end was still an end and that "The End" signalled the line between fiction and reality. Perhaps it was communism, or the atom bomb, or the advent of author/director films that resulted in this loss of certainty—for whatever reason, "The End" was simply no longer an option. Or perhaps it was because most stories were over

before they had even started, everything had already been told many times over—so why bother starting at all?

On the other hand, "The End" in movies did not signal a conclusion but rather conveyed the story book ending "And they lived happily ever after"—a sort of consoling reassurance that the hero and heroine were not only going to live forever but that their story is also universally applicable. And so it was. Perhaps Humphrey Bogart and Claude Rains are still together in their French garrison raising drink after drink, toasting their great friendship and their lost loves. Perhaps Vivien Leigh is at Tara waiting for Clark Gable "to give a damn" and come back to her. Anything is possible.

What is definitely not possible is that today's movie stars have a future after the credits have rolled. Their "shelf-life" lasts approximately the length of time it takes to eat a bag of popcorn and once the viewer has left the cinema, they are long forgotten. This could have something to do with the fact that long before the official end of the movie, viewers have already seen a number "The End's" themselves because, try as they might, they cannot possibly imagine what the real ending could be. After all, a dead enemy is only really dead when he's been killed several times over.

Nowadays movie characters are like cats—they have at least nine lives—which is probably because the story has to be drawn-out over the longest possible time in order to justify the viewers' expense for a babysitter, a parking lot and a meal. The studios seem to feel that audiences will complain that they haven't had their money's worth if a movie isn't at least a hundred-and-thirty-five minutes long. More often than not the price of a ticket actually includes about nine endings—of which eight are superfluous. The first doesn't necessarily signal the real end but rather the moment when one can happily leave the cinema (even though the movie has another forty-five minutes to run—forty-five minutes in which to work through the other eight endings . . .).

Never before has the film world had so many endings—but noone dares call it by its name.

[The End]

The Authors

Michael Althen (M.A.)
Film critic and currently film editor for the newspaper *Süddeutsche Zeitung*. Author of books on Dean Martin, Robert Mitchum, and Rock Hudson. Collaborated with Dominik Graf on two films: *Das Wispern im Berge der Dinge* (BR/WDR), *München – Geheimnisse einer Stadt* (BR)

Sibylle Alverdes (S.Al.)
German specialist and media journalist. Previously editor-in-chief of *Film-Manuskripte*. Co-authored the two volumes of *100 Jahre Kino*. Worked for, among others, *Blickpunkt: Film*, *Welt am Sonntag*, and the *Münchener Abendzeitung*.

Birgit Amon (B.A.)
Studied German language, literature and journalism (M.A.) at the Deutsche Journalistenschule (German school of Journalism), Munich. Founding editor, editor-in-chief and staff member of the Deutscher Fernsehdienst; co-authored the publications *Das große Album der Kinostars*, *100 Jahre Kino*, and *Das Buch vom Film*. Works as an independent journalist in Kiel.

James Attlee (J.A.)
Works for a London-based art publishing house and is a regular contributor to music and film magazines (among others, *Grammaphone Magazine* and *Songlines*).

Marga Boehle (M.B.)
Studied German language and literature with an emphasis on film. For the past 10 years has worked as an editor and editor-in-chief at Entertainment Media Verlag, Munich. Co-publisher of the monthly journal *Treffpunkt Kino*. Staff member of *Blickpunkt: Film*.

Klaus Christoph Dahm (K.D.)
Hamburg-based journalist. Studied English language and literature. Between 1985 and 1990 press chief of Warner Bros., Germany, before being appointed editor-in-chief of the magazines *Cinema*, *Max*, and (since 1998) *Petra*.

Peter W. Engelmeier (P.W.E.)
Professor of media-science and advisor to film production firms and television stations. Author of various books on film (including *Fashion in Film*, also published by Prestel). Engelmeier was head of the culture section of a Munich daily newspaper for many years. His picture archive relating to the history of film (1982–1997) is considered the most extensive of its kind in the world.

Wolf-Christian Fink (W.-C.F.)
Studied modern languages and literature. Journalist and author on the subject of classical music, cinema, art, and lifestyle; since 1991 he has been working as an independent editor for the pay-TV-channel, Premiere.

Arnold Hohmann (A.H.)
Film and television critic for the German daily newspaper *Westfälische Rundschau*, Dortmund. Author of the media section in the *Süddeutsche Zeitung*.

Andrea Kaiser (A.K.)
Literary scholar, freelance critic, and media journalist (*epd medien*, various daily newspapers, and the weekly *Die Zeit*).

Horst Peter Koll (H.P.K.)
Studied theater, film, and television (M.A.). Chief-editor for the magazine *Film-Dienst*, film journalist, and editor of several publications (*Lexikon des Internationalen Films*).

Josef Lederle (J.L.)
Film journalist. Studied philosophy and theology. Editor for the magazine *Film-Dienst*.

Hans Messias (H.M.)
Editor for the magazine *Film-Dienst*. Film journalist and editor (*Lexikon des Internationalen Films*).

Michael Radtke (M.R.)
Publicist and owner of the marketing firm 'Touch Medien Company.' Worked as editor-in-chief for the Axel Springer Verlag and for the publishing group Milchstrasse. "Docutainment" specialist, among others, director and author of the series *Herrenhäuser in Schleswig-Holstein*.

Susanne Rieger (S.R.)
Freelance film journalist and graphic designer. Worked in the editorial department of *Video-Woche*. Later editor-in-chief of *MedienMarkt* and *Film ab*.

Heiko Rosner (H.R.)
Contibutor to the Frankfurt publication *Pflasterstrand*, currently head journalist of the magazine *cinema*. Working on his first novel—which is not set in the world of film.

Ilse Schliekmann (Po.)
Studied journalism, German language and literature, and history. Writes movie critiques and editorials for the Munich daily newspaper *Abendzeitung* under the pseudonym Ponkie. Also publishes editorials and commentaries for, among others, the magazines *Stern* and *Cosmopolitan*. Awarded the Grimme-Preis in 1991.

Georg E. Vogel (G.E.V.)
Munich based professor of medicine who is also a movie-buff par excellence. He organizes regular movie sessions and invites directors and expert audiences to attend. Special attention is given to independent productions and non-mainstream movies.

Selected Bibliography

Bawden, Liz-Anne, ed. *The Oxford Companion of Film*. New York, 1976.

Bergan, Ronald. *The United Artists Story*. London, 1986.

Bock, Hans-Michael. *Lexikon Regisseure und Kameraleute*. Reinbek bei Hamburg, 1999.

Bock, Hans-Michael. *Lexikon Filmschauspieler international*. 2 vols. Reinbek near Hamburg, 1997.

Brown, Curtis F. *Ingrid Bergman*. New York, 1973.

Conway, Michael, Dion Mc Gregor and Mark Ricci. *The Films of Greta Garbo*. Secaucus, NJ, 1968.

Cook, Roger F. and Gerd Gemünden. *The Cinema of Wim Wenders: From Paris, France to Paris, Texas*. Ann Arbor, MI, 1988.

Curtis, Tony and Barry Paris. *Tony Curtis: The Autobiography*. New York, 1993.

Deschner, Donald. *The Films of Cary Grant*. Secaucus, NJ, 1973.

Dickens, Homer. *The Films of Gary Cooper*. New York, 1970.

Dickens, Homer. *The Films of Katharine Hepburn*. Secaucus, NJ, 1976.

Eames, John Douglas. *The MGM Story*. London, 1975.

Eames, John Douglas. *The Paramount Story*. London, 1985.

Engelmeier, Peter W. *Beauties—Faszination des schönen Scheins*. Augsburg, 1993.

Engelmeier, Peter W. *Das Buch vom Film*. Munich, 1996.

Engelmeier, Peter W. *Das große Album der Kino-Stars*. Augsburg, 1992.

Engelmeier, Peter W. *Hinter den Kulissen—Stars bei der Arbeit*. Munich, 1993.

Engelmeier, Peter W. *Traumfabrik—Die Kunst der Filmfotografie*, exhib. cat. Cologne, 1990.

Engelmeier, Peter W. *100 Jahre Kino—Die großen Filme*. Munich, 1994.

Engelmeier, Peter W. and Regine Engelmeier, eds. *Fashion in Film*. Munich, New York, 1990.

Filmschauspieler International. Reinbek near Hamburg, 1997.

Fischer Film Almanach. Frankfurt am Main, 1980ff.

Forman, Milos and Jan Novak. *Turnaround: A Memoir*. New York, 1994.

Francis Ford Coppola. Reihe Film vol. 33. Munich, 1985.

Hahn, Ronald M. and Volker Jansen. *Lexikon des Horrorfilms*. Bergisch Gladbach, 1985.

Hahn, Ronald M. and Volker Jansen. *Lexikon des Science Fiction Films*. 2 vols. Munich, 1997.

Hallberg, Jana. *Dogma 95*. Berlin, 2000.

Harvey, Stephen. *Fred Astaire*. New York, 1975.

Haver, Ronald. *David O. Selznick's Hollywood*. New York, 1985.

Heinzlmeier, Adolf and Berndt Schulz. *Lexikon Filme im Fernsehen*. Hamburg, 1988.

Hembus, Joe. *Das Western-Lexikon: Erweiterte Neuausgabe von Benjamin Hembus*. Munich, 1995.

Higham, Charles. *Audrey: The Life of Audrey Hepburn*. New York, 1984.

Hirsch, Foster. *Elizabeth Taylor*. New York, 1973.

Hirschhorn, Clive. *The Columbia Story*. London, 1989.

Hirschhorn, Clive. *The Universal Story*. London, 1983.

Hirschhorn, Clive. *The Warner Bros. Story*. London, 1979.

Höller, Josef. *Lexikon der Filmregisseure*. Munich, 1991.

Jewell, Richard B. and Vernon Harbin. *The RKO Story*. London, 1982.

Jordan, René. *Cary Cooper*. New York, 1975.

Katz, Ephraim. *The Macmillan International Film Encyclopedia*, new edition. London, 1994.

Kerbel, Michael. *Paul Newman*. New York, 1973.

Koebner, Thomas. *Filmregisseure: Biographien, Werkbeschreibungen, Filmographien*. Stuttgart, 1999.

Krusche, Dieter (assisted by Jürgen Labenski). *Reclams Filmführer*. 5., revised and expanded edition. Stuttgart, 1982.

Lexikon des Internationalen Films. Ed. Katholisches Institut für Medieninformation e.V. and Katholische Filmkommission Deutschland. Reinbek near Hamburg, 1997.

Marill, Alvin H. *Katharine Hepburn*. New York, 1973.

The Motion Picture Guide. Chicago, 1985.

Nichols, Peter W., ed. *The New York Times Guide to the Best 1,000 Movies Ever Made*. New York, 1999.

Payne, Robert. *The Great Garbo*. New York, 1976.

Peary, Gerald. *Rita Hayworth*. New York, 1976.

Quirk, Lawrence J. *The Films of Ingrid Bergman*. New York, 1970.

Stern, Lee Edward. *The Movie Musical*. New York, 1974.

Sunshine, Linda. *The Illustrated Woody Allen Reader*. New York, 1993.

Thissen, Rolf. *Howard Hawks: Seine Filme—sein Leben*. Munich, 1987.

Thomas, Tony. *Burt Lancaster*. New York, 1975.

Thomas, Tony. *Gregory Peck*. New York, 1977.

Thomas, Tony and Aubrey Solomon. *The Films of 20th Century-Fox*. Secaucus, NJ, 1979.

Toeplitz, Jerzy. *Geschichte des Films 1895–1945*. 2 vols. Munich, 1987.

Töteberg, Michael. *Fritz Lang mit Selbstzeugnissen und Bilddokumenten*. Reinbek near Hamburg, 1985.

Truffaut, François. *Correspondence, 1945–1984*. Trans. Gilbert Adair. Lanham, MD, 2000.

Vermilye, Jerry. *Cary Grant*. New York, 1973.

Weise, Eckhard. *Sergej M. Eisenstein in Selbstzeugnissen und Bilddokumenten*. Reinbek near Hamburg, 1975.

Werner, Paul. *Roman Polanski*. Frankfurt am Main, 1981.

Zondergeld, Rein A. *Alain Delon: Seine Filme—sein Leben*. Munich, 1984.

Zurhorst, Meinolf. *Lexikon des Kriminalfilms*. Munich, 1985.

Index

Part II. *Film Titles*

Page nos. in **bold type** refer to the 84 films presented in detail in this book. Original language titles are also listed.

191

Acknowledgments

A book such as this would not have been possible without teamwork. The Editor would like to thank the many people who were part of this team. Special thanks go to my editors, Gabriele Ebbecke (for the German edition), and Christopher Wynne (for the English edition), for their good-humored and helpful collaboration through all stages of the project, and their editorial expertise. Birgit Amon, author of numerous texts, was also involved in the completion of the documentory part of the book. With her unfailing knowledge of movies and the history of film she followed the book from the initial project planning through to the finishing stages. Special thanks also go to Sibylle Alverdes, who worked on the texts and assisted the Editor with the coordination of the project, and to Christian Schramm, who worked with enthusiasm on the biographies and who also assisted my wife in researching photographic material. The visual opulence of this book is credited to my wife, Regine Engelmeier, who worked closely with the designer, Rainald Schwarz. Finally, the Editor would like to thank all authors for their contributions to and suggestions for the contents of this book.   *P.W.E.*

Photographic Credits

Box Office Presseagentur, Nicole Kartes, Munich (53); Buena Vista International, Munich (1); Cinetext Bild und Textarchiv GmbH, Frankfurt a.M. (1); Domino Presseagentur, Munich (6); Dreamworks LLC & Universal Pictures, Frankfurt (1); *Filmarchitektur*, ed. by Dietrich Neumann, Prestel 1996 (1); Archiv KS, Frankfurt a.M. (74); Interfoto Pressebild-Agentur Bildarchiv, Munich (133); Kinowelt Mediengruppe, Munich (2); Nimbus Film, Hvidovre, Denmark (1); Prokino Filmverleih, Munich (1); pwe Verlag, Hamburg (19); Ullstein Bilderdienst, Berlin (1); Privatarchiv Georg E. Vogel (6). All other photographs have been taken from private collections or from the Publisher's archive.

The Editor and Publisher have made every effort to acknowledge all owners of copyright material and photographs included in this volume. Any accidental mistakes or exclusions will be rectified in subsequent additions. In this respect, the Publisher would be pleased to hear from any copyright holders who could not be traced.

Photo research: Regine Engelmeier
Assistance: Christian Schramm
Editorial assistance: Sibylle Alverdes

Front cover: Audrey Hepburn in *Breakfast at Tiffany's* (see p. 86). Inset, from top: *The Blue Angel* (see p. 24), *Gone with the Wind* (see p. 34), *Easy Rider* (see p. 104), *Star Wars* (see p. 122), *American Beauty* (see p. 182)
Back cover: *Le Samurai* (*The Godson*) (see p. 96), *Pulp Fiction* (see p. 166), *Down by Law* (see p. 142), *The Tin Drum* (see p. 128)

Page 1: *Singin' in the Rain* (see p. 60)
Frontispiece: *Casablanca* (see p. 42)
Page 15: Jim Jarmusch (Photo: Abe Frajndlich, New York)

© Prestel Verlag, Munich · London · New York, 2000

Library of Congress Card Number: 00-102982

Die Deutsche Bibliothek—CIP Einheitsaufnahme
Cataloging data is available

Prestel Verlag · Mandlstraße 26 · 80802 Munich · Germany
Tel. +49 (0 89) 38 17 09-0 · Fax +49 (0 89) 38 17 09 35
www.prestel.com
4 Bloomsbury Place · London WC1A 2QA · Great Britain
Tel. +44 (020) 7323-5004 · Fax +44 (020) 7636-8004
175 Fifth Avenue, Suite 402 · New York, NY 10010 · USA
Tel. +1 (212) 995-2720 · Fax +1 (212) 995-2733

All texts translated from the German by Elizabeth Schwaiger, Toronto, with the exception of the following: biographies, by John W. Gabriel, Worpswede; pages 6–15, by Stephen Telfer, Edinburgh; page 184, by Margaret Howie, Cape Town

Copy-edited by Courtenay Smith
Editorial direction: Christopher Wynne

Designed by zwischenschritt, Rainald Schwarz, Munich
Lithography by Repro Ludwig, Zell am See
Printed by Appl, Wemding
Bound by Kunst- und Verlagsbuchbinderei, Baalsdorf

Printed in Germany on acid-free paper

ISBN 3-7913-2394-6